SO
YOU WANT TO BE
A LOBBYIST?

The Inside Story of the
Political Lobbying Industry

by

CORINNE SOUZA

First published in Great Britain 1998
by Politico's Publishing
8 Artillery Row
London
SW1P 1RZ
England
Tel 0171 931 0090
Email politicos@artillery-row.demon.co.uk
Website http://www.politicos.co.uk

A catalogue record for this book is available from the British Library

ISBN 1902301005

Cover artwork courtesy of John Burrows

Printed and bound in Great Britain by St Edmundsbury Press
Typsetting by FSH.
Cover Design by Ad Vantage.

ACKNOWLEDGEMENTS

I would like to express my gratitude to Arthur Butler for reading the book and for his contributions to the text. The fact that *So You Want To Be A Lobbyist?* does not reflect some of the industry's significant achievements is due principally to the modesty, loyalty and discretion of its master. Posthumous thanks too, to Lt Commander Christopher Powell RN, the modern industry's founder. A procedural specialist and superb Parliamentary draftsman, he was a role model for us all – or would have been had public servants not tried so hard to deny his contribution to public life, and deliberately frustrated access to him, or knowledge of his achievements.

My thanks also to Mark Hollingsworth. For six years, he acted as trusted go-between, between myself and the late Bob Cryer MP, the commercial lobbying industry's scourge. Throughout this time, Mark's integrity and thoughtful understanding of both side's point of view sustained an atmosphere of openness and respect, if not acceptance, of some of the arguments.

As for Bob Cryer MP, he was kindness itself. While in the text I have, in general, been rude about many Parliamentarians, none of those comments apply to Bob. He was generous in his time, loyal to those who trusted him, even when he disagreed with their viewpoints, and anxious about their futures.

I am grateful too, to Richard Moir, an international relations specialist. His expert advice on the EU, the City and the implications for our foreign policy (and therefore trade) of the political risk industry, all explained with typical commercial pragmatism, was invaluable. These areas are only touched upon marginally in the text, and responsibility for superficial interpretation and explanation lies with myself.

My thanks to Simone Mondesir, Teresa Moriarty, and Jane Pasternak, for their insight and thoughtful comments on parts of the text. Particular thanks to Kauru S., now returned to her home in the Far East, for her expert instruction and interpretation of some aspects of the Japanese character. Thanks too to Les Pole, for his recall of pre and immediately post-War lobbying. Regrettably that story is for another book, although I was delighted to be able to include one anecdote.

My gratitude, as always, to Jo Sollberger, especially for her kindness and hospitality in Geneva, which enabled me to complete the book.

I would also like to express my thanks to my publisher, John Simmons. Over the months there have been times when feelings have been hurt, intentions misunderstood, and tempers raised. Throughout it all, John has been a kind mediator, keeping things steadily on track.

My greatest debt is to Iain Dale. Nothing can ever equal his generosity of spirit, or the fact that, as with everything else in his life, he has stuck to the project with loyalty, imagination and vigour. This, despite my belief that what has been produced is not altogether what he expected! This is partly due to the book's focus, and partly due to some of its inclusions and conclusions. However, despite the fact that these may have embarrassed him professionally, politically or commercially, he has been unflinching in his support. He has been contributor, 'translator' and, of course, editor. The latter was a particularly thankless task in view of what he calls sweetly my 'rather odd grammar and sentence construction'.

Finally, my thanks always to my mother, Julia, and Lawrence, my late father. *So You Want To Be A Lobbyist?* is dedicated to him.

FOREWORD

So You Want To Be a Lobbyist? is written partly for those who might be considering a career in the commercial lobbying industry and want to know more about it. Additionally, it is hoped that it will interest readers with a general wish to be informed on the subject or those who are thinking about employing a commercial lobbyist for the first time. It is not for idealists, those wanting academic definitions or a 'how-to' manual.

Its aim is to set commercial lobbying in a pragmatic context and throw up a few questions that the individual could consider before committing himself. It is written and edited from the point of view of ex-commercial lobbyists who believe that politics and commercial lobbying are an honourable mix, but recognise that picking a way through the arguments are difficult, particularly because some people, who can act as advisers in other situations, are either unsympathetic to the industry or inexperienced in the discussion.

The book is not about the whole lobbying industry, which would include information, for example, on pressure groups and single interest organisations (be they commercial or charitable). Nor is it about the one-man bands, often set up by public servants or former public servants, or about those, such as foreign 'Mr Fix-its', who are employed to lobby governments to influence commercial tendering and are paid a commission if such lobbying is successful.

More importantly, it is not about the significant influence of those commercial and other individual lobbyists, such as, for example, those working in the defence sector, whose work is not always transparent and who may have other links with unregulated industries or private bodies. Access to their story is impossible, although the extent of their power can be guessed at. This, for the long term good of democracy and probity, let alone the industry's reputation, is something for government to address with sympathetic public acknowledgement that not all that is discreet has sinister or cynical meaning or intent.

Sometimes discretion is in the public good. Sometimes also, discretion is no less than humility.

This book is written, instead, for those working for public affairs companies who seek to influence political forums in this country and on the Continent, on behalf of a range of fee paying clients. In the process, it is hoped that it will offer an insight into part of the industry and bring some understanding of that part to the wider public.

It is possible that in so doing some commercial lobbyists will be amused by what is said, others annoyed. If so, we have hit the spot! We are not arrogant enough to believe that we can make a difference – we do believe that we can set some of the industry in proper context.

We recognise that the book, for a variety of reasons (some legal!) is not necessarily as good as it could have been and apologise in advance for any obvious 'watering down' or any notable omissions. We hope that it at least has the merit of lacking the sterile caution of a corporate bureaucrat.

A not inconsiderable amount of time (as John Major might have said) has been spent on working out whether those employed by the public affairs companies should be called 'professional' or 'commercial' lobbyists. We have plumped for the latter for the simple reason that lobbyists do not have professional status – although many individuals in the industry have professional status from other disciplines – and because, unlike, say, accountants or lawyers, the work of the lobbyist is, or should be, invisible, albeit accountable.

We have started from the premise that the commercial lobbying industry is essential to the democratic process – not least because no public sector facility exists to run a political campaign across all the different countries of the EFTA or European Union – and because no credible organisation can afford to be politically ignorant and therefore excluded from the political network and consultation game that the commercial lobbyists know so well.

Any number of books have already been written on the subject. Nonetheless, we believe that the value of this book lies in the fact that:

- it is written on behalf of employees and smaller customers, rather than employers, corporate or private vested interest groups or salesmen
- it places the commercial lobbyist where he really is i.e. sometimes on the margins of politics – but, just as often, at the centre. This is not as obvious as it seems since the industry is more usually portrayed by those reluctant to accept the existence of the commercial lobbyists –

unless associated with 'sleaze' or anti-democratic practice – let alone, outside of the above, their sometimes central, and, crucially, legitimate role in political life; or by those, such as academics, who can be commercially unaware or, as often, may have a vested interest in ignoring or minimising the contributions made by the industry

- it is non-academic, therefore, it is hoped, it has avoided the academic trap of making politics appear terminally boring, and brought some aspects of politics to life for the so-called duffers at the back of the class!
- it is written and edited by those who do not believe that the public servant (who has written many of the lobbying books) has a monopoly on service to the country (although he appears to believe that he does) and, in consequence, has conveniently ignored the contribution made by commercial lobbyists to democratic life (unless of course he has gone into public affairs!)

and

- it is written and edited by those who, unlike, it seems, many journalists, want the industry to survive and prosper, not least because it offers employment to thousands.

Much of the book concentrates on the woeful conduct of great institutions of State and makes no attempt to hide a certain cynicism about the ways both the Westminster and European Parliaments operate, as well as both the executive and political arm of government. As a result, it could be that some of this cynicism could be regarded as seditious. If it is, we do not believe that apology is necessary.

We recognise that commercial lobbying has a poor reputation and that many of those who purport to speak for it are either unequal to the arguments or have underrated the antagonism. This has let down many in the industry who find their own reputations tarnished as a result. This book tries to redress the balance, although it recognises that, on the whole, commercial lobbyists have shown no commitment to dealing with their serious image problem, have allowed an information vacuum to develop and have appointed no credible spokesman to speak for the industry on a rolling, on-going basis or at a time of sudden crisis.

An example of this is the fact that, when the industry was still reeling from the aftermath of the 'Cash for Questions' affair, of which more later, a debate was organised by the Institute of Public Relations in a Committee Room at the House of Commons. The Motion was: 'That this House believes that professional lobbying is essential to the democratic process'.

Instead of fielding industry 'greats', the two put up to speak in favour of the motion appeared both callow and impertinent with only a rudimentary grasp of what commercial lobbying was all about. In addition, their knowledge of the arguments seemed non-existent. They did not appear to have any love for politics nor enjoyment in the debate (essential for all lobbyists), let alone any knowledge of how to conduct it or enthuse a fundamentally friendly audience.

They lost the Motion. The Queen might find it worrying to note that one of the proposers of the Motion was Mr Simon Lewis, her new spin doctor.

The industry was similarly found wanting during the July '98 'Cronygate' or 'cash-for-access' affair.

In complete disarray, it appears to have had no understanding of the outrage or the grief, far less the humility or sensitivity required, when both promoting and defending it. It lacks both respect for those who hold genuinely irreconcilable positions; and intellectual (let alone emotional) understanding of the need to establish its respectable credentials.

Perhaps this is because many in the industry, sometimes with good reason, genuinely do not care what people think of them. Unless, however, they do start caring they will attract into the industry only spivs, many of whom already predominate, and, crucially, pre-date 'Cronygate', who, like a magnet, attract other spivs into the political market. That can hardly be good for the industry as a whole or the democracy we all share.

An industry that is full of spivs drives out many of those who are both decent and of appropriate calibre. As importantly, it fails to attract and keep the right people in the first place.

Those who remain and who wish to conduct themselves in the correct manner find little nourishment. This is partially because some of the claims of the senior players, many of whom lack both education and skill, are bogus, unless the peddling of puff has a value; and partially because, for a variety of reasons, it is time for some of them to leave the stage, irrespective of their social standing or prestige. Arguably, some should not have been allowed to remain in public affairs at all, wherever their successful careers have taken them.

As importantly, it is because the industry's clients can be naive, unsophisticated in judging the product, greedy, or a mix of all three. The gist of the book, therefore, is not vanity or self-defensiveness but wounded anger over the humiliation many commercial lobbyists have felt in recent years. In writing it, there seemed to be no reason to be 'dull' or 'safe'. Nor was there any struggle to avoid wide condemnation of both the players and their standards.

As a result, at times, it will seem as if the book is anti the industry. It is not. It is anti those who have dragged, and continue to drag the industry down. In so doing, it has run the risk of ascribing impure motives to practically everyone and that is unjust.

There are plenty of idealists in politics – and that includes the commercial lobbyists. These make mistakes but also seek to find a way to transform. They deserve more recognition than they have been given.

The reason they have not been given appropriate recognition is because, with all their farsightedness and fair-mindedness, they are too often no match for their less distinguished opponents. Intelligent and innocent, they pop up from time to time reminding you of their existence. Super-articulate, warm, charismatic one-offs, they are just that, one-offs. Meanwhile, wide-eyed innocents, just starting their careers, find themselves entering a profession that exists in a twilight world of vulgar motivation and debased aspiration.

The book concludes that commercial lobbying, at the moment at least, is for the most part home to those with little initiative and not enough scruples. That is a tragedy for all of us who are predisposed to like the industry. It is also a tragedy for all those who love politics and recognise that politics is both the problem and the solution.

It is hoped that, having read the book, some people will be encouraged to learn more about public affairs, and why it is essential for them to do so. It is hoped also that they may discover for themselves that the modernisation of democracy is in their interest; just as it is in their interest to learn how to supervise democracy's servants and ensure that the spirit of democracy is observed in the 21st century.

Old mandarins who, in the wake of the collapse of the East/West divide, speak in terms of the death of ideology, seem to be unaware that there has long been a new ideology. It is called people power.

Or, even, Democracy.

Corinne Souza
August 1998

Note to Readers: Throughout the text, the word 'he' has been used in preference to 'she' or 's/he'. This may be politically incorrect but is one decision that the author and editor could agree on!

Readers wanting to know more about the industry might also like to consult the *Directory of Political Lobbying 1998–99*, also published by Politico's Publishing. Compiled and edited by Iain Dale and Corinne Souza, it contains detailed entries on all the lobbying companies in Britain, including client lists and biographical details of more than 200 people in the industry.

INTRODUCTION

Industry Defence – Political SERFS and KIPPERS –
How to Lobby – How to Use this Book – Lobbying Language –
Lobbying Background – Constitutional Reform – Present State of UK
Lobbying Industry – Intelligence Services – Is it for You?

Industry Defence

In recent years commercial lobbyists have had to defend their industry on the rather shaky premise that lobbying is at the heart of the British democratic system. This has been a difficult position to sustain since the system has only been democratic for some – it was never meant to be anything else – and although commercial and other lobbying has been at its heart, that heart has not been what the citizen has a right to expect from a modern democracy.

The commercial lobbyist has either kept as low a profile as possible or maintained the falsehood, usually against his wish, because he was obliged to do so by the political and administrative establishments, on whose good-will he depended.

Now, with constitutional reform at long last upon us, and no requirement to sustain both the establishment's apparent humbug and caste, the commercial lobbyist is released from all obligation to pretend. In addition, he need no longer be shy about his profession.

He can be straightforward about the industry and its future as the companion to modern democracy. In addition, he can offer his not inconsiderable communication skills to stimulate interest in the political world.

This is important not so much in questioning and exploring the intellectual basis of the discussion, but to assist the citizen in realising what he does not know and why he should. The commercial lobbyist has much to gain by this new openness, not least because it assists him to rise above the opprobrium the industry has attracted, allowing him to claim some rightful credit for the industry which has been at the forefront of the 'make politics relevant debate'.

So, firstly, what, exactly does the commercial lobbyist do?

Political SERFS and KIPPERS

Commercial lobbyists do two principal jobs, which are done badly or well depending on the individual's training and expertise. The costs for the client are sometimes considerable. The lowliest of these jobs, of which there are three grades, is described as the political 'SERF'. The other is the political 'KIPPER'. This book is written primarily for those interested in 'Serfdom'.

The junior political SERF **S**upplies clients with political information from various political infrastructures much of which is on-line, **E**ducates the client as to how such information may impact on his business, **R**efers the client to supporting or conflicting information from which a client may take a position, and **F**ocuses the client in the appropriate direction once such a position has been decided. This is usually achieved in tandem with the client's public affairs team and the SERF, often employed by public affairs consultants or public relations companies, is subordinate to the client's in-house department.

The next grade of SERF (intermediate) is the top grade in the public relations companies but the lowest grade in the political consultancies (which are often owned by public relations companies). These **S**tructure the client's needs into pragmatic targets, **E**valuate feedback, **R**esearch alternatives and **F**ind friends in the appropriate political systems and media in the relevant country/countries.

The intermediate SERF proactively seeks to in sert the client into the system and is adviser to in-house personnel as well as the supplier of a service i.e. the intermediate SERF is both adviser and salesman. This is an awkward mix and some political SERFs have not always been scrupulous in ensuring that the client is not sold a service he does not need.

The most senior political SERF, found only in the political consultancies, is a commercial lobbyist. He usually interacts at the client's board level.

He assists in the **S**ecuring of contracts (politics is about the awarding of commercial contracts whether at local, regional, national, European or international level. In addition, Government decides on grants, recommends tax changes and frames new laws) and/or **S**caremongers to see off opposition, **E**ffects by drafting, **R**aises issues and **F**raternises with selected personnel. In doing so, the senior political SERF invariably provides the client with a leadership role.

The top dogs are the political KIPPERS. Unlike the Senior political SERFS, their influence does not usually extend beyond national boundaries.

KIPPERS **K**ick/**K**iss **I**mportant **P**eople, are **P**ersuasive, **E**xpensive, **R**esourceful when spending other people's money and exceptionally **S**elective when it comes to bestowing their time and prestige. The word 'selective' is not always complimentary. They are often not commercial lobbyists at all but doyens of public relations companies.

By virtue of their largesse and patronage, some KIPPERS have become Peers of the Realm, non-executive directors, or sit on the board of prestigious charities. A few have been known to go belly up. KIPPERS usually sustain the status quo, in contrast to the 'pure' commercial lobbyist who more often challenges it.

Political Serfs do not consider the KIPPERS to be bone fide lobbyists and resent it when their roles are confused.

Neither SERFS nor KIPPERS are regarded as 'professionals' by those who consider themselves to be 'professionals'. This is often because the 'professionals' (such as lawyers, accountants and management consultants) envy the hired guns (commercial lobbyists) for making a great deal of money for doing very little, while they, apparently, are working their socks off and living on the breadline.

From time to time, three other groups also like to have a good sneer at the commercial lobbyist. These are politicians and Civil Servants (until they need a job and are desperate to join their ranks), journalists (of whom more later) and rent-a-quote academics, often commercially funded and therefore not independent, whose dissidence seldom rises above semantics, although they are invariably successful when it comes to monopolising the moral high ground.

It is, of course, not difficult to monopolise the moral high ground. SERFS seek to customise political infrastructures i.e. they try to customise politics for the convenience and cost effective benefit of their clients. Therefore, politics, and politicians are accessories, as it were, to lobbying. As a result, the industry is rightly vulnerable to the charge that their lobbying can limit the rights of others both in their own and other countries i.e. they can, and do, disadvantage those who cannot lobby.

In their defence, commercial lobbyists have also, at a price, provided those outside traditional interest groups access to the system as of right and effectively both accelerated modernisation and broadened the class base. That is to say, money rather than established privilege, has been the deciding factor, which at least has had the advantage of being more egalitarian.

Despite this, it must be admitted that commercial lobbyists (like the vested interests they seek to influence) have an interest in maintaining poor quality political infrastructure. A riposte to this, although not a particularly worthy one, is that the commercial lobbyist is running a business, not democracy, and is not responsible for the political systems of his own or other people's countries. Moreover, good political infrastructure would not deny h

im a role i.e. the commercial lobbyist has nothing to lose, and much to gain, by modernisation.

Nonetheless, the commercial lobbyists' present defence is frequently used as sheepish justification for servicing the needs of dubious clients or foreign governments. Another is that in such situations the commercial lobbyist is exposing the client to 'democracy' and thereby is performing both a public service and an educational role. The pieties are almost as offensive as the apparently exorbitant money with which the commercial lobbyist lines his pocket.

Commercial lobbying flourishes because political infrastructures are not democratically sophisticated, transparent, accountable or free of corruption. It succeeds particularly well because those same infrastructures are unregulated and wholly unexposed to the disciplines that are imposed on others. The commercial lobbyist accesses those systems for those who can afford to pay them and the whole, although not all of its parts, is manifestly wrong.

In dealing with such systems, the commercial lobbyist at best balances principle with pragmatism, at worst lacks all knowledge of what is or is not acceptable. He is not paid to provide a service for the greater good. Therefore he does not. Those uncomfortable with this should not be considering a career in the industry.

How to Lobby

There are a number of books around on how to lobby written by 'insiders' — a welcome change from the old days when industry practitioners, anxious to preserve their market, refused to write such books. *So You Want To Be A Lobbyist?* is not another such manual but offers the following advice.

There are really only three rules to remember. The first is knowing when to say 'No'. The second is that all politics, here, on the Continent and abroad, is the servant of its elites, elites which the lobbyist needs to identify; the third is that, all politics here, on the Continent and abroad, operates in much the same way as a dysfunctional family does.

In most dysfunctional families, 'religion' can play its part, if only by its absence. Agnostics or atheists have often been shaped by some religious culture or other, even though they have rejected it. As a result, the main branches of family trees can include a predominant group, as well as a not always comfortable mix of 'outsiders'. These can include Protestants, Roman Catholics, Jews, Muslims, Sikhs or Hindus. How a family treats its outsiders identifies the family's strengths and weaknesses. More importantly, it indicates whether it is likely to favour your cause or not and gives you an idea of its psychological profile.

Therefore, to lobby successfully, you must work out which 'religious' branch of the family you are dealing with, and which family members you least want to offend i.e. that which may offend the Roman Catholic branch of the family in Britain might be an acceptable risk – but not necessarily the case if you need to take your arguments to Catholic Europe.

Your arguments have no religious dimension? Fine – but in which case how are you going to motivate those unmoved by the secular? A knowledge of religion and religious culture may not be fashionable, but is essential for anyone wanting to be a lobbyist.

All dysfunctional families have a good mix of moral, immoral and amoral family members (all useful for lobbying); those who have no interest in family and wish to distance themselves from it; to those who wish to determine the family's direction (the wise, the disciplined, the fair-minded, or the libertines, opportunists, corrupt, ideologues and so on.)

In addition, all dysfunctional families are divided by politics, whether extremist or tyrannised by the centre. The result is fracture, or uneasy alliances that collapse and regroup as circumstances dictate, while putting on a good show at the political equivalent of the great religious festivals e.g. the State Opening of Parliament.

If you, the Political SERF, view Parliament (Westminster & European) as 'Mother', Whitehall or European Commission as 'Father' enduring a long-suffering and frequently unhappy marriage of mixed religious beliefs, you will not go far wrong.

National Government, or in Europe the Council of Ministers, and its Departments of State, are the Catholic (Anglo and Roman) patricians and favoured children of the marriage who squabble among themselves but usually close ranks when their lesser siblings (e.g. regional/local government) start trying to assert their authority and prove themselves (especially in the future) unwilling to accept the role of lesser sibling.

They are assisted by urbane diplomats who, recognising the stresses and strains within the marriage, and, anxious to protect the value of the assets, fulfil the role of family lawyer to ensure that there will be no divorce.

Her Majesty's Opposition are less favoured children, and therefore invisible, who want what the other children have and who meanwhile similarly squabble when they are not dabbling with alternative religion; Standing Committee Chairmen are ruthless maiden Aunts (very Protestant!) steamrollering legislation through the system on behalf of their favourite patrician nephews whose 'religious' faith they do not share but who, nonetheless, have captured their maidenly hearts; backbenchers, MEPs, Select Committee Chairmen, Peers and Councillors are the 'poor relations' (all religions and none) − more so these days given the plethora of quangos, task forces and focus groups, the wishes of which, in terms of influence, take precedence over theirs, and, very often, ministers as well.

Quangos, task forces and focus groups are almost always the first port of call for lobbyists these days and should be regarded as the 'taxman' (very agnostic!) with the lobbyist acting as family accountant or financial adviser (!) for the client. The 'taxman's' achievements can be fairly hit and miss − he sometimes gets things wrong, sometimes gets things right. Ditto the quangos, task forces and focus groups.

As the 'accountant', the lobbyist is brought in by the client to make a deal if he can. Sometimes, the 'taxman' will over-compensate, and the client's views will be too successfully met, increasing the hostilities of others. To prevent this, the lobbyist will advise the client not to be too greedy and make concessions. On the other hand, the 'taxman' can take too much i.e. from the views of others and not accurately reflect your client's interests − in which case it is up to the lobbyist or 'accountant' to claw things back (with interest!).

Clawing things back stands a chance if the lobbyist recognises from the outset that the client, like the quangos, task forces and focus groups, belongs to the same dysfunctional family, albeit different branches.

To lobby the dysfunctional family you have to work out whether your client is better off with 'Mother' because she will pressurise 'Father', or, the reverse. Sometimes, you are better off never letting 'Father' find out what you have put 'Mother' up to; or allowing her to chose the timing as to when she tells him, leaving him to inform the 'taxman'.

You also have to work out on behalf of your client who your client is − a long lost 'relative', a 'cousin', or not even 'family' at all? 'Mother' and 'Father' might unite in the face of a forgotten 'relative' particularly if the 'relative' is after money. Therefore, you, as the lobbyist, will have to find a friendly 'Uncle' – the Press? Or, if your client is a 'cousin', is his kinship determined by 'Mother' or 'Father'? If there is no kinship, could your client pose as the 'family' skeleton in the cupboard or as the 'family' uniter?

Apply all the stereotypes and you will know, instinctively, how to lobby.

How To Use This Book

While naturally it is hoped that you will read the whole book, different parts will appeal to different readers. If you are considering a career in commercial lobbying, or, are a parent or careers adviser, the key chapters are 'How To Become a Lobbyist'; which tells you something about the life and how to select an employer; 'The Lobbying World' which identifies some of the companies; and 'The Clients'.

However, any young person considering a career in the industry should also know something about its modern history. As a result, one of the most relevant chapters is 'The Industry Overview'. This chapter includes guestimates as to where the industry is going in the future, essential for those thinking about entering the profession.

Also recommended is 'The Wrong Scandal' which gives an outline of the 'Cash for Questions' affair, and touches briefly on 'Cronygate'. Although already dated for some, the former, rather than the latter, is responsible for putting commercial lobbying under the public spotlight and a knowledge of it could be useful for those entering the profession. Many in the industry – until 'Cronygate' – tried to dismiss what happened either as a 'one-off' or on the basis that it was part of the 'excesses' culture of the 1980s. That, as we all know, is a myth.

Excesses are not part of a single decade but run continuously. The 1990s are no better or worse. Moreover, those who talk about the excesses of the 1980s imply that such excesses were all embracing. That is not the case and many commercial lobbyists did not, and do not, conduct themselves as some of those involved in 'The Wrong Scandal' appear to have done.

It is also important to stress to those entering the industry, that on the whole, commercial lobbying is fairly corruption free – certainly more so than, say, some of the shenanigans that have gone on in financial and corporate public relations, aided and abetted by some members of the allegedly reputable press.

In addition, lobbying in the UK is not a euphemism for something else – in the Elf scandal in France, for example, its chairman secretly hired a senior Minister's lover as a 'lobbyist'. If the industry is full of tarts and temptresses they are being kept well hidden!

Finally, those readers looking forward to a few indiscretions, might like to read 'The Lobbying World', most particularly the 'Tour of the Lobbying Companies' section. However, since there are various indiscretions throughout the book, there seems no reason to labour this point! The chapter entitled 'Product Policing' takes a look at regulation. It also includes some suggestions for joint ventures with both the press and political institutions to assist address some aspects of the democratic deficit; as well as, in an informed and user-friendly manner, bringing some aspects of the political system closer to the people.

Lobbying Language

In order to bring the industry to life, a lobbying 'language' has been invented. It is important to remember that these are inventions, and not official Parliamentary words or terms. Some of these inventions follow below.

As we have already seen above, those working in the industry are called Political **SERFS** and **KIPPERS**. In addition, the reader will come across the **'Political SCALPS'** – a term for the Party Whips, and the **'Political GALLOWS'** – a term for some members of the Press whose reputation as a whole is only just saved by the excellence of the **Political HAWKS** and **SEAGULLS**.

These are all part of the **Political CUMMERBUND**. Clients of the industry are referred to as **Political PILGRIMS**, companies as **Political POPPETS** or **BOGGLES**.

Lobbying Background

Before launching into the book, it is important to set the immediate past and present political scene.

Here in Britain, and following the change of Government in May '97, the old Conservative order, and more importantly the Establishment, seemed to become undermined with astonishing speed. The collapse of both were interrelated and in the case of the Establishment long overdue, since the Establishment's representatives and institutions had fudged or deliberately frustrated democratic change for decades. This is hardly surprising. Most elites are obsessed with the desire for permanence and fear the destruction wrought by change on their own lives, even though such change benefits others.

Until recently, the Political Establishment defended both its refusal and inability to deliver democracy by ill-considered and specious arguments such as (erroneously) talking in terms of people's political apathy. At the same time, and in order to have it both ways, it cited their rising political expectations.

This cut little ice with the people, who demonstrated their political activism by joining pressure groups and proved that the reality was not that their expectations had risen but that the Political Establishment's ability to deny them had diminished.

Similarly, the Administrative Establishment also tried to defend its inability to deliver by positioning itself half-way between irrelevance and sentimental twaddle. It spoke with nauseous reverence about the Mother of Parliaments without apparently realising that 'mother' dumped the 'children' long ago. It spoke of a people losing its way and Britain's lost identity. Again, this too cut little ice with the people, since they had not lost their way, far less their identity, although the Administrative Establishment had. The commercial lobbyist took advantage of this.

This was not particularly difficult since neither Establishment felt itself under any obligation to change its ways or catch up with the people. Jealous of its rank and privilege, it proved adept at knowing what was best for itself but could not be trusted to do what was best for the country. To fortify its position, it denied the contribution of those who both cared for the country and wanted to make it better. These people, motivated by an uplifting desire to take part in an honourable endeavour the sum of which was greater than themselves, lost heart. The commercial lobbyist, on the other hand, prospered.

Others also prospered, notably the country's largest minority. These, because of the nature of the voting system, were able to elect and re-elect a government that denied the citizen civic responsibility or participation in national life, in exchange for providing the economic framework that promoted social mobility based on the opportunity to gain money and prestige. The partnership was acceptable because a sufficient number of people voted for it.

A sufficient number of other people, however, who collectively formed the majority, were frustrated, enraged and bitter. Some of these looked at the services offered by the commercial lobbyists and employed them if they could afford to. They wanted change, and in the meanwhile, access to the system that denied them change.

Accessing the system did not come cheaply, principally because the UK plc is not a democratically run or modern institution. Some would say there is a fiction of democracy.

It supports a Chairman and Board of Directors no longer in charge but expensive all the same (the Royal Family, House of Lords); a President that has no Oval Office (Prime Minister); a management that cannot manage (Government, Departments of State); an Executive that cannot execute (local government, Whitehall, European Commission); a scrutiny body with no forensic skills (Select Committees); a servicing department that is unaccountable (Quango, task force, focus group) and a sales force (Councillor, MP, MEP) that can neither sell, provide, influence nor maintain the product of democracy.

The commercial lobbying market boomed. But some members of the largest minority ran into trouble. Negative equity, collapsing small businesses and redundancies took their toll. Some of these swelled the ranks of the different minorities that formed the disenchanted majority. Numbers increased further when government exhorted the scrupulously well-behaved to become 'good citizens' when a few of its own supporters or political appointees had better need of the lesson.

A rash of scandals followed in the government party, Whitehall and the business community (to which government was linked through its privatisation programme) – which led to almost universal outrage and acknowledgement of injustice.

The result was a change of government, the incoming party of which was elected in the same way as the previous i.e. by the largest minority. The commercial lobbying industry weathered the change by giving jobs to those who had helped, however marginally, the now political party of government secure the change. In this the industry received an unexpected fillip – the new government, in order to access commerce, was intensely commercial lobbying friendly. The commercial lobbyists and their clients, while positioning themselves to absorb the non-stop constitutional revolution underway, were also growing accustomed to their position as bridge between the government and corporate worlds.

Constitutional Reform

Constitutional reform has as its goal the administrative provision of a modern state, apparently on the citizen's terms. However, one expression of this goal are the new task forces and focus groups which influence government and which are themselves undemocratic in their appointments criteria and accountability. Another is the establishing of modern councils and regional government, freeing up national government for other duties, and, you guessed it, leaving the citizen even further out in the cold.

While, as part of the modernisation process, the citizen is being encouraged to engage in the body politic, as long as he is willing to pick a political party to do the engaging on his behalf, government is taking the politics out of politics by itself engaging task forces and focus groups i.e. short-circuiting politics and replacing it with corporatism.

Duping the citizen further, government offers proportional representation, reinforcing the political party system by bringing smaller parties into the game and denying the citizen expression of apolitical voice, while government itself is doing the reverse by seeking to follow a centrist, apolitical line. This is not wholly government's fault – the global economy demands it – but this is a denial of the modern democracy that it apparently is seeking to offer.

The pretence, however, that 'democratic modernisation' is on offer is vital to government for two reasons. First of all because of the diminution of national power in politically world forums and secondly because of the technology that now exists to enable the citizen to vote directly on all issues that interest him rather than electing a middleman (politician) who is the placeman of one particular party or another i.e. the reason why government got elected in the first place. In other words, to maintain its legitimacy, and, incidentally, the political party system and the jobs of countless politicians, government needs the citizen as never before.

As a result it offers modernisation without explaining the journey's inevitable end i.e. a King's Republic (the only style appropriate if the citizen wishes to retain the Royal Family as an institution and the family itself is willing to offer such service) or all the features of what government considers to be a modern state.

One of these features encompasses the increasingly privatised political machine – whose stated objective is to incorporate greater fairness into the system – explains its relationship with the commercial lobbying industry which operates, or will soon operate, at local, regional, national, European and international government level. The debate is sensitive because government itself routinely employs lobbyists for the winning of major contracts, for example in the defence or construction fields overseas, or, closer to home, in the current round of privatisations, regulation and legislation.

Government's ignorance of business both in the UK and further afield is the cause of this, as is its need for money and business sponsorship. In addition, the operation of the global economy imposes other strains. National government is unable to beat the drum for commerce, or curb its excesses, since business is more impressed by international pressure group than it is by national government. In addition, national government does not have the time nor the ability – for the most part, politicians and Civil Servants are commercially inexperienced – to act for individual industries. These frequently face several regulatory authorities at the same time, which need to be accessed and steered. The commercial lobbyist provides such access and frequently the steer.

In so doing, and much to the horror of press and public alike, he proves himself integral to the system rather than at its margins i.e. the relationship between business, commercial lobbyist and policy maker becomes symbiotic in much the same way as it is in Washington, where the lobbyist is very much part of the process, playing a role in making the whole machine work. Taken too far, however, this alters the traditional role of the commercial lobbyist which has been to act as challenger to, rather than sustainer of, the status quo. And, taken too far it makes the United Kingdom an importer of Washington Lobbying Practices. This, without the regulation, negates the whole modernisation of the state argument.

How the policy makers insert the appropriate checks and balances into the system has yet to be decided. Moreover, there is a tendency to ignore the problem on the basis that national government, along with other governments, is proving itself increasingly willing to reassert its authority by absorbing some of the arguments that motivated pressure groups thus going some way to fixing itself as the protector of the citizen's environment and property.

That is to say, to protect itself government has forced itself to become more relevant. This, in turn, diminishes the power of pressure groups. It acts as a spur for them to seek insider status, and, just as importantly, ensures that business, with its commercial lobbyists, shifts its focus back to government.

To establish a more level playing field different options are being considered. One is the provision of state lobbyists, as in Canada, so that the citizen or small groups have a public sector facility operating nationally and beyond, equal to that provided by the private. Another option is a 'lobbying tax' i.e. a levy on fee income to train and pay for public sector lobbyists.

However nothing has yet been given the go-ahead so the reality therefore remains that for the most part there are no options other than doing the job yourself, or – wait for it – employing a commercial lobbyist.

Present State of the UK Lobbying Industry

The commercial lobbying industry today has come a long way since 'lobbyist' Sidney Stanley (a Polish gentleman who changed his name to Stanley because it was the surname of the most distinguished family in

England) hit the headlines offering a bribe to a government minister soon after the Second World War. It has also come a long way since the late Lt. Commander Christopher Powell, the modern industry's founder (see 'Product Policing'), lost his office inside Parliament.

It came of age during the Conservative 'privatisation' years and is certainly ripening well under New Labour. British commercial lobbyists are the market leaders on the Continent, increasingly successful in eleven different languages and fifteen different cultures. In commercial terms, the industry is one of the country's unsung success stories and could be borne in mind every time politicians whinge about Britain's lack of influence across the Channel were the media, politicians, Civil Service and academics sufficiently switched on to developments in the industry, to look beyond immediate 'scandal'.

In the 1970s and 1980s the commercial lobbyists were a small but select fraternity. The industry received its first important boost in Britain in the early 1970s thanks to the Heath Government's decision to have a major reform and shake-up of local government. Faced with threats to their power bases and jobs, local government big-wigs sought help from PR/lobbying companies.

One of the first to do so was the City of Cardiff, a Tory controlled authority which the Tory Government proposed to hand over to a surrounding Labour controlled local government area. With the Tories and Labour in alliance, the task of defeating the proposal appeared virtually impossible. But a PR company, Partnerplan, recruited the ex-political editor of the *Daily Sketch*, Arthur Butler, who helped to devise a campaign linking grass roots activity, media work and lobbying.

This was so successful that it forced the Government to think again and grant Cardiff independent local government status. The *Financial Times* commented on 5 November 1971:

> 'The apparently prosaic announcement by Mr Peter Thomas MP, Secretary of State for Wales, that in the forthcoming re-organisation of local government, Glamorgan is to be split into three rather than two new counties is in fact the culmination of a novel and perhaps precedent-setting political public relations campaign run by the City of Cardiff...

> 'The Cardiff Council voted £15,000 to fight the proposal that they should be merged into a large new county and hired a London public relations company, Partnerplan, to conduct the campaign...

> 'Cardiff's example of professional political lobbying will not, I imagine, be lost on interest groups all over the country.'

It was not.

Campaign, the journal of the advertising and PR world, commented: 'Cardiff won its fight because Partnerplan articulated and assembled those reasons of expediency which enabled the Government to change its mind. It is just the kind of professional worldliness that is currently rare in the PR world.'

Soon, other local authorities were beating a trail to Partnerplan's small front door in Fleet Street. And, repeating Butler's tactics of mobilising local grass roots activity linked to media coverage and lobbying at Westminster, Partnerplan chalked up more successes, notably persuading the Government to drop its plan to hand over Colchester and a large part of surrounding Essex to Suffolk; and establishing a new county, based on Teeside, which, at Butler's suggestion, was named Cleveland.

One of the problems in the past for lobbyists had been to prove that they had actually achieved something at the end of a campaign. Now everyone who took an interest in local government affairs could see the clear results of a lobbyist's work.

One of the first non-local government organisations to see the significance of this new style campaigning was the British Road Federation, covering road construction and road user organisations, which employed Butler in 1973 to put muscle into its battle to get a strategic motorway network built in Britain.

Riding high on the local government wave, Butler was persuaded to leave Partnerplan to help set up a new operation for John Addey Associates, then the fastest growing PR company in Britain. There, he joined Partnerplan's former Vice Chairman, David Powell, a superb PR specialist who had conceived the idea of a local government specialist unit which, with the assistance of a merchant bank, would provide local authorities with low interest finance for developments, PR for promotional work – and lobbying.

The financial package offered attracted a great many authorities – but also the attention of the Treasury. Whitehall, operating a credit squeeze at that stage, told the merchant bank that although it was not breaking any rules, its local authority scheme was not favoured. However, the scheme at the top of the list for a new conference centre for Brighton was allowed through the net.

The Brighton Conference Centre, of course, has a special place in the heart of politics – and lobbying for it plays host to political party conferences. While many condemn the centre for its ugliness, and, these days, its somewhat ageing facilities, they could do well to remember the battle to build it in the first place, and the prosperity it has brought to the town.

Alfred Sherman, later Sir Alfred, who had left the *Daily Telegraph* to work with Butler, devised Partnerplan's new unit's name – LOGOS (Local Government Services).

At about this time, 1976, there was another significant development. Impressed by the publicity gained for PR/lobbying in the local government field, the Corporation of the City of London decided that, for the first time in its history, it would employ a consultancy to assist it with its PR and political problems.

Faced with a short list of two, the Corporation chose John Addey Associates, one reason being that the other firm employed a well-known Tory MP and the City thought that could lead to a conflict of interests and other problems. Meanwhile, other companies, in an attempt to compete in the now fast-growing lobbying field were looking for MPs to employ – and MPs were looking for consultancies.

These days the lobbying market has exploded to such an extent that you are lucky if you recognise the names of all the major players. In due course it is likely that there will be more lobbyists in Brussels than the present number of European Union Civil Servants and the market could overtake Washington although the range and sophistication of the latter's products are likely to remain ahead of Brussels for some time, not least because the Americans are operating in one language, one currency and one homogeneous political system.

Much of the industry is influenced, owned by or has close links with American communications firms. This has contributed to what some euphemistically term 'lazy' standards over here. The Americans can take a 'softer' line on ethical commercial practice abroad, except when it is commercially expedient not to do so, and this, to a certain extent, has translated across the Atlantic. Commercial lobbyists accept, however, that it is too easy to blame others for their own shortcomings.

The industry has prospered principally because the United States cannot deal with Europe in one 'phone call. Because it is more established in Britain than anywhere else in the EU, Anglo/US lobbyists have swept all before them. How the industry settles down once the other European countries catch up is uncertain. At the moment at least there is little evidence of serious challenge although the Dutch and Germans are beginning to come through. Some commentators however are now arguing that since the Europeans are forming the bulk of staff of the Brussels based Anglo-Us owned lobbyists, they will soon be setting up copy-cat companies.

Anglo/US lobbyists have established themselves in the Far East (although it is possible that the market here will eventually be challenged by the Australian lawyer-lobbyists) and countries of the former Soviet Union where they are both training and in joint venture with local staff. In so doing, some claim that commercial lobbying, alongside vast EU projects, is raising the standard of political debate in newly emerging democracies and fostering loyalties to the West in general or Britain and America in specific.

It is difficult to accept this premise. The most that is being fostered is a fondness for the piggy bank. There is talk of a need for a Code of Conduct for those operating in Eastern Europe, but since such debate is 'unsophisticated' in the UK, there is not much hope of one for Eastern Europe in the near future, if ever.

Some believe that, in view of their networks and business bias, those British commercial lobbyists not employed in American companies could in future assist either national or EU government in establishing trade offices abroad, a role currently and not particularly competently, undertaken by HM Diplomatic Corps and EU Civil Servants.

This point of view is usually lost in the arguments for and against the retention of some of our Embassies.

Those against remind the public that EU Member States are our competitors – without apparently being aware that whether we like it or not most business these days is undertaken by multinationals which are no respecter of national boundaries.

Here it is probably appropriate to ask the question whether a commercial lobbyist can work for a foreign-owned company, or have such a company as a client, and be loyal to the national or greater good. In addition, can the commercial lobbyist, in these circumstances, be a patriot and/or represent the nation?

The answer is 'not always'.

Intelligence Services

Following on from this, it is important to mention that a few commercial lobbyists can be approached to assist the intelligence services on either a voluntary or remunerative basis. This is because, as intelligence services swing away from technology and back to human intelligence, the commercial lobbyist is ideally placed to offer assistance or act as a source either in his own country or abroad. This is partially because of the environment in which he works, and partially because some commercial lobbyists possess many of the characteristics essential for espionage i.e. languages, inter-personal skills, a buccaneering, courageous spirit and detached loyalties.

Moreover, multinationals, who depend on lobbyists, and who have been dependent on the intelligence services for many years can facilitate such contacts. This dependency exists because, for example, government is anxious that the commercial sector does not lose out to those they deem to be 'extremists' such as environmentalists who may be 'right' on many issues but are not responsible for finding the money to put things right; and secondly because of a growing threat of organised crime.

Here, a word of warning, although the issue is more fully explored later on. Commercial lobbyists working in the EU or beyond are inevitably tied up with the intricacies of foreign politics. This means they can, either inadvertently or because they have been seduced by surface excitements, be sucked into situations beyond their wishes, ethics, or capabilities. Such situations can be personally dangerous as we ll as dangerous to unknowing friends and contacts who may be drawn in by association. In these circumstances, involvement in clandestine national government agencies is unlikely to be helpful. Advice is to resist acting as a source for such agencies unless, rather than wanting to be a lobbyist, you really do want to be a spy.

Lobbyists are also advised to steer clear of their clients' individual intelligence networks, whether this be provided in-house or by outside agencies such as private security companies. This is not always easy since many commercial organisations have managed to develop an intelligence service and a global contact network to rival that of many sophisticated countries. Enormous sums of money – bribery, oiling the wheels – can change hands and can end up in offshore and/or murky bank accounts. This, it should be made clear, is not the norm but does occur principally because commercial or industrial espionage (sometimes with the agreement of national governments) – which is usually a euphemism for theft – is on the increase, and outsiders, such as commercial lobbyists, are not always able to distinguish what is, or is not, against the law. The commercial lobbyist gets involved in such activity at his peril.

Is it for you?

The commercial lobbying world is fascinating, and can be exceptionally financially rewarding and seductive. For some, it offers a life of privilege and many opportunities. For others, it is a constant battle of awkward moral choices – it is not always possible to afford ones principles – and thinking for yourself becomes both a habit and a tyranny.

At best this is because of pragmatic horse-trading between what can and cannot be achieved in order to arrive at a common position. At worst it is because of empirical knowledge that that which one can be required to do is wrong. Those who compromise – and many do – can progress their careers without recognising the emptiness at the centre of their work and imagination.

This is a tragedy for the commercial lobbying industry because it means that many within it are not driven by informed argument, let alone a powerful sense of morality, but by self-interest and detached conscience. As a result the industry finds it hard to overcome justifiable prejudice, continues to contribute to its own as well as the political world's catastrophic image problem, and falls increasingly into the hands of the powerful, conscienceless and despised.

There is another way forward and this depends crucially on the quality of those now entering the profession. If they have high standards, their employers and colleagues will have to address their concerns in order to attract and keep them.

This does not mean that the commercial lobbyist's function is to use politics to translate social and international ideals into action – that is for campaigners, including politicians. It does mean that the commercial lobbyist's function is to ensure fair play so that he can continue to take a legitimate and welcome role in political life.

We all, of course, wish to succeed. We all fear being discovered as not as good as we present ourselves, and we all secretly have our doubts about our abilities. However, in commercial lobbying, one mistake and you end up over your head, digging yourself into an ever deeper hole.

This book is about how to avoid that hole.

THE WRONG SCANDAL

The 'Cash for Questions' Affair – The Political SCALPS – What is Corruption? – Lt Commander Christopher Powell RN – The Public's Responsibility – The Press – The Commercial Lobbyists – Implications of the Al Fayed affair for the Foreign Business Community – Mohammed Al Fayed – Ian Greer – House of Commons Select Committee on Members' Interests – 'Cronygate'

The 'Cash for Questions' Affair

In the long months prior to the May 1997 General Election a high profile story riveted the attention of the media, public servant and the business community.

This was the case of former Conservative Ministers Neil Hamilton and Tim Smith, who, before they became ministers, were alleged to have accepted cash or gifts from a prominent London-based businessman, Mohammed Al-Fayed. For his part, Mr Al Fayed is alleged to have believed that Parliamentarians could assist him to reverse the findings of a DTI Report into his purchase of Harrods.

He became a client of commercial lobbyist Ian Greer. At a subsequent stage, and, dissatisfied with what he believed could have been the standard of care he could have received from the politicians he said he had paid, he approached the *Guardian* newspaper. The consequences for all concerned were immense, not least in personal terms for their families.

More important, however, were the public consequences. This proved to the electorate, who had always found the involvement of politicians and rich businessmen shocking – as a rule, the citizen does not like his public servants feathering their own nests – that some politicians were apparently abusing their positions of trust by accepting money to promote the interests of the rich and powerful. In addition, it drew attention to the unregulated commercial lobbying industry.

Such proof could not have come at a worse possible time for a Conservative Government widely believed to have been too long in office, since it confirmed a general perception of (non-related) 'sleaze'. This included anxieties about the triumph of the free market at the expense of the less well off; the hypocrisy about the personal lives of some politicians; the individual cases of corruption in the Inland Revenue and Ministry of Defence; the remuneration paid to the bosses of privatised companies; the lucrative employment of public servants after retirement; and the perceived problems in an allegedly politically biased Judiciary.

Anxious to minimise the developing political scandal summarised by the term 'cash-for-questions', not least because of the impending General Election, the Government tried to boil the problem down to a few wayward MPs, a commercial lobbyist who, it could be argued, allegedly put temptation in their way, and his businessman client who had the means to provide such temptation, even if he had not viewed the offering of such temptation as a bribe, or, those to whom it had been offered, had accepted it as a bribe.

For a variety of reasons, the then Government failed. As a result, it cast around for other villains – such as commercial lobbyists – who were blamed for creating the market that 'tempted' politicians in the first place (not true) and exploiting the market in the second (true). In addition, it also blamed the Press for misrepresenting the facts (often true) and using the story to deliberately distract the public's attention from what it considered to be the main issues of the General Election (certainly true).

At no stage did the Government accept any blame of itself, nor was it prepared to recognise that individuals do not corrupt Parliament by putting temptation in the way of the greedy unless Government or Parliament itself is somewhere at fault. This conclusion was indirectly supported by Lord Justice Nolan, the senior judge subsequently invited to inquire into and report on misconduct in public life. In other words, Parliament and Politician stood condemned rather than the 'outsiders'.

A Symptom not a Cause

Informed and disinterested political observers have generally recognised that the Al-Fayed/Greer/Hamilton/Smith affair was a problem waiting to happen. In the same way, although for different reasons, 'Cronygate' could similarly have been anticipated.

In the case of the former, this was because the Conservative Party, and therefore Parliament which, by virtue of its large majority it controlled, had, throughout its long years of uninterrupted office, steadfastly refused to unravel the growing number of relationships between public servants and 'outsiders'. The reasons it had not done so were due, in equal measure, to lassitude and moral cowardice. After all, no-one knew where the 'unravelling' might end. The system had operated like that for generations, so why, they successfully argued, risk opening up a can of worms? Instead, it relied on the Political SCALPS to maintain good order.

The Political SCALPS

Parliament's business managers are known collectively by the antiquated title of 'The Whips' or, in some circumstances, 'the Usual Channels'. A more appropriate and up-to-date style (though completely unofficial) would be Political SCALPS for one party or another. The primary duty of all SCALPS is to maintain discipline, and, if need be, to criticise savagely.

The SCALPS below refer to those from the Conservative Party (the Conservatives were in office at the time of the 'Cash for Questions' affair) although they could apply equally to the Labour Party at that time.

The junior SCALPS **S**niff around Westminster; identifying **C**anoodlers and the **A**wkward squad; **L**iase upwards in order to **P**re-empt problems; and, if possible, **S**mooth over any problems.

If this fails, the intermediate SCALPS take over. These **S**equester some hapless individual, who may or may not be innocent, and question him closely; identify the **C**ross-fire; organise, if necessary, the **A**mbush; **L**urk around for further trouble; determine additional **P**rey; and, if they can, **S**quelch.

If this also fails, the senior SCALPS take over, usually led by the Chief Whip. If the problem is large enough, any number of unofficial senior SCALPS are also called upon to assist – many of them not necessarily MPs but important people in the victim's life.

The senior SCALPS have two functions. On the one hand they seek to **S**afeguard the **C**abinet by identifying possible **A**ttackers; **L**imit the dangers they pose by offering **P**atronage or, more commonly, attempting to **S**abotage. On the other hand, they also police Westminster by **S**haming the **C**ads, **A**dvising **L**osers, and deciding whether or not to **P**rotect or **S**acrifice them.

In effect, the Political SCALPS regulate Parliament.

Self-regulation i.e. internal policing is common practice in many walks of business life. For example, major banks do not always alert the police if they detect internal fraud even though a criminal offence has been committed and it is a criminal offence not to report such misdemeanour. For a variety of reasons (some cynical) they prefer to identify culprits themselves, who are then slung out, although not always prosecuted. That, in theory, is also the function of the Political SCALPS.

However, in the 'Cash for Questions' affair, and other examples, the SCALPS, despite having all the necessary information, failed to do their duty. They were specifically informed by senior members of the commercial lobbying fraternity of:

- The financial relationship existent between one or two commercial lobbyists and several politicians.
- The alleged conduct of an officer of the Conservative Backbench Trade and Industry Committee, who is said to have received 'introduction' fees from Mr Greer and was therefore perceived as being diligent in promoting Mr Greer's lobbying company at the expense of those commercial lobbyists who refused to pay 'introduction' fees and who in consequence allegedly found their clients unlikely to be called before the Committee (see footnote below).
- The acceptance and demand for free airline tickets by countless politicians, offered by British Airways, a client of Mr Greer.

The commercial lobbyists who complained to the Political SCALPS received short shrift. Their criticisms were regarded as an assault on the proprieties of Westminster and, accordingly, the guardians of Westminster spat back reminding them that the commercial lobbyists themselves were there on sufferance.

Next, the commercial lobbyists took their complaints to members of the Select Committee on Members' Interests. Again their criticisms were stone-walled.

This had the effect of denying the strict codes of conduct that some commercial lobbyists were seeking to enforce, encouraging sharp practice and offering no encouragement to the well-behaved. Any commercial lobbyist persisting in his accusations could have damaged his career by being frozen out of Westminster.

The commercial lobbyists also advised some members of the Press (not for nothing are they known as the Nation's Fourth Estate) of their anxieties, some of which were investigated. For the most part, however, the Press (who are considered in greater detail later in the book) also offered no welcome, preferring instead to follow their own agenda. This was for three reasons:

- The Press were generally hostile to the commercial lobbyists, and therefore, despite happily devouring the stories lobbyists fed them on behalf of their clients, not anxious to be seen to be assisting them. That is to say, they denied the legitimacy of commercial lobbying because they did not like many of the commercial lobbyists, and despite the fact that a senior commercial lobbyist had strong links with them and was personally respected by them. In denying the industry's existence, it refused to offer nourishment to good commercial lobbying practice.
- The operation of the lobby system meant that some members of the Press were not always as assiduous as they could have been about rocking the boat.
- With rare exceptions, the Press allow no criticism of themselves. To have covered the complaints of the commercial lobbyists, some of these would have been implicit.

As a result, the Political SCALPS were able to get away with doing nothing. Meanwhile, Ian Greer (and several others) continued to pay 'introduction fees', and some of the commercial lobbyists continued to complain.

Closing Ranks

Political life is a sophisticated world and the Parliaments of most countries are sophisticated 'companies' run by worldly people. The UK Parliament, however, as an institution, is too insular to be worldly – although many individuals within it are – and its officers, including the Political SCALPS, are seldom good for anything other than the closing of ranks.

Closing ranks is awkward, however, when a commercial lobbyist, in this case, Ian Greer, has hitherto had a symbiotic relationship with the Conservatives and for one reason or another, none of which were criminal, has found himself in trouble and all over the newspapers.

It is even more awkward because, although in the past every attempt has been made to deny the importance of the commercial lobbyist, Mr Greer's career proves exactly the opposite.

The SCALPS found they could not contain the problem. As a result any number of people and institutions ended up with egg on their faces. These included:

- some politicians who had made a life for themselves ingratiating themselves with commercial lobbyists;

- some politicians who had written books about "influencing Parliament" and, in order to maintain their own authority, or, in some cases, their own lucrative sidelines outside of those opportunities provided to them by some commercial lobbyists, had omitted to mention the commercial lobbyists;
- some academics who had built their careers claiming that commercial lobbyists were ineffectual, some of whom were commercially funded and/or locked into Think Tanks;

and

- some journalists who had assumed that the commercial lobbyist was democracy's demon and needed to be stamped out, without mentioning the close relationship between some journalists and some editors and some of the commercial lobbyist's clients, let alone the requirement to toe the politicians' line by some journalists who did not wish to fall foul of the lobby system.

With the scandal exploding all over the place, the political moralists had a field day.

At the same time, the commercial lobbyists were left utterly bewildered by both the hysteria and humbug that distinguishes the pious everywhere. As the entire media ranged against them, it seemed as if everyone was trying to have things both ways. On the one hand people were at best seeking to deny that commercial lobbyists had any influence. At worst they were claiming that they were ineffectual.

On the other hand, they were being told that they were responsible for all democracy's ills and therefore did have influence and were not ineffectual.

The truth of course, like so many truths, was somewhere in between. Commercial lobbying can influence and can get results although Mr Al Fayed may argue to the contrary. The scandal is that the vast majority of the public were unaware of commercial lobbyists and their long history, far less their involvement with some politicians.

That was not, and has never been, the fault of commercial lobbyists nor does it deny the industry's legitimate role within the political process. Doubts however remain because some Parliamentary conditions, with or without commercial lobbyists, can favour corruption, even if, for the most part, the system is remarkably corruption free.

What is corruption?

After two decades of centrism, the Constitution has become radically unbalanced. Intermediary institutions have been almost terminally weakened. Local government is now barely worth its name. Serious problems have arisen because of conflicts between public duties and private interests and public bodies, their members, patronage and quangos. These have all contributed to growing anxieties about corruption in the UK. Parallel with this is awareness of lesser evils such as slackness and ethical lassitude.

For example, many consider it 'immoral' for hereditary peers to draw a 'salary', or daily allowance merely for turning up in the House of Lords, paid for by the tax-payer, when they perform no public duties. Many consider it equally immoral for hereditary and non-hereditary peers to draw a 'salary' paid for by the tax-payer once they have retired from public life and are already in receipt of a pension also provided by the tax-payer. As unemployment/retirement clubs go, the House of Lords is surely among the cushiest – one reason, no doubt, why reform of the Upper House is at long last on the agenda.

Many others consider it immoral to hire out Parliamentary catering facilities to some outside bodies who may know a sympathetic MP or Peer, and deny it to others, equally or more worthy, who do not have the same contacts book. Others consider the practice of up-grading a public servant's rank (from Brigadiers to diplomats) immediately prior to retirement so that the tax-payer will provide him with a higher pension, equally immoral. Others again find the remuneration and other benefits offered to MEPs and Euro bureaucrats unacceptable. The list is endless. These examples contribute to the public's perception of a gravy train, even if the instances are not themselves always corrupt, if ever.

More crucially, corruption is fostered by general economic weakness and low public sector salaries. The tax-payer, however, has little sympathy for the latter for two reasons. First of all because in their view senior public servants are, for the most part, well paid. Secondly, if others in the private sector are overpaid, it is hardly an excuse for the tax-payer to over-pay his public servant so that he avoids the temptation of putting his nose in the trough.

In addition, corruption is fostered by feeble political institutions, excessive use of patronage, nepotism, secrecy and lack of accountability – all of which have applied at some stage or other to the UK.

Commercial Lobbyists Rebuffed

To combat Parliament's manifest inadequacies, the commercial lobbying industry, representing outsiders relevant to the country's economic and social interests, offered on numerous occasions to improve the situation by making formal presentations to Westminster, as long as it was, in return, offered either transparent facilities or a seat at the debating table in recognition of its work in widening access to Westminster, and, more recently, the EU. The offer was consistently rebuffed.

To ensure that the commercial lobbyists were kept out, the Political SCALPS ignored those commercial lobbyists wishing to improve matters. They were joined in their efforts by the Civil Servants running Westminster. These, despite many of their claims, in practice can appear to dislike the public, let alone commercial lobbyists who were often representing various collective 'publics' whom they equally disliked.

Those commercial lobbyists who persisted in their criticisms could have faced professional ruin. In addition, they were forced to accept a variety of insults, such as:

— commercial lobbyists were exposing the political system, opening doors to countless numbers, therefore making it more accessible to the corrupt and/or corrupt practice (i.e. the increasing demands on democracy as well as commercial lobbyists were responsible for corruption)
— Those piling in were the 'wrong sort', a class-based judgement and an astonishing excuse to keep the 'toffs' who, apparently, were less corrupt since they spoke 'better'
— Not only were those piling in the 'wrong sort' but they were also encouraging a less deferential attitude to Parliament. Meaning that, deference, apparently, protected Parliament from corruption!

At no time did the SCALPS recognise that the main reason that corruption flourishes is if there are no means of catching up with the culprit. Or that correcting such faults can take years.

Commander Christopher Powell RN

The most distinguished offer of assistance came from the father of the modern commercial lobbying industry, the late Lt.Cdr. Christopher Powell RN. Powell, much against the wishes of the Political SCALPS, specialised in taking Private Members' Bills to Statute, outside the Private Members' Ballot, for modest commercial fee. The Parliamentarians in whose name the Bills were piloted were unpaid and indeed would have been insulted had they been offered payment, which they were not.

Anxious what the public would say if they heard about Powell's work, the SCALPS forced him to carry out his business in conditions of secrecy and subterfuge. His colleagues in the lobbying industry, meanwhile, were warned about his behaviour and the dire consequences of him 'bringing things tumbling down'.

These neurosis were in marked contrast to the demeanour of Parliamentarians (from both the major parties) with whom Powell worked, who were generous in their praise of him and embarrassed at being forced into taking credit for his work. They were horrified that the SCALPS were only (just) stopping short of intimidation, which they extended to a young female member of Powell's staff (the author) who was his assistant in the 1980s.

What were the Political SCALPS so afraid of?

Three things.

Powell's skills, if they had become known to the wider public, would have shown the public what was available, at what price (substantially cheaper than hiring a politician) and to whom and why; and, as importantly, proved to the public what they were missing, why, and what their own public servants were frequently incapable of delivering.

For this reason, Powell was never allowed to advertise his services. All his clients – including charities and small trade bodies – came to him by word of mouth. Such was the conspiracy to deny his work that even the fulsome obituaries in the newspapers following his death made no mention of his principal achievement i.e. the body of technical, social, and charitable Bills he drafted and saw to Statute. Obituaries in national newspapers often lie!

Who Else Was Responsible?

Commercial lobbyists cannot exist in the political world and not be aware of its excesses. It is an urbane world and all those in it – politician, Civil Servant, journalist, client and commercial lobbyist – usually know what is going on. All five know that there are various levels of proof and that grey areas need to be looked into.

In the 'Cash for Questions' affair, all were aware that there were various office holders, notably the SCALPS, who could have intervened, or followed up rumours of alleged wrong-doing once, however informally, these had been reported. As has already been explained, this did not happen.

However, it is not merely the Political SCALPS who were to blame.

The Public

For any number of reasons, the public as a whole is indirectly to blame for what happened principally because of its disinterest, complacency and ignorance in both the political process and public affairs. This is in part because the political process deliberately excludes them, and in part because the Media refuses to empower them.

In greater part, however, it is because the public itself is passive unless that which it perceives to be in its own immediate interests are directly involved. That is to say, selfishness, and individualism, is the norm. As a result, it has allowed some politicians and public servants get away with far too much.

Large numbers of professionals, who claim they 'have no time' for civic responsibilities (e.g. jury service), find the time to run their residents associations if in doing so they can maintain the value of their properties. They could equally well turn their attention to the political world if they were so minded or public spirited and if the media and political process encouraged them to do so.

In truth, of course, neither public servant nor media has wanted the public involved in politics – and many members of the public have willingly complied with such exclusion.

In addition, the public has a tendency to lean towards smugness – corruption is what happens to foreigners who, the argument goes, have a lower threshold than the British to such things, or cynicism – for example, local councils are run by the corrupt and the stupid and nothing can be done about them. Neither arguments are true – corruption hurts everybody and is no respecter of nationality or community. Moreover something can be done about them, with the assistance of an investigative press (bring back local government correspondents and specialist reporters!), a vigorous judiciary, and modernised political selection procedures and criteria, if there is a collective will to do so.

The public, therefore, who, for whatever reason have opted out, are as much to blame for their tolerance of a political system that can be corrupt, as they are for any ignorance of such system or corruption in the first place. Taking a politician 'on trust' is an honourable, considered and active decision if it is made with a knowledge of the political system's indefensible limitations.

The Press

As already indicated, the Press is considered in greater detail elsewhere in the book. However, in so far as the 'Cash for Questions' affair is concerned, there are some 'truths' which must be addressed. The first is that, for the most part, the Press as a whole has had a narrow and even distorted perception of commercial lobbying. As a result, and taken as a whole, they have closed their minds to whistle-blowers from the commercial lobbying community, doubting their integrity and treating them, their work, and their industry, with intellectual contempt and outright hostility.

As a result they have not collectively tackled the problem at source i.e. by shaming the Political SCALPS for not policing the system.

This was for three reasons. Firstly, because of the operation of the Lobby system. Secondly because of the conduct of some of their number, and thirdly because, for the most part, their sole interest has been in sensationalist media exposes. From these they have built up arguments based on particular instances, such as the 'Cash for Questions' affair, by which time it has been too late to prevent enormous damage, not least the employment prospects of innocent employees.

Meanwhile, those commercial lobbyists the Press were prepared to meet, were always anxious that, in their exuberance to tell a sensationalist story, the press would get some of their facts wrong thus leaving the lobbyist legally liable or subjecting private people to unwanted media attention.

The Commercial Lobbyists

The peers of any industry or profession are always responsible for the standards, ethics and good conduct of their industry and those who work in it. For a variety of reasons, few of which do the commercial lobbying industry any justice, the failure of the senior political SERFS and KIPPERS (i.e. senior commercial lobbyists) to put an end to the conduct and practices of some of their number, meant that they failed in their responsibilities. Had they done so, the 'Cronygate' cash for access affair could have been avoided, or, could have been more effectively landed at Government's door, rather than that of the industry.

Instead they let down the public, the industry itself and a whole generation of young political SERFS already in the industry or those tempted to try a career in it.

Foreign Businessmen and the Implications for the Foreign Business Community

Throughout the 'Cash for Questions' scandal, the views of the foreign business community resident in this country were either ignored or insulted. Therefore, before looking specifically at Mr Al Fayed, it is important to make some general observations.

Firstly, that a largely hostile press makes no allowance for the fact that all outsiders, irrespective of nationality or wealth, learn how the British system operates from insiders and the company they keep.

Secondly that many 'outsiders' rightly consider they 'belong', even though they are not Anglo–Saxon (i.e. white), because of the many years they have lived in and contributed to the country, even though the press not only does not recognise them but appears to deliberately ignore their cultural existence. As a result the Press either have no knowledge of, nor respect for, the cultures and cultural backgrounds of many who live in this country.

Thirdly, that many in the foreign business community were hurt by some of the comments in the national press during the 'Cash for Questions' affair. For example, a Japanese businessman, interviewed before the collapse of the Japanese economy, and who did not wish to be named, told the author:

'What happened to Mr Al Fayed shattered many of us. We have been employing commercial lobbyists both in the UK and in the European Commission for years. We have always been assured that this was the British way. Moreover, if we were asked to assist a British politician financially, and thought him good value, we would do so. Firstly, it is good manners to help your friends. Secondly, it is good business – a combination that the Japanese like.

'However, we would never do so if we thought it against the law – and those who advise us assure us that it is not. We are very sensitive about such matters and are always anxious not to offend our host countries. Now, because of what happened to Mr Al Fayed, we do not know what to do.

'What did he do that was so wrong? He wanted British nationality, like thousands before him who have not made the contribution to the country that he has made. As for this business in Parliament, we do not believe that he bribed British politicians even if he has been forced to say that he has. Most foreign businessmen have, at some time or other, 'paid' a British politician for advice both at Westminster and in the European Parliament. If Mr Al Fayed was in the wrong then so is the entire foreign business community as well as half the Conservative Party.

'Actually, the feeling amongst my colleagues is that there was another agenda, where Mr Al Fayed was concerned. They feel he was probably an unknowing victim of a branch of British intelligence. Which is probably why, as a rule, the Japanese stay clear of intelligence agencies, especially the CIA and MI6. We don't want to get involved.

'The problem for Mr Al Fayed is that no Establishment strand in this country is self-standing – each one supports the other. Then along comes Mr Al Fayed and explodes the hypocrisy of it all – something that many (British) people would have liked to have done if they had had his money.

'If he is still hanging in there it is because many believe him, including some of the establishment. The result is that several British worlds are in conflict with each other, not least Government's awareness that to insult Mr Al Fayed is to insult the Arab world.'

The same Japanese businessman continued:

'The British press have also not helped, acting as they have as a branch of the Establishment. They are deeply prejudiced against 'wogs' (Arabs or Japanese!) and that, despite the fact that someone like Mr Al Fayed' has been here thirty years, feels British and has British children. He is very hurt.

'I can't speak for that but I do know that the British Press offers the foreign business community no welcome. The public feeds on these prejudices. Yes, we are in business in this country to make money and maximise profits. But we did not invade – we were invited to make money here by Mrs Thatcher. Besides, there is something in it for your country and your citizens too.

'Why don't the Press point this out instead of constantly harking back to what the "Japs" did in the last war? I don't remember the War and I resent being held responsible for events that occurred nearly fifty years ago. I resent even more being told that because business in Japan is corrupt, we "corrupt your politicians" when we are scrupulous in taking advice on such issues, and try to ensure that our Japanese colleagues also over here are the same. It is as if it is only the "foreigner" who behaves badly – when the reality is that there are more Britons in jails overseas than there are Japanese!

'The treatment of Mr Al Fayed has left us nervous. In view of his close friendship with the Egyptian Ambassador to London, we reckon the matter must have been taken up at diplomatic level too. That makes all the Embassies nervous. As a rule, Embassies try to stay out of the limelight. But they would not have done so on an issue like this when one of their prominent nationals was involved which means that the Court of St James' has been involved too.

'And why? Because the xenophobic British press has hit upon three phobias – two of which we did not even know were phobias because no-one, least of all our British friends, told us they were phobias. This is the melding of British politicians with foreign businessmen and commercial lobbyists. But that's the way things are – and, more importantly, that's the way the British created the system. It was not the other way around. If there is criticism, it must be criticism of yourselves.'

There are some home truths there which we may deny but which are true nonetheless. Unless we recognise our own culpability, and take responsibility for it, not only will problems remain but new ones will be added.

This is because London is a magnet for many foreign businessmen who make their homes here. Historically, those businessmen who are of a certain age (post 55) learned about the UK because part of their education had been undertaken in Britain; because they may have been educated by the British Council in their countries of origin (and are invariably shocked to find that educational standards in Britain are often lower than those in their own country); or because they have grown up with the BBC World Service on the radio. Such lessons they glue onto their own cultures.

In addition, some have also learned about the UK through their professional advisers (e.g. lawyers and accountants) or the service industries they employ (e.g. advertisers/public relations companies).

Others, again especially the over-55s, have learned about the UK through the behaviour of :

– British businessmen overseas
– British diplomats and officials
– Visiting British dignitaries (including Royals)
– Visiting British politicians on private visits or those arranged by Select Committees and All Party Groups
– British commercial lobbyists, sometimes, although not always, accompanied by politicians
– British businessmen and politicians met on the cocktail party circuit in London, sometimes under the auspices of chambers of commerce or All Party Groups at Westminster.

All the above, in one way or another, were stuck in a time warp. They reinforced a dated British cocoon of self belief and, frequently dazzled or amused the foreigner with the bureaucracy and paraphernalia of a bygone age. Subsequently, an extra heady mix was added – the deliberate targeting of some foreigners for political party donations.

The older generation of the foreign business community, therefore, learned their conduct from the then ruling elites of this country. As a result, they absorbed the system they believed existed. In addition, they had a view of Britain, and the officials that run the country, that for one reason or another the British citizen did not have.

They witnessed the conduct of British diplomat; they witnessed the behaviour of British politicians; they witnessed the practices of British businessmen. Some of these were hardly role models.

Many were on a gravy train and parasitical in their 'requests' for hospitality, contracts, contacts or money. Many others thrust wives and daughters forward for jewels or other gifts. The foreign business community were encouraged to believe that this was the norm. They learned what they had good reason to believe was the British system from 'insiders'.

Complaints were often made, notably to some British ambassadors overseas. Some of these tried to wage a bitter campaign against Westminster based politicians, making it clear that there was no need for national or foreign businessmen to hire them since the service they were apparently offering was available free of charge at the Embassies.

They were unsuccessful for a variety of reasons including the fact that, unlike the politician, they were not elected (something the dodgy politician is always keen to point out) and therefore not in a position to dictate to the politician; and because of their own lack of standing or knowledge of the commercial world.

The author's father, Lawrence de Souza, who died in 1986, a foreign born British businessman decorated by this country, gave a graphic description of former public servants, throwing themselves, and being thrown, in his direction, in the 1970s.

'I could not believe what was going on. They were absolutely shameless in their demands and convinced of their own superiority. It was shocking. It was as if I was expected to fund their retirement, by providing them with so-called employment, in exchange for which I would receive certain benefits. I was expected to feel gratitude that they had noticed me – not least because of the colour of my skin, and my country of origin.

'I did not employ them, firstly, because I am proud of the colour of my skin; secondly because I regarded them as parasites, thirdly because I had worked for my money, and fourthly because I resented the pressure (some of which was Masonic – I am a freemason) under which I was placed. I have no idea whether my business career would have prospered further if I had given in. I know that my Masonic network was diminished.

'So far as Westminster was concerned, I was offered no informed help, although I asked for it. Up until my first dealings with politicians I had always believed that the British MP was corruption free. Now I was coming up against politicians wanting commissions! It was, I was assured, perfectly normal.

'Maybe it was, maybe it wasn't. I only know that there was no-one around to explain the limits of the relationship, help me determine whether I was being taken for a ride and crucially, help me to work out whether or not I would get value for money if I employed any of them. One of the arguments they gave me in favour of employing them, I remember, was because the Press was so hostile to businessmen such as myself. In those days all wogs began at Calais – and dark-skinned wogs were the worst of all! Politicians used this as a reason why we should appoint them to help with our businesses – rather than calling in the editors of newspapers to clean up the racism. Quite apart from anything else, such racism was losing British companies foreign contracts.

'I was not alone in my criticisms. Any number of other foreign businessmen were complaining about it – although we had no-one to complain to, except to each other. We had certainly not heard of commercial lobbyists – had I known of such people, I can certainly see myself employing one of them, if for nothing else to help me pick my way through the British system which in reality works very differently to the way we are told, or the country's citizens believe.

'Without such buffers, we were on our own. We felt that politicians were foisting themselves on us – especially at cocktail parties hosted by various Chambers of Commerce and Westminster Groups – when we had no way of judging either their knowledge or influence, let alone whether the relationship was legal – and all this while the Press were implying we (because we were foreign) were the crooks.

'There were also the gripes of those who could not afford to pay them, and thus saw contracts going to those who could. Then came the rumours about a businessman who had complained – only to find himself blacklisted and rubbished in Parliament by the very politician he had complained about. Apparently, the politician was protected by Parliamentary privilege and could say what he liked!

'We were acutely aware that, as foreigners, we had no rights and that, if a problem arose, we would get dumped with a not necessarily fair judiciary and press joining in the dumping. Prejudice is such that the public always believe that, but for the foreigners, there would be no scandal. As a result, I always took the view never to employ a British public servant if I could possibly avoid it. On the other hand, I gave countless valuable gifts – it was expected of me and, culturally, I found it very difficult to say no.

'One way of assisting the foreign businessman would have been a formal Parliamentary Statement, which both businessman and public servant would have been required to sign under formal conditions, clearly setting out both sides' obligations under the law. In effect, a 'public health warning'.

'I do not for one moment think that this will ever happen.

'The British public servant likes to think himself a 'gentleman' and therefore above such statements. Besides, Government itself does not want to spell things out in black and white since this does not always work in Government's favour.'

Mohammed Al Fayed

The foreign businessman at the centre of the 'Cash for Questions' affair was Egyptian born Mohammed Al Fayed. Over a long period of years, Mr Al Fayed had come to believe that the Conservative Government had insulted him, had failed to appreciate what he had given to the country in terms of employment and substantial charitable donations and had denied both him and his brothers citizenship although their children were British. In addition, he had had an on-going disagreement with a rival businessman over the purchase of a London department store.

By his own admission, he made payments and offered hospitality to MPs. But such hospitality must be seen in the context of the hospitality that he kindly offered to countless others who were by no means powerful or important people. For anyone who knows the Middle East, this is very much in keeping with conduct in the Arab world where there is a culture of generosity, which behoves a rich man to pay for a poor man, especially if he considers him to be his friend.

Only cynics and those who do not understand or, more importantly, do not respect the Arab culture, could twist such conduct into something other than it was. Mr Al Fayed believed that the politicians to whom he had been introduced were indeed his friends, as a result, in keeping with his culture, he was generous. Moreover, some of those from the wholly British world in which he moved, allegedly assured him that it was not inappropriate to be so, although only the principals know the extent of the hospitality and what each believed to be the courtesies expected in the giving and accepting of such hospitality.

35

In addition, some of his British intimates also encouraged him to employ a commercial lobbyist. Regrettably, however, neither some of his friends, nor the commercial lobbyist, appeared to recognise what was widely understood to be one of Mr Al Fayed's major character flaws – i.e. an inability to be kept on a tight rein. In powerful men such a flaw is not uncommon.

Since Mr Al Fayed's character was well-known, arguably such a need could have been anticipated, if those surrounding him had been able to thwart it and if the commercial lobbyist had been both kept at the centre of events and strong enough to enforce it. This was all the more important because, as a foreigner, Mr Al Fayed would not have had an instinctive notion of how far he could go and when to draw back – not least because English was not his first language. Nor was the extent of the hospitality he was providing known to all – hospitality he allegedly eventually came to consider to be poor value.

In due course, some would say naively, he turned to a newspaper to air his complaints. Since then he has been blamed for:

– the collapse the Conservative Government (and incidentally destroying the good name of Parliament);
– bringing down the system; and
– bringing in a senior member of the Judiciary (Nolan) to report upon standards in public life,

in much the same way as a then twenty eight year old carried the can for bringing down Barings Bank. (It should be made clear that, unlike the Barings Bank case, there is no suggestion of criminal wrong-doing by Mr Al Fayed. The comparison is used merely to point out the absurdity of heaping blame on a single individual.)

All could have been avoided if the Political SCALPS had been doing their job in the first place. Instead, and to draw fire away from themselves, they failed to police their own and allowed opprobrium to be poured on the outsiders.

Mr Al Fayed was one of them. The other was commercial lobbyist Ian Greer. Both men were soft targets: Mr Al Fayed because he is a controversial figure, and because there exists in this country a subliminal deep loathing for all that is Arab, including a distaste for Islam. Mr Greer, a long-standing Conservative supporter, because of, at that time, an increasing loathing for both the Conservative Party and the commercial lobbying industry which had flourished under it and which he in many ways came to personify.

Ian Greer

Mr Greer's career flourished for several reasons, not least because Tory Government lasted nearly two decades. Having been a Party worker, he knew most of the mainstays of both the Thatcher and Major Administrations and had been a loyal, sincere and devoted friend of the party since his youth. Because of the longevity of Tory rule, his position as lobbyist-in-chief was unassailable. Unlike most commercial lobbyists, he was an 'insider' – until he became an embarrassment.

In his defence it should be noted that he says in his book *'One Man's Word'* that he reported his anxieties about the conduct of several Parliamentarians whom, out of loyalty, he refused to name, to the Chief SCALP. However, this went nowhere since he refused to name names.

His insider status, meanwhile, made him several enemies in the commercial lobbying world – in the same way as post May 1997 insiders i.e. New Labour Lobbyists, attracted the same jealousy, and the same crowing when they were embarrassed. In the case of Mr Greer, however, many believed, and still do, that he let the industry down before the 'Cash for Questions' episode catapulted him into the headlines.

Criticisms of him included:

– His close identification with the Conservative Party – in the same way as 'Cronygate' is identified with New Labour – which swung the industry away from its traditional position of political non-alignment.

(It is interesting to note that since the Labour Party secured office, many ex-Tory MPs seeking to set themselves up as lobbyists are self interestedly trying hard to turn the industry back to its previously non-aligned position. They are right to do so albeit for the wrong reasons. This has received extra impetus following 'Cronygate'. Moreover, during the last twenty years any number of the industry's clients have deliberately developed their in-house departments to avoid identification with the governing Party of the day.)

– His alleged lack of procedural knowledge and predilection for 'hospitality' lobbying.

This is often the case when much of your business has been built on the basis of the 'contacts' you know – New Labour Lobbyists did not event 'cronyism'. Since, however, throughout the 1980s and, courtesy of 'Cronygate', as we now know, well into the 1990s, the key to some ministerial doorways was what some lobbying was undeniably all about,

Mr Greer – and New Labour Lobbyists subsequently – can hardly be blamed for trying to use that key; nor can they be blamed if the key worked. It is up to Government to get its links with outsiders sorted out, not the reverse. More particularly, it is up to Government to come clean about what it wants from the industry's clients – money – and what it is prepared to give in return.

In Mr Greer's case, however, his reliance on his contacts, coincided with some moves in the industry as a whole to get away from commercial lobbying's image of offering no more than cocktail party skills and hospitality, or, in the case of both Mr Greer and New Labour Lobbyists, acting as a political dating agency. However, in view of the large numbers of inexperienced New Labour youngsters offered jobs in commercial lobbying immediately after May 1997 the hypocrisies are apparent.

It also coincided with the belief held by some journalists that targeting lobbyists – appropriate during 'Cronygate' as well – would eventually secure a bigger prize.

– His relationship with various politicians, in particular with a Tory backbencher who chaired a backbench committee. (See footnote 1)
– His clients, one of whom, whether or not Greer approved or encouraged, offered free airflights to a large number of politicians.

Ian Greer himself has since explained this retrospectively as being part of the 'excesses of the 1980s' – air flights being no different to the corporate hospitality offered by many commercial lobbyists on behalf of their clients at venues such as Glyndebourne, Ascot and Wimbledon. All of course who offered such hospitality penalised those not in a position to offer it.

– His alleged decision to act for the Serbian Government, which, if true, it is understood, he did not reveal to his employees.

In his defence it should be made clear that as owner of his company, Mr Greer was under no legal obligation to reveal the alleged client to his staff. In addition, it should be noted that former public servants are similarly involved in Serbia through post-retirement employment with an international bank. While many might find such involvement distasteful, it is not against the law.

– His homosexuality.

This has always been an issue in the commercial lobbying industry although the industry itself is far from homophobic. Some of the prejudice is due to the industry's earlier image when some commercial lobbyists and public relations consultants (but assuredly not Mr Greer) were rumoured to have procured young people (of both sexes) for their clients.

In so far as Mr Greer is concerned, it is a matter of record that he has lived a blameless, discreet private life with his male companion. Moreover, it is important to point out that he displayed remarkable courage in being open about his homosexuality at a time when many gays, in both public affairs and public service, were closeted.

For the reasons described above, few if any commercial lobbyists came forward to defend him when his career collapsed, although 'There but for the grace of God' must have been a thought that passed through the minds of some of his competitors. Many of these seemed not only to glory in his demise but could hardly wait to gorge themselves on the bones of his ailing company. Within a few hours of it going into liquidation other consultancies were on the 'phone to his clients selling their wares. It was like vultures feeding on a carcass.

He paid a terrible price for a man who had committed no criminal offence. His company disintegrated. His staff, whom he idolised, either deserted him or were forced to move on. Old friends, some of them politicians, dropped him – neatly forgetting that over the years they had done very nicely out of him. In addition, his private life was shredded by a homophobic press.

But was Greer – and, subsequently, those involved in 'Cronygate' – so much to blame? In the case of Mr Greer, what he did was show the public the excesses of political life. He confirmed what they had always believed anyway – that politicians are on the make. He exposed the fact privilege creates its own morality.

It is true to say, however, that as a man of age and experience, Ian Greer should have known how far he could/could not go and resisted going beyond the point that is acceptable.

So, could the Greer scandal, and subsequently, 'Cronygate', have been avoided? The answer is a categorical 'yes'.

House of Commons Select Committee on Members' Interests

Prior to the Greer affair, and, as has been shown, policing the House of Commons was one of the duties of the Political SCALPS. In theory they were assisted in this task by the now defunct House of Commons Select Committee on Members' Interests, a minor committee set up in the 1970s to inquire into the business interests of Members of the House of Commons. Its remit was subsequently extended to include the commercial lobbyists and All Party Groups. See Footnote 2.

This sort of scrutiny and response to public disquiet was not new – a House of Lords Committee had tried before but, as an unelected body, had watched its reports gather dust – and, like every single previous Committee inquiring into lobbying, its conclusions resulted in either failure or cover-up.

Its principal problem was the intellectual competence of some of its members, as well as the fact that some who sat on it had substantial business interests of their own and were therefore not disinterested parties in the outcome of any decisions or recommendations made. As a result, its reports (usually minority) were as bland as they were banal.

For the most part, the Press played into their hands by ignoring them. Here it should be said that the majority of the Select Committees lack sufficient forensic skills and, for various reasons, are unable to comprehend the complicated nature of modern life. This, as much as anything, is the reason why many are demanding outside and independent scrutiny committees. As a result, and in order to claw back some authority and establish reputations, some select committees are today dictating a faster and more modern agenda, no doubt hoping to imitate the clout of US Congressional committees. As a result they are belatedly attracting some worthwhile press attention. This, however, was not the case with the Members Interests Select Committee.

Although the Committee's composition was not always of the highest calibre, an exception was one of its number, the late Bob Cryer MP (see 'Product Policing'). Cryer, who died in a car crash in 1994, was the scourge of commercial lobbying throughout his years of public service. A former Labour Minister and MEP, he was scrupulously even-handed in his condemnation of both Labour and Conservative MPs who had outside business interests, and assiduous in his campaign against commercial lobbyists.

In this task he had the backing of many in the then Labour Party, although today Labour's official position, (somewhat to its recent embarrassment), has shifted in the direction of tacit approval, if not outright acceptance of commercial lobbyists.

Despite Bob Cryer's efforts, the Committee went nowhere. This was because it was anxious not to unravel the relationship between politician and outsider. Firstly because many had a financial interest not to do so. And secondly because the unpicking of such employment practice meant a journey that would lead towards electoral reform and reform of government, which in itself meant to question the nature of representation, the role of government and how it is elected in the first place.

This was not a journey on which the Committee was prepared to embark, even though it was in the public interest for them to do so. Nor, in fairness to the Committee, did it receive any encouragement to do so from the Political SCALPS.

Instead, and in order to be seen to be doing 'something', it spotlighted the activities of some MPs (but not members of the House of Lords, Civil Service or Special Advisers who were deliberately left outside their remit) and tried to attack easy outsiders – commercial lobbyists. i.e. it tried to ring-fence problems in order to draw fire away from the wider problems.

For a while, ring-fencing worked. It always does in a deferential society, most particularly when some members of the Press sustain such society for a variety of reasons, not always honourable. But, in targeting the lobbyists it soon became apparent that this would also set off the chain reaction it was so desperate to avoid. Instead of being honest and establishing, for example, a Royal Commission on Democracy, which was what was needed, the Committee declared an uneasy truce. This bought them time but little else. The 'Cash for Questions' episode, or something like it, was by now almost inevitable.

It is impossible to escape the conclusion that, because of the business interests of some, the Committee found it awkward to sit in judgement on the business interests of others. As a result, the Committee:

– denied its responsibilities to the citizen;
– absolved itself from regulation of the Parliamentary product and the political market;
– denied its responsibilities to the market's clients (the citizen as well as fee-paying interests);
– refused to determine the limits of contact/access with government or representative of government
– refused to take a lead or provide a role model on ethical practice; and
– refused to protect the staff who worked in the industry.

Had it done even a modicum of the above, the 'Cash for Questions' scandal could have been avoided. And, arguably, also 'Cronygate'.

Instead, the Committee left the clients of the commercial lobbying market unprotected by even basic consumer protection (even rich men and their companies are entitled to this). It failed to make clear what access could be anti-democratic, if only because it allowed some to 'jump the queue', even if, once access had been secured, queue jumpers had no influence. And it made no acknowledgement that the public had a right to expect a certain standard of conduct from both those elected to or appointed on their behalf to serve them; and clients and staff working in a wholly private sector unregulated business require protection and product monitoring until the market is demolished at source – an unlikely eventuality.

Neither the Committee nor the Political SCALPS could bring themselves to accept the truth – that access and contacts can mean cronyism. A Private Members' Bill taken to Statute has a price. Political information has a price – and that the public deserved to be told what that price was, and where they could obtain such service for free until reform of Parliament meant that there was a credible alternative to 'going private'.

Instead, and on behalf of the Political SCALPS, the Committee asked the industry to self-regulate, ignoring the public's needs, and further absolving itself of any responsibility to define the product standard or base cost, leaving the public, and consumer with the worst of all worlds.

They offered:

– no truthful picture of Parliamentary democracy to the public
– no guidance on standards or pricing, exposing the vulnerable to charlatans;
– no guidance on how to avoid the incompetent or greedy commercial lobbyist or politician;
– no guidance on how to find, let alone judge, the effectiveness of Parliamentarians who steadfastly refuse payments above those already provided by the tax-payer;

and, crucially,

– no guidance to citizen or foreigner alike, as to what is or is not corrupt practice, or assistance in seeing a way through some fairly blurred areas.

Once the 'Cash for Questions' affair exploded, resulting in Nolan, the public, of course, had a right to expect that many of the lessons had been learned. Not a bit of it – as 'Cronygate' proved.

'Cronygate'

Labour lobbying arrived in large numbers following the change of government in May 1997. Any pretence the commercial lobbying industry might have had that it was not a political dating agency went out the window as any number of untrained youngsters were offered jobs and silly titles. In addition, the salaries offered were considerably higher than those paid to existing employees, thoroughly irritating many staff and creating a thousand jealousies.

Meanwhile, a number of lobbying companies enjoyed the facilities of

Millbank Tower, the Labour Party Communications Centre, to which they had moved prior to the general election. Gossip was the order of the day. In addition, government got stuck in with commercial lobbyists in order to access their corporate clients. The corporate world welcomed the approach and responded, beating a path to the door of some of the commercial lobbyists acting as conduit.

Rumours circulated for months about the goings on and much more besides. These were fed by disaffected lobbyists no longer in the loop; and by members of the Parliamentary Labour Party who loathed lobbyists and New Labour, and, in particular some of the flash young men associated with it. However, the young entering public affairs and lobbying were hardly setting a precedent – Frank Barlow, the Secretary of the Parliamentary Labour Party, for example, 'retired' into the business in the early 1980s. Selective amnesia always prospers at a time of Parliamentary piety.

In July 1998 *The Observer* revealed that:

- Karl Milner, who, until May 1997, had worked for Gordon Brown before being employed by GJW, had given them an advance copy of a Parliamentary committee report.
- Derek Draper, who had worked for Peter Mandelson, before joining Market Access, was claiming that he could get clients into Downing Street, and
- Ben Lucas, formerly in Jack Straw's office, and now a co-founder of LLM, was boasting of passing on inside information.

The most serious of these turned out to be the second because of Derek Draper's close connections with Downing Street Adviser Roger Liddle. All the lobbyists involved had played a role in modernising Labour prior to office, and, more importantly, were close friends of many still playing a key role with the now governing party.

Not all of the matters arising were as serious as, on the face of it, they appeared. For example, the 'leaking' of Parliamentary documents is established practice and is often done without cynical intent, when, for example, a member of the press, who is legitimately entitled to an advance copy, shows it to someone whose opinion he needs, prior to the embargo being lifted. As a result of this, the public often has the benefit of such opinion at the appropriate time.

Where it is wrong, however, is if such documents are 'sold', most particularly if they contain information, early receipt of which could lead to unfair advantage.

'Cronyism' was one of the severest charges made by *The Observer*. Commercial lobbyists solicit meetings with Ministers on behalf of their clients. If they, and the arguments they present, are any good, they usually succeed in this aim. However, the unfair advantage apparently being offered to some of the clients of New Labour Lobbyists, in the same way as the unfair advantages offered to some under the previous Government by Old Tory Lobbyists, is something that should have been both anticipated and avoided.

Because it was not, clients of the commercial lobbying industry used as their entrée some rather brash young men who knew the new gate-keepers.

Government's immediate response was to close ranks and distance itself from the problem. However, rather like Ian Greer, it was difficult to close ranks since those thrust into the limelight were loyal party supporters. Some apologists then tried to limit the scandal by putting it down to inexperienced new government and too much testosterone. It deceived no-one. 'Cronygate' was born.

Elected officials need to police themselves, as do those appointed by them such as special advisers. Since they cannot always be trusted to do so, legislation is needed to avoid problems in the future. However, we also need to recognise that people have a right to earn their living after they have helped a political party secure office, or have retired from a career in public service. Therefore, if a period of 'gardening leave' is to be recommended, they must be financed during such leave.

As for the charge of cronyism, the product is easy to identify and the solution equally easy. Those who seek high office make many sacrifices – and receive many rewards. The sacrifices that they must be encouraged to make once they secure office is the dumping of old friends who are or are likely to become fatcats on the strength of their association. In view of the fact that as a society we can dump an honourable spouse with enormous ease, this is not likely to be difficult.

For example, it is not appropriate for Chancellor of the Exchequer John Bloggs to have as a close friend banker Bit of the Lad Flash, or indeed, banker the Good Lad, even though such friendship predates high office. Purdah is required. Had those associated with the present Government observed such purdah, an exceptionally likeable so-called 'lobbyist' would not have dominated the national press for as long as he did, lost his job and his newspaper column to boot. (He appears to have picked up another one.)

In addition, had such purdah been in operation, lobbying companies wishing to take advantage of foolish young men would not have been able to puff them up in the first place. Nor would such young men have been able to deliver – which they did – puffing them up even further.

The value of commercial lobbying depends on what it means. Young men who have no experience of the industry and are not lobbyists at all (newspaper columnists may be campaigners, but they are never lobbyists) but are employed by a commercial lobbying company, cannot be expected to observe the hypocrisies, let alone know the rules if they are not explained to them in clear and concise fashion.

And why should they? In the case of Draper he was paid to deliver, and did so. If what he perceived to be his role was wrong or different to that envisaged by his employers, it should not have taken a newspaper to tell him and his employers so. From whom do the young launched into commercial life learn? The answer is obvious. Someone takes them in hand and teaches them. When the product is democracy such mentors could also mention something about humility.

Here, of course, there is proof, if proof is needed, of the compelling requirement for regulation. This is explored later in the book. In the meanwhile, what could have prevented the problem was mentoring. This, however, is non-existent in the industry, not least because few have the appropriate mix of experience, social standing and an uncompromised past to act as mentors. Moreover, given the arrogance of many New Labour Lobbyists it is unlikely that any of them would have accepted such mentoring even if it had been offered in the first place.

With 'Cronygate' came other questions too, not least the links between some commercial lobbying companies and some Think Tanks/foundations, although their influence on the government process is debatable; the political motivation of some of these, where they are not transparent; and various matters pertaining to funding. Some solutions for these matters arising are offered under 'Product Policing'.

The most important issue flagged up by the Press lies in the Government's relationship with commercial lobbying companies in general, their clients, and the appointments it is making to Task Forces. That is a matter for the country (Parliament claims it is a matter for it, on the country's behalf) – although Government does not agree. It is all about democracy and what sort of democracy we want. It is up to Government to be transparent about what it wants from the corporate world, and what it will give in return, with or without the public's approval.

Since we are not being asked to give an opinion, let us hope that when Government give us its answer it will not merely do so by finding the right words to say. Democracy is about citizens, but citizens are not being consulted about how it is to work.

Conclusions

Much of the above makes deeply depressing reading. However, those considering a career in commercial lobbying should recognise that every industry has its problems – and those in the commercial lobbying industry are no worse than many. Moreover, they can take heart in the fact that the source of the industry's problems is the 'market' – for which they are not responsible. If the 'market' cleans itself up, which is to say by setting standards in public life, much else will follow.

In fact, it is possible to argue that given the industry's lack of regulation, and the large sums of money known to slosh around political forums, commercial lobbying in the UK is, as its history in the following chapter shows, fairly corruption free.

FOOTNOTE 1:

Official Committees of Westminster (Backbench or Select Committee) cover areas of considerable commercial interest to many businesses and industries. In addition, the whole of Westminster is a 'tendering house' i.e. the offering of considerable commercial contracts is within its gift, from small private security contracts to billion pound franchises. Despite this, there is very little scrutiny of competition criteria within Westminster. Therefore, the suggestion that a senior Backbencher was allegedly or could interfere with access to one of these Committees was shocking in the extreme.

FOOTNOTE 2:

Select Committees have a fairly patchy history. Since May 1997 enormous strides have been made to tackle many of the criticisms. Prior to May 1997, most divided along party lines and their reports carried little weight with Government. Those chaired by party hacks, such as the Select Committee on Members' Interests, carried even less weight. A few of such Committees had been rumoured to offer Masonic protection to miscreants, others had been 'careful' about whom they called to give evidence. Others again had been careful about what inquiries they held. This contributed to increasing cynicism with the whole Committee system. Many businessmen refused to give evidence to them because politicians on them were paid consultants of their competitors. In addition, members of the public were dismayed at the field trips undertaken by some of the Committees, at the tax-payers expense which amounted to little more than 'freebies'. Travel rules have since been tightened up – as has the system of instigating inquiries.

INDUSTRY OVERVIEW
1978 – 1998 Past-Tense; Future-Imperfect

Introduction – Pre Thatcher Commercial Lobbying – All Party Groups – Party Conference – Post Thatcher Commercial Lobbying – Greed – Multinationals – The Press – The Civil Service – Back to Business – House of Lords – Deregulation, Privatisation, Foreign Businessmen, EU – Pressure Groups – Changes in the Commercial Lobbying Companies – 1990+ – The Future: Where are the Commercial Lobbyists Going? – In UK – In Europe – Global – Political Risk Companies: Do they threaten Commercial Lobbyists? – Conclusion

Introduction

The myth of democracy was based on our right to free speech, supported by a free press, and our right to represent such free speech without fear or favour by virtue of a vote. This vote along with the votes of others, implemented the will of the majority, with consideration for the minority.

The myth has been exploded by recognition that the majority are disenfranchised because those that represent, act upon their representations, execute, and their respective forums, are neither representative of majority nor free of favour.

This is because the limited democracy that we have been offered evolved out of, and was maintained by, the hierarchies, professions, needs, vested interests and so on, of the day. That is to say, lobbies. Lawyers rather than civil engineers, aristocrats rather than businessmen, churchmen rather than social workers, landowners rather than town planners, men rather than women, white rather than ethnic, Christian, and latterly, Jew, rather than Muslim, Hindu and so on...

As one group or other achieved prominence or recognition by lobbying, they diminished or excluded those already represented, becoming in their turn both lobby and vested interest.

The electorate's lack of representation was masked by the fact that the voter was allowed to cast his vote in favour of a political party which most closely represented his views. As a result, one party or another took possession of government by forming a Government from party representative elected by the largest individual vote, rather than by majority vote.

Government was sustained by outside undemocratic financiers i.e. lobbies – The City; Trades Unions – and their respective activists and sympathisers, as well as an unelected upper tier of politician (Peers in the House of Lords) who themselves represented lobbies (e.g. landowners).

This had the effect that while the political minority and their outside supporters were temporarily disenfranchised until they won power, the majority were permanently disenfranchised.

The only way into the system was lobbying, including financial patronage and favour. Lobbying was not out of character since those already in the system had arrived by the same route.

In effect, the United Kingdom plc – with or without its new subsidiaries (National Assemblies) – like other plcs, was not, and is not, a democratically run institution.

Much to the disapproval of the majority, its governance is decided by culture, patronage, nepotism and wealth. Those who became disenfranchised included private individuals, representatives of 'new' commercial interests (e.g. technology), single issue interests (e.g. environmentalists) and 'foreigners' i.e. the representatives of large corporations paying tax in this country and employing large workforces, but who, unlike traditional business groups, are unrepresented officially – as opposed to unofficially – within our political system.

Most plcs do not pretend to be democratic. Some even resent the suggestion that small shareholders or non-shareholders have rights and resent even more the fact that they are required to be transparent internally and externally as well as accountable (report and accounts; disclosure). However, they are required by law to be financially accountable, both here and abroad, and 'corruption' is appropriately policed and punished.

The UK plc, on the other hand, in business because of democracy, is not accountable, nor, by law, does it have to be although it pretends otherwise. As a result, various subsidiaries of the company (e.g. Scotland and Wales) have pushed, and now succeeded, in organising a management buyout.

Its junior 'staff', (MPs, MEPs), unlike most staff of commercial enterprises, are able to accept money from several employers, even though their primary employer (i.e. the citizen) is, for the most part, unaware of this, or has no say in such employment if he is. Therefore, the lobbies that they assist, and who sustain them, may be anti-democratic.

Its senior 'staff' (Whitehall, Government Minister, Special Adviser) behave similarly although this is disguised since they do not accept money from other employers until after they have left government. Money comes from those who wish to influence government. Again this can be, and often is, anti-democratic.

The 'staff' of UK plc and its subsidiaries (e.g. Civil Servants in the proposed new Scottish Assembly) are not answerable to their 'shareholders' – that is to say, citizens – since they are unelected (Whitehall, Quangos, the current House of Lords), or appointed by political party (Minister, MP, MEP, Councillor, Assemblyman). As a result, and so that they are answerable, the citizen has long demanded modernisation of UK plc.

Any number of 'staff' are sympathetic to the 'shareholders' point of view, including some of the 'staff' of the traditional lobbies (e.g. inherited Peerage) who have a great deal to lose by modernisation. All are aware that the 'management' of what currently constitutes UK plc operates within a structure that evolved out of previous managements, precluding modern management and demanding short-termism to keep the show on the road.

The 'chairman' (i.e. Prime Minister) of UK plc is having to operate with two proposed subsidiaries (Scotland and Wales) while shutting his eyes to the fact that a management buy-out has been organised; a third subsidiary (Northern Ireland) that the shareholders of the parent group wish to be rid of; additional subsidiaries e.g. a Mayor for London; a joint venture with the EU that does not have the support of all the Directors or company shareholders; a management that is structurally unable to keep both the show on the road or add the extra lanes and dual carriageways needed to free up chairmanship from management, thus stunting modern chairmanship and the demand for long termism, as well as limiting the executive's ability to execute.

Life is made more difficult for the 'Chairman' because:

– he cannot 'patriotise' the money markets, or those who, to the detriment of UK plc and its 'shareholders', speculate on those markets;

– those who own and or invest in UK plc (including foreign investors and multinationals) who do not necessarily have the interests of the component parts and/or the UK as a whole, as a priority or even as an interest and, excluded from political responsibility, do not need to. (Many argue that had the chairmen of Japanese multinationals sat in the House of Lords during the 1980s, the country's design skills at that time would not have been lost overseas);

– he does not have overall control of UK plc's 'staff', some of whom are more respectful of private service (i.e. kickbacks) than they are of public service, nor does he have control of the political machine that elected him (which is one reason why ignoring his backbenchers, while perfectly understandable, is not such a good idea.).

Therefore, while the 'Chairman' is telling the citizen that the citizen is an equal 'shareholder' in what will be left of UK plc, he is also having to admit that some have a bigger bite of the cherry than others, while others again have none at all.

Meanwhile he is becoming bogged down by the internal management problems of UK plc as described above, as well as the modernisation of the state, including:

– the need to redefine his own office (currently being translated as a desire for the presidential system of government);

– the need to restore confidence in political institutions (hence constitutional change) and other examples such as Parliament's inability to conduct investigative inquiries, essential if the backbencher is to retain some importance in the political system (the present discussion about turning Select Committees into imitations of congressional committees, despite the known inadequacies of politicians, has as much to do with maintaining an undeserved role for backbenchers as anything else);

– the establishment of regional assemblies and strengthening of local government in order to breathe new life into local democracy. This is well nigh impossible given that these will be staffed by party hacks or political re-treads;

– the need to convince the citizen that closer involvement with Europe is the citizen's wish, when such decision has already been made

– the need to convince the citizen that the 'Americanisation' of politics is not on the cards – at a time when the Americans themselves apparently wish they did not have, for example, a politicised Civil Service – although the evidence proves otherwise instead of being free to:

- recognise the practicalities of the market place without problems from his own party (i.e. recognition that a global economy forces all governments to follow a centrist line even though this denies valid argument from both left and right) and pilot UK plc, including the subsidiaries if they will allow it, into the 21st century;
- dictate its relationships beyond the immediate market-place (EU); yesterday's (Commonwealth), or position it for tomorrow's (China);

with even less time to address other expressions of the market i.e. ethical commerce and foreign policy (despite making all the right noises); or issues such as the need to establish a modern 'lobbying' framework encompassing both monetary reward of government servants as well as ethical considerations.

The latter is likely to be covered in promised anti-corruption legislation. However, this is unlikely to address the whole problem.

For example, how ethically correct is it for politicians and Whitehall Civil Servants to lobby Government to promote, for example, the construction industry in China, when the Chinese political system does not conform to Western ideals? Similarly, how ethically correct is it for politicians and Whitehall Civil Servants to lobby Government to promote the defence industry in Saudi Arabia for the same reasons? Or, for that matter, accept hospitality for themselves and their spouses from such foreign governments.

The whole lobbying issue cannot be seen in terms of regulating the private sector industry (i.e. commercial lobbyists) without government imposing on itself similar regulatory constraints.

So, where did the private sector come from?

Pre-Thatcher Commercial Lobbying

There is always a danger of imposing a new interpretation on recent history. However, in general, it is fair to say that prior to the Thatcher decade, commercial lobbyists were few and far between.

On the whole, big business had little need of the services of a commercial lobbyist because they relied upon their old boy network (which included Commander Powell who refused to call himself a commercial lobbyist) to influence government policy.

Such influence was a mixture of pulling strings, hearing confessions and bailing (usually Tory) politicians out of various financial difficulties so that they could continue at Westminster, leaving Powell to do most of their legislative drafting when needed, and usually on an ad hoc basis.

Foreign companies, individuals and organisations which had no such network relied on informal arrangements, such as the assistance of Masonic friends or organisations such as chambers of commerce.

Both communities tended to fear the Labour Party. This fear was tied into communism and the perceived threat of the then Soviet bloc. The Labour Party's manifesto commitment to nationalise banks, construction companies, insurance and pharmaceutical industries, as well as countless other privately owned businesses, confirmed such fears.

To protect itself, the commercial world relied on and was adept at dealing with, the secret state (intelligence services) with whom they had a long history (intelligence work was as much about the protection of British commerce as anything else), as well as financing right-wing business organisations. Both the intelligence services and the right wing business organisations shared the prejudices of the commercial world, and included in their remit the profiling of politicians, trades unionists and journalists regarded as enemies of the state. Christopher Powell, incidentally, had a low opinion of such conduct.

Those businesses that did employ commercial lobbyists, many of whom at that time were sole practitioners, usually took no more than a cuttings service of the political documents from them. Such business was usually won on the basis of the lobbyists 'class' i.e. the ability to waste considerable man-hours with various client companies, as well as representatives of the secret state, at, for example, the races, or, it is rumoured, on his ability to provide client or politician with young men and women for extra curricular activities.

Dedicated public affairs companies in Britain were slow to develop. The PR companies getting into lobbying in the mid-1970s replaced a smaller band of old-style PR linked lobbyist who had run out of steam.

One such company was Voice and Vision, which had been active in the late 1950s on behalf of the Central African Federation, organising trips for MPs to see the Rhodesian problems on the spot. It had also worked for Imperial Tobacco in the early stages of the Parliamentary battle over anti-smoking legislation.

Another company, Traverse Healy and Lyons, which combined the expertise and contacts of a Tory and a Labour supporter, sought to give itself more muscle by buying, in the early 1970s, the highly respected and long established Parliamentary consultancy, Watney & Powell. However, finding Commander Powell's modest fees and deep interest in Parliamentary procedure not to their taste, they soon sold it on to the old established City PR and advertising company Charles Barker.

In the late 1960s, the firm had taken on Conrad Voss Bark, a BBC

Parliamentary reporter, to carry out discreet political contact work and it now set up a strong Parliamentary subsidiary with the name Charles Barker Watney & Powell. With the break up of John Addey Associates in 1977, Arthur Butler, the head of that company's public affairs division, moved across to Charles Barker Watney & Powell, taking with him an important batch of clients to which were soon added some that had temporarily gone astray, such as the Corporation of the City of London and Tesco, now a client of New Labour lobbyists LLM.

Charles Barker Watney & Powell now towered over all its rivals by dint of its astonishing blue-chip client list and its considerable expertise. But, due to the influence of Commander Powell, its fees remained modest and its style discreet.

Relationships with the companies and political world were usually confined to friendships with individuals. As a result, and for the most part, the lobbying companies operated deferentially, anxious not to upset their friends or their political masters.

Within their limitations, however, the companies made politics and the political system, accessible to those not traditionally part of it but which offered no threat to the state (e.g. small businesses or professional groups and charities which usually had a patron in the House of Lords). As a result, some interest groups, charities, local authorities, and small trade associations, learned about politics from them. Most subordinate staff of the lobbying companies were scrupulous in ensuring that their clients upheld good conduct and none of the politicians with whom they worked were paid.

They drafted or assisted in the drafting of Parliamentary questions, clauses to government, private or private members bills, and found the requisite supporters to table them. They sought to interest Parliamentarians in taking on apolitical and non-controversial bills to statute or becoming responsible for giving issues an airing either by adjournment debate or early day motion.

The Parliamentarian, for the most part, found his own supporters for an issue that he believed in and for which he wanted support either by blocking or assisting. The calibre of the commercial lobbyist's Parliamentary and client knowledge dictated the depth of the link between Parliamentarian and outside body. And the calibre of the commercial lobbyist's friendships dictated both the spread of the link and its influence. The commercial lobbyists went to party conference to meet existing friends rather than to make new ones.

For a variety of reasons, including the slow erosion of the deferential society and a growing awareness of the fact that there was money to be made, as well as a democratic need, from a more aggressive assault on the political status quo, things began to change in the mid-1970s.

Into the industry came personalities such as commercial lobbyist Doug Smith who founded his lobbying company with Peter Fry, the then Conservative MP for Wellingborough. Five years after forming it, Peter Fry became a member of the House of Commons Transport Select Committee. Specialising in transport affairs, the company soon added local government to its Westminster service – local government was the 'Cinderella' of politics principally because of the attitude of the political centre (Whitehall).

Traditional commercial lobbyists, who had followed an unwritten code of not employing politicians, were both aghast and wrong-footed by such developments.

With Britain's entry into the European Economic Community in 1973, the world of commercial lobbying changed again. In addition to monitoring Westminster and local government, the commercial lobbying companies found that they were having to take Europe seriously. In its 1973 brochure, Partnerplan, for example, boasted of a network of offices in the Common Market.

Those with sufficient funds soon established European divisions. These, for the most part, were principally for 'show' and ran at a loss, since the vast majority of the industry's clients, and, indeed, commercial lobbyists, had not yet realised that the pace of legislation was being dictated by Europe, rather than national, government.

Meanwhile, traditional interests were fragmenting, and businesses that had once relied exclusively on their chums in Westminster or representative organisations such as chambers of commerce recognised that they needed more. Most, by that time, recognised that any group that could be touched by government could not afford to be without representation.

This explosion of needs pole-axed Westminster and doubled representation by commercial lobbyists. In addition, more politicians joined the industry claiming that in so doing they were better able to represent business interests, and therefore the interests of their constituents.

At the same time, a similar number of politicians complained about the commercial lobbyists operating at Westminster, without apparently realising that the political system, rather than the commercial lobbying industry, was at the root of the problem, and, crucially, without linking it to the growth in the commercial activities of politicians, some of whom were similarly being condemned.

All Party Groups

Accepting the acknowledged judgement that Westminster was too cut off from the business world, some commercial lobbyists ignored the murmurs of disapproval, and, at the request of Parliamentarians or client industries, went on to greatly enlarge the network of specialised Westminster All Party Groups. Industry had no other real voice or forum. These All Party Groups had a secretary, usually the commercial lobbyist, and joint chairmen, who were always politicians representing both the major parties.

The groups acted as a catalyst familiarising more outsiders with the system. In setting them up, commercial lobbyists were subjected to enormous hostility – not least from Commander Powell, representative of the previous generation of lobbyists, who felt the plethora of new groups devalued the prestige of his own, notably the Parliamentary and Scientific Committee.

However, the problem for the Parliamentary and Scientific Committee was that it sought to cover such an enormous area of science and technology that in any one year there was only time to have one meeting on information technology or minerals and energy. MPs active in the Parliamentary and Scientific Committee with particular interests in such fields, therefore, asked for new specialist IT or minerals/energy committees to be set up.

They asked the then Secretary of the Parliamentary and Scientific Committee, Arthur Butler, to take action to meet the needs and so the Parliamentary Information Technology Committee and the All Party Minerals Group were established. The growth of such Committees – as Christopher Powell had feared – meant, however, that the Parliamentary membership of the Parliamentary and Scientific Committee ceased to expand.

Notwithstanding hostility, the 'new boys' pressed on. The All Party Groups dealing exclusively with commercial matters acted as a forum for business representatives and trades unionists to meet with politicians to discuss the leading issues of the day. At the time, such a forum, offering informal meetings and discussion groups with both employer and trades unionists, was a revolutionary idea, and certainly not one that commercial lobbyists such as Commander Powell (then approaching his eighties) had ever intended.

In due course, the All Party Groups began to be recognised by some to be of value because employer and employee (usually represented respectively by management and trades union) found it difficult to meet politicians from across the party divide. Similarly, many politicians, anxious that they were ignored and consequently uninformed about important component parts of the community they represented, regarded the groups as a welcome method of introduction, while they were out of office, which introductions, without cynicism or self-interest, would stand both sides in good stead once office had been secured.

Basically, politician, worker representative and businessman lived in non-touching worlds and the All Party Group was a way of bridging those worlds. The feeling was that it was to everybody's benefit that both the major parties knew something about the business world before they became responsible for legislating for the business world.

As importantly, the All Party Groups gave politicians the opportunity to question the heads of multinational companies, either in this country or on the continent, about their intentions in the UK, specifically the consequences for employment. The multinationals were usually, although not always, pleased to receive an invitation to address the groups.

However, an inevitable consequence of many years of uninterrupted Tory government, was that in due course, Tory politicians began to be favoured by them, seriously imbalancing the all-party nature of the groups. As a result, one of the few avenues by which the Labour Party could remain in the consultation game, however imperfectly, ineffectually and, indeed, reluctantly, was undermined. The commercial lobbyists, notably Arthur Butler, believed it to be a public duty to keep the Labour Party involved, even though pursuing such a duty was often a thankless task.

The undermining of the Labour Party within some of the Groups continued. Such undermining made it particularly difficult for the Labour joint chairmen of the groups (who were already having difficulties justifying the groups to some of their colleagues – many in the Labour Party were bitterly opposed to the groups because they were ideologically opposed to industry). – As a result they came to lean on the commercial lobbyist as trusted middleman even more. For a while, such lobbyists were their sole link with the business world. Nonetheless, often misunderstood by both sides of the House of Commons, opposition to the groups grew as many politicians started to use the groups as an opportunity to market themselves to the groups' often wealthy clients.

To co-ordinate the industry groups' activities (i.e. meetings, local and overseas visits, and agenda) more commercial lobbyists became secretary to them, while their companies ran the Secretariats with limited funding provided by client and client industries. Today, many of the groups no longer employ outside lobbyists.

The politicians, which is to say the more powerful Conservative Joint Chairmen, kept control of the agenda. This sometimes meant that those whom they agreed to meet were not necessarily the most worthy, although they were most usually able to offer (sometimes lavish) hospitality.

The lobbyist accepted such bias for two reasons. Firstly, because otherwise it was impossible for him to keep the groups' numbers up; and secondly because if he crossed the politician the latter usually threatened to switch the Secretariat to a rival lobbying company. Scrutiny of tendering criteria was, and remains, a grey area. Because the all party nature of the groups – and therefore their credibility – was largely maintained by the lobbyist acting as secretary, the result was usually an uneasy truce between politician and lobbyist. Not that providing the Secretariats to the Groups offered lobbyists large sums of money – in fact they often ran at a loss. They did, however, provide access to a large number of politicians – the lobbyists bread-and-butter, and therefore their value was incalculable.

For obvious reasons, the calibre of the groups varied – many were no more than badly run jollies or marketing vehicles – as did the calibre of the lobbyists and politicians involved with them. Tightly run Secretariats maintained records of attendance, meetings and questions, hospitality and expenditure, all of which were available for scrutiny and could have been made available to the public, without damaging client confidentiality, had the politicians agreed to do so. This would have protected the 'good' groups from criticism and distanced them from the 'bad'. The politicians however chose not to make such records available, their motives not always being the most

honourable, which gave the funding client, and often the commercial lobbyist too, the way out he wanted.

The Groups' records gave a detailed and useful snapshot of an industry's concerns, including the personalities from all its worlds, the appointments, promotions and knighthoods. These snapshots were not always complimentary to the politicians' response to their concerns.

They often indicated the number of politicians (in both Houses of Parliament) tabling Parliamentary questions for a particular company or another, having first visited the company with the All Party Group, without the Secretariat being in a position to bar those politicians charging for such Parliamentary questions, or from membership of the Group.

Other records showed some of the Groups' bias in favour of larger companies. This always angered smaller clients of the sponsoring organisation, usually trade associations, who felt that they were subsidising the Secretariat through their subscriptions, without getting any of the benefits.

In addition, any number of smaller companies who presented to the Groups in Parliament (without the means to offer hospitality) and devoted hours of valuable time in the preparation of their presentations were frequently outraged to find that no politician could be bothered to turn up and listen to them on the grounds that they were "too busy". These politicians, however, were not too busy to go on an overseas visit, also organised by the Group, or attend a lavish 'working' dinner.

Similarly, trades unionists who addressed the Groups were often disappointed by the turn out at the meetings. Unlike those above, these were always full (given the number of MPs sponsored by trades unions) but usually only included a sprinkling of Tories, if any at all, thereby negating the all party point of the groups and the trades unions desire to influence dissident Tories and/or make some impact on (Tory) government thinking.

Despite these drawbacks the records of the Groups faithfully recorded the issues of the day – large and small – as well as the anxieties and attitudes of the politicians who took part in the groups and those they met, be they employer, trades unionist or designer. They were an industry history and, over the years, developed into useful source reference material devoid of commentary or bias.

Attached to these histories were commentaries from the national press covering the same industries. These usually indicated the support given to the Conservative government's national programme – for example the trumpeting of new jobs created by Japanese and American multinationals, without apparently understanding that such investment usually only provided short-term non-skilled employment gain, as well as giving both countries an entree into Europe. British multinationals were, of course, doing the same thing overseas themselves. As a result, the groups' records, free of bias or analysis, were 'purer' than the information offered by the press.

The records could be anecdotally funny – such as the occasion when industrialist Ian MacGregor was due to speak to one of the groups about the British steel industry but could not persuade the Palace of Westminster police to let him jump the tourist queue; or when a (West) German company, anxious not to offend its visiting British MP dignitaries, dismantled a sixty foot world map to 'remove' the island of Cyprus in order to insert it where the Falklands were; or when the same group 'teased' the West Germans as they pretended they were snatching photographs of a new car, a hitherto unseen model that had not yet had its official launch.

Equally, they could be anecdotally shocking, for example the Parliamentarians who pointed the soles of their shoes at Far Eastern dignitaries, causing untold offence, despite the fact they were on a goodwill visit to beat the drum for British trade; or talked about the 'Paki' vote in their constituencies.

Occasionally the groups hit the spot exactly. John de Lorean was due to address, and be questioned by one of the Groups on the day that he was arrested.

The trips abroad were frequently an eye-opener. In former West Germany the unions were more management than the management and shared the platform with them. They were particularly sympathetic about the then unemployment problems in the UK and were happy to organise apprenticeships and work experience for young British unemployed.

In France things were completely different. French management did not know why the Groups had to meet the French unions since the French unions had not organised the visit. Their objection was not that they should not meet British politicians, just that they should organise it themselves. When the Groups did meet them the French unionists were sufficiently straightforward about their links with Moscow for the (British) Labour politicians not to want to meet them again in case the British Press came to hear about it.

In Italy and Spain the unions scarcely seemed to exist. Management did not even make a show of wanting them involved in the discussions. Moreover, in Italy the 'management' that greeted the Groups at the beginning of a visit, were not always the 'management' that said good-bye to them at the end, because, apparently they had decided to 'go on holiday' – a euphemism for 'helping the magistrate with his enquiries'!

A visit to Spain was cancelled on the basis that the subsidiary of an (American) multinational could not make time for the Spanish unions to meet the Group. This was a disappointment to both Labour and Conservative politicians since, at that time, the Spanish unions were often better informed about the multinationals' employment intentions than anyone else.

Some of the Groups were stuck with some of their Chairmen (always politicians) until they lost their seats. This was often a handicap because, as a result, some of the Groups began to be run like personal fiefdoms – particularly the case when the politician recognised that he was not going to be voted into Government or senior shadow cabinet responsibilities. As a result, those who wanted their own fiefdoms – usually to meet business and pick up consultancies – set up their own groups.

Justification for the genuine All Party Group fell upon the Secretary, i.e. commercial lobbyist, because of the fee that was charged by his company for providing the Secretariat. This was frequently difficult because many client-industries did not know the purpose of the groups and in consequence were often disappointed.

For their part the officers of the groups continued to have difficulty in keeping up attendances especially on the Labour side. (It is one of many ironies that, today, the Labour Party not only publicly favours commercial lobbyists, but is desperate to access the commercial world that had once been offered to it on a plate by the All Party Groups. The All Party Groups, in effect, were ahead of the game. Arguably, had the Labour party been mature enough to recognise the importance of the business world, its fortunes, a nd the conduct of many of the All Party Groups, might have been better.)

That not being the case, the commercial lobbyist was left having to keep the groups going. In order, therefore, to drum up more support, the hospitality programme, funded by client and (often) reluctant client industries, was extended.

Party Conference

A parallel development to the All Party Groups was limited hospitality at party conference. (Party conference had, historically, been ignored by the commercial lobbyists until those coming into commercial lobbying from journalism who were used to attending the conferences and saw their value – principally Arthur Butler – included it.) This enabled the clients of the commercial lobbyists to develop political friendships, sometimes for the first time, while their lobbyists deepened many of their existing friendships by bumping into friends they had nurtured, often through the All Party Groups, now newly appointed to government or shadow cabinet responsibilities, or by thrashing out matters of policy with friends that now had input into the party machines i.e. conference resolution or manifesto commitment.

It should be noted here that present reliance on the input from quangos, task forces and focus groups, has radically altered the importance of party conference. 'The Fringe' is likely to be the only area of interest to serious lobbyists – unless networking with their colleagues and other public affairs specialists counts.

Those lobbyists that were well organised, involved their subordinate staff in party conference as well. That is to say, while they entertained politicians, they ensured that their subordinates entertained the politicians' secretaries/research assistants in London. Links with the

Labour Party, for pragmatic reasons (the Labour Party were not in government) but also reflecting business' prejudices and short-termism, were still left largely to the lobbyists, unless the clients had large, unionised workforces.

To recap, pre Thatcher, the commercial lobbying industry was offering a Westminster and fledgling European Service, limited local government coverage and the opportunity to meet politicians through meetings organised at party conference or the All Party Groups. 'Whitehall' was not part of the remit although some of those entering the commercial lobbying market were beginning to have it within their sights – and some were making bogus claims about their ability to influence Civil Servants.

Parallel to all the local developments, a well established tradition by some companies of working for foreign governments and corporate entities also flourished. Although companies such as Charles Barker had a house rule not to work for foreign governments – or employ any MPs – others were not so particular. Examples included a whole range of PR/Public Affairs consultancies from the 1950s onwards working for states such as the Central African Federation, the Greek Colonels and the Middle East States. The list could go on.

Lobbying under Mrs Thatcher

In 1979 the business world heaved a huge sigh of relief when the Tories came into office. This did not reflect their respect for Tory politicians (negligible) nor Parliament (irrelevant/time consuming/ out of date) but their assumption that by virtue of a Conservative Government they would be able to conduct their affairs without interference, in tandem with a government that was keeping the workforce, and trades unions, under control.

Traditionally, business had tended to regard government and politics as a remote activity concerned with macro issues unrelated to business. However, the winter of discontent and paranoia about anything to do with the Socialist party had made business more proactive. Many business people, most of whom were Conservative party supporters and funders, dealt directly with politicians who were very accessible to such party supporters.

For the most part, they did not recognise that European Community (now European Union) issues affected them. Those that did (for example, those involved in 'doorstep selling' – insurers, cosmetic companies – and therefore interested in the relevant EC directive) assumed, wrongly, that national government would be able to assist them.

'Newer' industry and foreign-owned companies made no such assumption. As a result, the latter, familiar with the American model of lobbying, hunted around for public affairs specialists and lobbyists, which specialists they were usually introduced to through public relations companies or politicians they had met through either official or unofficial committees (e.g. All Party Groups) or party fund-raising activities.

Although relieved to find the Conservatives in office, 'newer' industry, long aware that they were not part of an old boy network and therefore had no access to Government (partially because they were not predisposed to fund the Conservative Party, even if they had the means to do so, which most did not) sought out the most cost-effective way of being brought into the consultation game.

Originally, this was via their trade or other representative organisations. However, many found themselves again squeezed out by older or more established business. As a result, they hunted around for Parliamentarians willing to represent them on an ad hoc basis (no money changed hands) or permanently, either by accepting paid directorships (no more than one, or, at most two) or yearly retainer. Those politicians appointed usually had a thorough grasp of their problems, and were modest in their demands for money.

For the most part, such politicians were the only protection the small organisations had against the resources and influences of larger and perceived priority operations. As a result, they frequently tabled Parliamentary questions on their behalf. The point of these was not that such questions were important or influenced but that the statistics they uncovered via Civil Servants were of value. (The use of Civil Servants in this way was subsequently to become an issue – in the early years it could be defended by the fact that access to information was severely limited and a good MP was expected to assist in securing such information for his client who more often than not was his constituents' largest employer and did not have the resources to conduct such research.)

In addition to their own efforts, the politicians often recommended that their clients take a Parliamentary information and monitoring service from the old-style commercial lobbying companies. For the most part, these were not working for foreign owned companies – some 'traditional' commercial lobbying companies always refused to act for foreign interests – as those owned by the large public relations companies were, thus creating the beginning of the fees imbalance problem.

The politicians who introduced their small clients to the traditional commercial lobbyists received no 'introduction' fee – one reason why some members of the commercial lobbying fraternity were so outraged by the conduct of some politicians subsequently involved with Ian Greer Associates or similar companies.

The politicians recommended the commercial lobbyists for five reasons:

– they needed the back-up the commercial lobbyists provided
– they were scrupulous in reminding their clients that, unlike the commercial lobbyists, they could cover "only half the House. The lobbyists know Tories and Socialists and follow them to party conference"
– they were the first to admit that, unlike the commercial lobbyists, they had no knowledge of legislative trends in Europe which were beginning to intrude upon their client's working environment
– they were anxious about their Parliamentary procedural knowledge and often appreciated that the commercial lobbyists' was better
– the work demanded by their clients was becoming substantially more than they had anticipated, and, since the clients invariably did not have the money to offer the politician a larger fee or appropriate secretarial assistance, he wished to off-load them, arguably allowing him the freedom to accept more lucrative and less time consuming work. This reinforced the fees imbalance in the commercial lobbying industry.

The traditional commercial lobbyists, small and politically non-aligned, came into their own on occasions such as Budget Day in particular (Government's priority was getting the information to the Press, and not the business community). Therefore, their clients were grateful to have someone to stand in the rain for them, usually for several hours, outside HMSO, to collect the Budget's background notes. These were only available once the Chancellor had finished speaking.

They were also grateful to have someone speed-read those same notes – sometimes two hundred pages worth – to select those pages which were relevant to them as employers and traders.

They were even more grateful when, having selected, photocopied and despatched them, their lobbyists drafted a two-line response for them to give to the Press when they rang up to get their reaction, and, eventually, when it was published, began work on drafting amendments for the Finance Bill i.e. the translation of the Budget into legislation, because they, their lawyers, and the politicians they employed, were untrained in Parliamentary drafting. In addition, they found their lobbyists even more useful, when, coming up to the reporting of their annual accounts, their lobbyists provided them with a selection of political questions the Press might ask in order to embarrass them.

Most clients of the traditional commercial lobbyists were also additionally appreciative of the fact that provision of such service was modestly priced, (essential given the state of their own finances) in sharp contrast to those services provided by other professionals such as their lawyers and accountants. They were also happy to accept their lobbyists as confidantes who offered respite from their own working environments which were often characterised by feuding, carping and penny-pinching.

Greed

Recognising that much of the work undertaken by the traditional commercial lobbyists was poorly paid, time-consuming, specialised and low-profile, many politicians cast around for more lucrative, high profile employment. In addition, some of them eschewed the old tradition of taking on only a couple of outside commercial interests. Instead, they began to sell their public 'office', rather than their expertise, to as many as would pay them.

The Parliamentary units, meanwhile, were owned by consultants some of whom, for one reason or another (mostly financial) decided to throw in their lot – and their staff – with public relations companies. These were often owned by the advertising giants. At that time, advertising was the big story. After all, advertisers had 'won' the election for Mrs. Thatcher.

Initial interest in the small commercial lobbyists however soon waned, when the advertising and PR agencies found them adhering to old-fashioned values. Their specialised skills, low profit margins and equally low profile both distanced and diminished them in the eyes of their new owners whose psychology was high profit and high profile.

Thus was devalued the useful job of:

- Parliamentary drafting
- providing private reports, written on request, rather than as a marketing document;
- reading and monitoring the documents of Westminster and the EU;
- supplying information based on what was read by telephoning a Parliamentary clerk, European bureaucrat or Parliamentarian in both institutions;
- and digging around for further information in order to save somebody else the bother.

As was their steady development of contacts with Civil Servants who were themselves beginning to specialise in the European institutions. All that the traditional commercial lobbyists were deemed to be good for was the provision of interesting tittle-tattle to the clients of the advertising/PR agencies i.e. the chairmen of major companies who wanted to impress their guests in the corporate hospitality tent at Henley Regatta and other such venues with political gossip.

1980+

Big business, dated and unwieldy, watched its world fall apart as economic recession gripped. In addition, many industries, such as construction, which were traditional Tory supporters, found themselves ignored by a government who, although it valued their political donations and was happy to acquiesce in the granting of various knighthoods and, for some, large commercial contracts, rightly believed some of them to be dinosaurs.

The foreign business community however came into its own. As access to Downing Street was increasingly made available to it – government favoured this type of businessman both because of the (admittedly low skilled) employment he offered, as well as for the large donations they made to Conservative Party funds – the original commercial status quo found itself marginalised. Those able to swing behind the government e.g. the defence industry/larger construction companies remained favoured friends. Everybody else dropped by the wayside.

Staff in the commercial lobbying companies meanwhile witnessed the worst of the recession as their clients made countless staff redundant. Their own jobs were secure because, despite high overheads, salaries were traditionally low. In addition, their clients, now having to grapple with redundancy and unemployment legislation, needed the cheap services of the lobbying companies, not least because the information they were providing was considerably cheaper, and arguably better, than that provided by their lawyers.

Their clients' problems trebled the workload for the commercial lobbying staff. In addition, the emerging picture of money-grabbing managements presiding over human misery and chaos began to define many of the younger generation of commercial lobbyists' political viewpoints – particularly those subordinates in touch with the Labour Party and trades unionists through the All Party Groups.

The result was that some of the staff of the commercial lobbying companies, but usually not their proprietors, were increasingly divorced from the political culture of the industry that employed them, as well as the clients that paid their salaries. Sensitive to the arguments being made by some of the politicians they admired they saw their client managements, often categorised by incompetence and lack of skill, dump skilled staff in order to sustain their status quo. At the same time, Tory Government was bolstering management's position through employment law and offering lucrative additional employment on quangos, as well as dishing out the knighthoods.

Disillusioned, the staff finally acquired professional maturity by comparing *Hansard* reports of debates on industrial action with that which they read in the press. The two did not tally since the majority of the press were reflecting heavy government bias. The knowledge that the press was not free and independent, shattered many of the more innocent.

Back in the All Party Groups, traditional thinking was being challenged. While Government was extolling the virtues of self-employment, the freeing of entrepreneurial spirit and the setting up of new businesses (the majority of which collapsed), politicians on both sides of the House were pointing out that established businesses provided the greater employment, and these needed the skills and vision of some of those who had been so ruthlessly jettisoned, had the status quo not been so anxious to sustain itself.

The All Party Groups began arranging meetings with 'outsiders', including academics, i.e. embryonic focus groups, which, in many respects, today fulfil the function that All Party Groups should have been allowed to do had their value been recognised at the appropriate time and they had not been allowed to dwindle into marketing vehicles.

These outsiders encouraged wider thinking, for example viewing the growth in self-employment as an opportunity to knock the age of retirement on the head, instead of the system that scrapped men and women at fifty; as well as looking at salary structures and the appointing of (lucratively rewarded) non-executive directors, who decided the pay of their main boards, who in turn decided theirs.

Crucially, however, the All Party Groups started challenging the 'group think'. As thousands lost their jobs, some Conservative politicians, subsequently dismissed as 'wets', sacrificed any hope of political advancement by joining with Labour to criticise government policy.

In effect, they were saying that "management does not know how to lead", implying that those remaining in the traditional industries were unequal to the task of modernising them, or running the modern businesses that were so essential to the country, while those that could had been scrapped. Self employment and the enterprise culture, they continued, was not an expression of financial health but the reverse.

Government responded by ignoring those deemed to be Tory 'wets', (the 'cull' in the Labour Party today of non-Blairite MPs is almost identical to the Conservative 'cull' of twenty years ago) and ignoring the Opposition altogether. It added insult to injury by lambasting the trades unions for being out of date (very true) without any recognition that management was equally behind the times, nor that the costs of unemployment, in human terms as well as economic, would mop up all the cash the government was acquiring from the sale of the country's assets.

As the recession deepened, reports reached the All Party Groups that decent industrial foremen were losing their jobs and being undermined by appalling shop stewards, allowing management, with government's blessing, to get away with ducking the social responsibilities conferred upon it by 'Butskellism'.

The Labour Party began to hone its opposition skills (something the Conservatives, now in opposition themselves, are having to learn while Labour learns about government). The Tory 'wets' on the other hand, isolated and depressed, (wrongly) anticipated their government's defeat at the next election. As a result, some of them became more active in the All Party Groups and interested in the commercial lobbyists who provided the secretariats. They were joined by opposition members who realistically viewed their chances of reaching the government frontbench as negligible even if the Labour Party won the election, which it did not.

The uniting element therefore became shared anxieties about re-election, which depended on constituents, or family members, who were unemployed. The All Party Groups began to take on a more 'human' face, as politicians vied with each other to get the groups to visit factories and plants in their constituencies where the remaining workforce could see them on parade. In addition, both Conservative and Labour politicians began to take an interest in the European divisions of the commercial lobbyists running the groups, asking them to provide them with information on the accessing of industrial and/or regional grants provided by the European Community (now Union) which could assist or ameliorate conditions in the areas that they represented.

The attention of commercial lobbyist, client and politician was temporarily diverted when all three began following developments in the newly formed Social Democratic Party, which, for a brief time, looked set to unseat the Conservatives. The SDP was seen by many in the commercial world as the better of two evils – i.e. the Tories were unpopular and 'loony' Labour was unthinkable.

Instructed by their clients, lobbyists began to factor in their concerns to the SDP. Despite this, there was some panic in the commercial world. Such panic was exacerbated by growing realisation of the importance of (Socialist) Europe and the belief that the SDP was European socialism – with all the protection that such socialism offered workforces – in all but name.

As it happens, following the Falklands War, it was the Tories who were returned to office.

As a result, many Tory MPs who, for whatever reason, would never sit on the government benches, began to seek outside commercial employment. So did some of their colleagues in the Labour Party. One way of making contact with such outside commercial interests was via some of the All Party Groups. In addition, some businesses, including public affairs companies, because of the increasing importance of (socialist) Europe and awareness of the growing popularity of single issue causes, were becoming interested in appointing Labour MPs whom they believed, wrongly, had greater access to Europe via British Labour MEPs and/or could give a token impression of political balance. The result was the start of an unprecedented growth in the commercial interests of politicians on both sides of the House, but principally on the Conservative side. This was replicated in local government with countless numbers of councillors enjoying the gravy train.

Meanwhile, those businesses weathering the recession, and looking for future growth, diversified. Again, the staff of the commercial lobbying companies bore witness to this, as, for example, component clients purchased waste disposal companies, tacking yet more interests on to the monitoring lists and exposing the staff to environmental concerns. As a result, those following environmental developments became heavily engaged in European Union issues, joining those staff already specialising in them. The day of the 'straddle' lobbyist had arrived.

This widened an already visible divide between some of the lobbyists and their subordinates. That is to say, subordinates began to over-take their superiors. These, rather than their superiors, began handling the new demands. This included the provision of information pertaining to so-called 'enemy activities' (competitor or single issue group); commercial and new market intelligence culled from national and EU political documentation , and political and legal guestimates in both the UK and EU.

In addition, clients were waking up to the fact that legislation could be introduced via affirmative/negative statutory instrument rather than by primary legislation as well as making use of private bill legislation. (The Law Lords eventually levelled the playing field.)

Meanwhile their superiors were either trying to catch up with their former staff or trying to keep control of them by minimising their value – 'My dear, you can learn Europe in half day' – apparently unaware that EU work was the staple diet of all Whitehall departments. Others, however, began funding the newly developing European lobbyists in offices in Strasbourg and Brussels where they joined countless others jostling to take advantage of a now growing market. The bleed of the staff began.

Those that stayed exclusively with Westminster put together more and more ministerial delegations with the attendant duties; and widened their coverage of Party Conference. Lavish hospitality programmes were devised. Wining and dining became an industry in itself as did the acquisition of political contacts and opinion formers outside of politics in Whitehall, quangos, the press and non-governmental organisations. Many of these were profiled by the public affairs companies, as well as by the still functioning right wing organisations, and their newer manifestations, with their attendant connections with the secret state.

As the commercial lobbying industry was exploding, the vast majority within it were unaware of the new arrivals and what they did, including many foreign 'Mr Fix-its' who acted as commission agents on large government contracts. These were happy to see the known commercial lobbying industry hijacked by noisy hospitality and conference specialists, attracting the attentions of the press, which distracted the press from their own activities.

As the hospitality business boomed those lobbyists running All Party Groups found themselves ahead of the pack. Many Ministers and Opposition Shadow Secretaries of State had enjoyed their hospitality via the groups which gave them a lead on other companies. Meanwhile staff trawled Party Conference Fringe Meetings (few of which were covered by the Press) to monitor the 'Alternative Voices', which 'threatened' their clients since some of the 'Alternative Voices' were receiving a fairer hearing in Europe than they were in the UK and therefore growing increasingly more powerful.

The staff, many of whom were no more than green girls delighted to have their first jobs, were under instruction not to draw attention to themselves, or engage in any dialogue with the Press.

Simultaneously, a new breed of 'traditional' commercial lobbyist arrived on the scene, such as Gifford, Jeger and Weekes (GJW), formed by three former aides to leaders of the three main parties (Steel,

Callaghan and Heath). These were much more up front about lobbying, and, as proven by their press launch, both actively encouraged and did not fight shy of media attention. In addition, Ian Greer, once the other half of the successful partnership Russell-Greer, and who was to come to grief in the 'Cash for Questions' affair, broke up with John Russell and set up another company, Ian Greer Associates successfully capitalising on his Conservative background.

To match the competition, fees in some of the lobbying companies began to rocket as a service industry turned itself into a consultancy industry overnight. Exclusively a marketing ploy, this began to attract more of the multinationals. These expected their consultants to be expensive. Fees rose without an appreciable rise in standards.

The Multinationals

Mostly from the United States, the multinationals (who were used to working with lobbyists) were anxious about legislative developments in the European Union. Other nationals, principally the Japanese, who felt culturally disadvantaged, were similarly interested in Europe. Both were anxious about protectionism. Both saw the UK as their sole entree into European markets. And both paid their newly acquired lobbyists large fees to get results.

As a result, client demands became more sophisticated and began to evolve at a considerably faster pace than the lobbyists themselves. By this time also, lawyers were beginning to follow their clients to Westminster (private bills) and working ever more closely with Parliamentary agents; as well as following their clients to Europe. Management consultants, or the management consultancy arms of large accountancy practices, soon headed off after them. The UK Parliament was viewed from Europe rather than the reverse, a development not recognised by the Press for at least a decade afterwards.

Despite the strictures of the traditional lobbying companies that staff should not talk to the press, their own lavish hospitality programmes soon brought them to their attention. Up until then, disapprobation had been concentrated in the hands of one or two in the written press. 'Hospitality' however made good television. The limited relationship between the two began to deteriorate further.

The Press

Some people in The Lobby and Parliamentary Press Gallery had had links with commercial firms – providing information etc and breaking

Fleet Street and Press Gallery rules. As a result, many commercial lobbyists were incensed to find themselves singled out by the press for some of their habits.

Most lobbyists at that time had a policy not to engage with the press, therefore those that did were few and far between and, for the most part, only knew the anti-Thatcherite print press, reflecting their own personal political opinions, and either a marginalised or a minority view. Very few lobbyists had been working journalists and therefore had problems getting some of their stories placed, which annoyed those predisposed to get on with the Thatcherite newspapers.

The print press, who were aware of commercial lobbyists, i.e. the minority, themselves refused to cover their affairs (see 'The Political Gallows') principally because they believed themselves to be upholding the status quo and the commercial lobbyists embarrassed such status quo. They had very little opinion of the television press and the new breed of TV investigative reporter.

These, with little knowledge of the background to the lobbying industry, had a steep learning curve. The result was that television programmes, often as an excuse to attack individual companies/multinationals, began to learn more about the industry, most of which was hostile. They were soon querying the morality of lobbyists as propagandists, and their skills. They began to query publicly what the lobbyist actually did for his clients.

This was followed by arguments about the morality of lobbying in general, and influence, which appeared to be based solely on the size of the wallet. For some there was also a hidden agenda – i.e. attacking the commercial lobbyists was a way of attacking the Conservative Party, given the stranglehold the Conservatives had over much of the press machine.

Those making the television programmes, however, appeared to be wholly unaware that some of their colleagues, for a variety of reasons, had sustained the status quo. Nor, apparently, did they know anything about the (discredited) lobby system, or the fact that some of their colleagues had willingly subscribed to the conventions. As a result, the commercial lobbyist became demonised without being given the right of reply which would have bounced the arguments back into the political system which provided the market.

Even more astonishingly some members of the press appeared to be unaware of the existence of the distinguished former Labour Minister, MEP, and MP, Bob Cryer, who had single-handedly led the campaign to crack down on the lobbyists years before they had arrived on the scene. (Reluctance to promote Bob Cryer's valid arguments had a great deal to do with the fact that he was viewed as a 'left-winger' – a prefix which always preceded his name in order to diminish him – and many of the press refused to air the views of such left-wingers.)

The press as a whole became more obviously interested in commercial lobbying when the industry's clients' relationship (and political donations) to the Conservative Party became a more public issue.

The perfect foil to company donations, historically, had been trades union donations to the Labour Party. Such foil however was found increasingly wanting in view of the large sums of money allegedly pouring into the Conservative party from unaccountable and untransparent sources.

Not that the Press were able to get at the full picture – their stories tended to concentrate on what could be seen and did not highlight the 'gaps', that is to say money spent by individuals on partisan advertising, 'research' institutes, donations in kind, major loans and offshore accounts.

This brought in yet more investigative reporters who were prepared to cut across cosy press relationships in order to expose what was going on. For the most part they were also hostile to commercial lobbying, still unaware that the politicians and political infrastructures were the source of the market. In addition, and for the most part, they did not recognise that many of the commercial lobbyists had nothing to do with other more sinister lobbying activities and the rumoured involvement of Whitehall in some of those activities, or any knowledge of party funding.

The media attention saved the commercial lobbyists the necessity of advertising. Advertising was, in any event, frowned upon by the old guard at Westminster, if not by the European Parliament who, at that time were oblivious to the extent of the lobbying in both Westminster and Europe. (The Germans do not even have a word for 'lobbying').

More new business came flooding in.

Civil Servants

Behind the scenes, all were waking up to the commercial implications of privatisation and de-regulation. And the need to start cultivating Civil Servants (i.e. Whitehall). These were seen to be key because junior officials draft legislation and are interested to meet those with a genuine interest in the field that they are covering – indeed, a substantial amount of a lobbyist's time is spent dealing with Civil Servants who ring the lobbyist for advice; and middle and higher ranks who have enormous ability to sway/award commercial tenders.

Traditionally regarded as secretive and impervious to external influence and lobbying (but not impervious to those already enjoying insider status), parts of the Civil Service was changing out of all recognition.

This was in part due to the interaction between Civil Servants and their colleagues from other EU States which intensified, doubtless playing a major part in encouraging a more open relationship with all the attendant lobbying possibilities; in part due to government bouncing outsiders (usually businessmen) on to them as 'special advisers'; and in part due to conflicting cultures, lax conduct and poor policing of such conduct.

The political world began to explode.

Meanwhile, government was bravely seeking to assert its authority over some industries and professions with a varying degree of success. These were bloodied when Ministers called their bluff (e.g. Kenneth Clarke/pharmaceutical lobby) or challenged (e.g. Nigel Lawson/oil cartels) or actively took the part of the consumer (e.g. Richard Tracey/tobacco lobby and Edwina Currie/food lobby).

At the same time, those who had assumed that Government, with the assistance of the Civil Service, would always bail them out were finding that this was less and less the case, and the financial community were warned that they were going to get de-regulated and investment fund managers could suffer.

Back to Business

By the mid-1980s large corporations were finally persuaded that they needed lobbyists. Those employing them were no longer the sort of people who read the book reviews in the Sunday papers and discussed them in a mannered way over a silver service tea. Instead they were the sort who bought race horses in their company names but either never went to the races, or, if they did, spent their time networking/seducing favourite clients, politicians, journalists and commercial lobbyists, in hospitality tents sited at racecourses in order to further the self-interest of everyone present.

Those, incidentally, with an interest in the stock market, were ideally placed to judge commercial trends by trawling through the political documentation as well as scrutinising the lobbyists' ever changing monitoring lists.

Meanwhile a flood of public servants were entering the market e.g. ex Ministers Keith Speed and Marcus Fox who established their lobbying company Westminster Communications in 1982. At much the same time, everybody started hunting around for additional/alternative sources of influence and started splashing out the directorships, opera tickets and lunch invitations.

Back at Westminster, politicians were having to deal with a very heavy legislative programme.

House of Lords

To cope with everything the House of Lords were required to play a much more active role than had become customary. Firstly on science and technology (the House of Commons had very little interest in science); secondly on Europe where their Lordships bore the brunt of scrutiny; thirdly as Opposition (the government called up the previously non-voting peerage as a result); and fourthly as unhappy judge with an increasingly anxious Judiciary establishing legal precedents determined by blatant politics.

Lobbying the House of Lords became big business. Their Lordships responded vigorously. To date their business interests are not fully transparent, one reason why wholesale reform of the Upper House is now on the cards.

De-regulation, Privatisation, Foreign Businessmen and the EU

Next, the politicians had to cope with de-regulation, privatisation, and acknowledgement that, whether they liked it or not, the EU was controlling much of the agenda. The latter brought in more of the multinationals. These believed in aggressive lobbying. They were also used to arranging the terms of the agenda, and rubbishing anything that threatened it.

Meanwhile, staff in the commercial lobbying companies were watching the rise of men in the privatised utilities who had risen through the ranks and were now in comfortable retreat from the rigours of real life. Unequal to their new positions, they elevated their public affairs advisers to the boardroom. Many of these were known to commercial lobbyists (who, while liking them socially, often found them intellectually weak), reinforcing links between the business and commercial lobbying world, as well as providing commercial lobbyists with an ability to judge the level of competence (or lack of) of the new chairmen, which helped, among other things, to know which politicians to put their way.

Simultaneously, as before in the early 1970s, there was a mergers and take-over boom. This funded the rise of the financial and corporate public relations companies and the spin doctors. Fees went off into the stratosphere. Political consultants, with substantially lower fees, became the poor relations in the worlds with which they were linked.

And linked they were as financial and corporate PRs planted stories in the press (sometimes with the editor or journalist's collusion) which enabled politicians to run with the story in Westminster talking up/or talking down various companies and individuals with the attendant repercussions on share prices. Cosy relationships and inducements became the name of the game as colossal fortunes were made.

The City press did very little publicly to expose what was going on any more than the political press publicly exposed one-time commercial activities in the Parliamentary Press Gallery. However, the heat remained on the commercial lobbyists, who, with a few glorious exceptions, were not party to such conduct, although their company's proprietors might have been. The politicians rounded on them and started 'investigating' their activities via the never very credible Select Committee on Members' Interests.

Meanwhile, many businessmen became ever more detached from reality, sliding, along with those who assisted them, into what many believed to be corruption, although the word was seldom used.

The Multinationals

The multinationals soon recognised that the British government was not up to controlling any of the fiscal or legislative decision making in Europe, and were even more aware that Europe was concentrating far too hard on the 'Alternative Voices' i.e. pressure groups such as environmentalists.

To keep tabs on the pressure groups, and events in Europe, some believe they started to call upon the services of the secret state again, some of whose personnel were happy to moonlight with or without their employers' consent. In addition, rumours were heard all over Westminster and the European Parliament that the flood of American research assistants offering to work for no pay were funded by the CIA.

What was to become nearly two decades of uninterrupted Tory Government eventually resulted in an unprecedented expansion of business activities in the lobbying field. Countless public servants set up or joined companies to take advantage of the vast opportunities created by the privatisation programme. Many became millionaires.

In addition, many joined the lobbying industry and many went freelance. Some of the freelancers were naive, desperate or greedy (sometimes all three) and ended up servicing work that either the main agencies had turned down, or, had accepted because of the moneys involved but wanted an outsider to be seen to be doing the work (e.g. political promotion of the tobacco substitute Skoal Bandits).

Public servants scrutinising legislation in Standing Committee were picked up by commercial interests on a regular basis. Rubbing shoulders with stock brokers, merchant bankers and investment companies they and/or their commercial lobbying companies became prized assets.

Meanwhile, foreign governments, companies and individuals also wanted influence. Hundreds of Peers, MPs/MEPs, many of them members of Committees which travelled widely at the national/European taxpayer's expense, were happy to accept lucrative consultancies from them. These were paid either directly to them or via lobbying companies. Favourite countries included China, Israel, Nigeria, East Germany and the Middle East.

The 'loadsamoney' philosophy dominated public affairs and public servants alike. The latter seemed oblivious to the fact that as holders of public office they had a duty to conduct themselves as role models for the community.

Pressure Groups

The electorate, with the help of a more confident and capable Opposition frontbench, began to wake up to the responsibilities and implications of privatisation. In addition, they were growing uncomfortable with media coverage of so-called 'yobs' e.g. anti-nuclear waste, animal rights, road, and environment protesters, whom they recognised as themselves in all but name. The voters arrived in Westminster – only to find that there was no meaningful way for them to express their discontent.

As a result, single issue pressure groups began to make greater headway. They recognised that much of what was being decided by national government was not being decided by Westminster at all but by Whitehall and 'discreet' offices of major Departments of State, as well as by Europe, which, at that time, was considerably more sympathetic to single issue interests than were national Parliaments. In consequence, some of these groups also began to employ commercial lobbyists.

Even more of them began to look towards MEPs, particularly Labour MEPs, who revelled in the divide between (Tory) Government, the European Parliament and, indirectly, European Commission. To balance this, many of the multinationals began employing (Tory) MEPs and accepting consultancy services from former European bureaucrats. As a result, the lobbyist was yet again up against public servants making a fast buck, this time in Europe.

Changes in the Political Consultancies

As the workload at Westminster and Europe increased, so the role of the staff of the commercial lobbying companies changed. Those that could not cope with the new demands fell by the wayside. To follow the market, those that remained were appointed to different aspects of the market. Meanwhile, newcomers patrolled the market with increasing gusto.

Westminster groups with foreign connections began to be wined and dined. Those politicians, both here and in Europe, with strong business links with foreigners were particularly in demand. Established country pressure groups and old-fashioned Parliamentary groups suffered in consequence, as did old Masonic networks. These gave birth to a plethora of Think Tanks and foundations some of which were pursuing undemocratic political agendas with un-transparent funding arrangements. It should also be said, of course, that any number of such Think Tanks were fulfilling a much needed, and often maligned role.

The All Party Group system exploded, with countless politicians using them as a marketing vehicle and agreeing to 'employ' 'research assistants' from commercial companies whose only role was to promote the private interests of the company. And they were even given passes giving full access to the Palace of Westminster, a fact which was to become a focus of media attention in the future.

As a result, the traditional lobbying companies were eclipsed. New companies were being created all the time. These included SGL, which, with an insider knowledge of Whitehall, helped firms win MoD contracts; and Michael Forsyth Associates which went on to assist cleaning and catering companies win political influence in battles for privatised NHS services.

In 1988 commercial opportunities provided by electricity privatisation (the Bill became law in 1990) brought swathes of foreign companies in hoping to provide heating systems. Privatisation and deregulation of television, and the winning of cable TV franchises, spawned another group all wanting inside knowledge of government plans and policies. All of these companies employed commercial lobbyists.

Defence interests became an even bigger earner as the UK allegedly acted as export conduit for countries such as America whose stated policy was to adhere to various embargoes imposed by the US Congress. Next, the defence unions, anxious about the privatisation of the Royal Ordnance Factories wanted lobbyists. These had learned the lessons of the miners strike – case studies had included the mobilisation of government supporters, to tactics used by 'lobbyists', to the contacts needed to control press coverage and the requirement for spin doctors. As a result, they wanted 'professionals'.

Other unions began to take an interest in using the services of the commercial lobbyists. However, for the most part they could not afford to employ them – and subsidised and pro-bono work had not yet become fashionable. The result was the establishing of smaller lobbying companies catering to the needs of those on the left of politics.

Next, head-hunters moved in to find public servants – from former Ambassadors to ex-Secretaries of State – to go on main boards of companies the latter had either privatised or assisted in the post-privatisation spoils. Former public servants, from senior personnel in the armed services to diplomats and spies, had traditionally found post-retirement employment in the City.

The head-hunters broadened, and formalised their position in political life. Pretty soon, countless public servants were knocking on their doors. Whitehall mandarins, their subordinates and former Ministers, as well as those injected into the system from outside, all wanted a share of the spoils, promoting the market and dictating their price in the market place.

The lobbying market finally boomed when more and more politicians became willing to acquire business interests and therefore actively pursued them. The privatisation programme and the injection into Whitehall of non-Whitehall personnel fuelled the psychology of the market place. The sheer scale of the privatisation programme, and the army of lawyers, merchant bankers and accountants serving the programme meant that it was unstoppable.

De-regulation brought other pressures. Big companies found themselves dealing with 'Civil Servants' on placement from their competitors. Some of these had the power to award contracts to their old employers. No complaint could be made in case complainants were blacklisted. Nonetheless, letters of complaint were drafted by commercial lobbyists for their clients, the decision whether or not to send them being left with the client.

An unregulated industry, long out of hand, was now off the Richter scale. No-one in authority, least of all Government, appeared to recognise that the raw pressures of the market could not be left to operate unhindered. While political public relations never commanded the financial weight of corporate, financial and crisis public relations, it was catching up fast.

In the lobbying companies the boom years saw two developments. Firstly that they could pump up the profits and profile of their mainstream PR agency owners by offering a political service if they had one; and secondly that they could buy a consultancy that offered such a service if they did not. If the former, they could make an existing overhead 100% more profitable for no extra cost.

In both cases they could start offering their clients packages without investing in the training of their existing staff. Desperate to attract further big accounts, the lobbyists brought in over the heads of their existing staff, new 'consultants' or high-flyers, who, by virtue of their previous employment (usually government service) were seen as good marketing ploys. Since, however, they were not lobbyists they added to already overstretched workloads. In addition, they cost heavily, draining resources away from staff and, in consequence, knocking on the head their last vestiges of loyalty. Standards and morale sank.

Staff were having to distribute their time between new clients coming via the PR agencies, new clients coming via their consultants, and their existing clients, all of whom had priority but none of whom had the same rank, product knowledge, requirements (real, perceived or created) or paid the same price for their services. Also, they were having to be in Brussels or Strasbourg, while their superiors wanted their assistance with their solely Westminster based clients.

In addition, senior personnel from the main PR Agency, without product knowledge but with substantially larger budgets and with an eye on the profits, believed they could do a better job themselves and sought to do so. In this way major clashes of interests were absorbed and funds required by the political units were pumped elsewhere.

Meanwhile, more and more individuals, groups of individuals and other professions or service industries were purporting to give a political consultancy service covering the UK, Europe and USA. Those specialising in, and set up solely as a response to, deregulation and privatisation made further millions.

Standards of both lobbyist and staff slid dramatically further as 'getting results' was no longer necessarily based on good lobbying skills but on 'kickbacks' and 'spin'. As a result, those in a position to offer staff sound management, ethical employment and financial security picked up the few good subordinates around who willingly flopped exhausted out of the agencies or private consultancies.

This left the lobbyists running around without the protection and support systems previously offered to them by their departing staff while for the first time government relations and European affairs became the responsibility of their clients' main boards, and the demands became both more sophisticated and confidential in nature.

Those lobbyists with the appropriate skills became integral advisers, the social divide between the service industry and the customer breaking down, those without them being found increasingly wanting. As a result, the agencies started losing clients since expertise was increasingly being moved in-house.

This loss of business was masked because there was so much business coming in.

Employment increased but those being employed were untrained. Moreover, some of those clients remaining with the consultancies or acquiring lobbyists for the first time were, for the most part, politically unsophisticated. This often meant that they did not know what they wanted and were therefore offered the service the lobbyist could provide, not the service they needed. The wide-boys had arrived.

The agencies, meanwhile, went public in order to raise finance for other purchases, mostly of companies abroad. They therefore continued not to invest in their existing or subsidiary companies. In addition, staff salaries remained low since they were having to provide their new shareholders with a dividend (a burden carried by the staff who were already subsidising the original shareholders and the newly acquired so-called 'high flyers').

Waking up to the need to keep their staff, and apparently embracing Conservative legislation making it easier for staff to purchase shares in the businesses that employed them, the PR agencies began to offer their staff shares in their companies. As a result, some staff managed to pay off their mortgages when their companies merged or were purchased elsewhere, irrespective of their skills, while other staff watched the status quo cream off the profits before they themselves were able to purchase shares. Pay, for those excluded from (but sustaining) the status quo, remained poor.

1990+

Come the early 1990s, many of the agencies had over-extended themselves. To service their businesses they were having to both spend money on staff and the then new technologies. But they did not have any money because of their global purchases.

The few high-calibre lobbyists remaining were now supporting the deficiencies of other lobbyists, to the detriment of their own career growth and profit share, and to the detriment of the next generation of lobbyists who were learning on the job, and working for people who did likewise, within too short a space of time to have the experience necessary to learn on the job.

Simultaneously, there were increasing complaints from Parliamentarians about the countless numbers of 'lobbyists' who were trying to contact them, as well as complaints about the explosion in financial interests of many of their political colleagues. The result was a minor inquiry, conducted by a minor select committee of the House of Commons (see 'The Wrong Scandal') and increasing demands on the industry to self regulate, as if the industry, or government's relationship with clients of the industry, and not the public servant, were the problem. The next development was the setting up of a fledgling regulatory body, the Association of Professional Political Consultants, which, to date, has been ineffectual.

The agencies continued to take on new business for which they had neither the expertise nor the staffing. Next, the market moved on principally because major issues in Europe required either non-party alignment or all party support. Most of the agencies, however, could not offer such all party support since so many of them knew only Conservative politicians.

As the privatisation and de-regulation work dried up, and European Union and local government business increased, they found themselves exposed. They were even more exposed when links with Whitehall became chiefly the preserve of those commercial lobbying companies specialising exclusively in Whitehall or because, used to dealing directly with client industries, Whitehall itself booted them out, in order to cut out the middle man.

Finally, the 'obvious' commercial lobbying market exploded when the 'Cash for Questions' affair hit the headlines. It unravelled much of the whole, leading to the Nolan Committee into Standards in Public Life; and the promise of anti corruption legislation to be announced in November 1998.

Meanwhile, the secretive newcomers (mostly, but not exclusively, specialising in defence lobbying) began to lose influence as public servants grew anxious about press inquiries and where such inquiries could lead. Not of course that this mattered to many of them since vast fortunes had already been made – and incalculable damage done to innocent civilians overseas.

The PR agencies links with local government were also increasingly found wanting. Locally employed Civil Servants often did not share the lobbyists goals (and, for years, had been incensed to find that Tory-controlled quangos wielded more power than they did). Moreover, councillors were just as likely to be Labour or Liberal/Social Democrats than they were Tory – and the agencies had very little knowledge of or contact with either of them.

As a result, some of the larger lobbying companies began to look more favourably at some of the trade unions. These had more money to spend, and, however reluctant, they were to accept working with 'anti democrats' such as commercial lobbyists, were willing to pay for their skills. The companies accepted the work – some of which was subsidised – because, following the deposing of Mrs Thatcher, some of them had an axe to grind with those who had opposed her i.e. they loathed the new Conservative Government. In addition, they needed contacts in the Labour movement. The relationship with the unions worked well for both sides.

As the century closes, the Labour Party has come full circle. Now the governing Party, it is proving itself as much the creature of lobbyists as the previous government. Some commercial lobbying companies have become central to all its privatisation, regulation and legislative work. Because of the commercial lobbying industry debate, and government's dishonesty in not shedding light on the debate and extent of connections – this has led to some embarrassment and even more vociferous demands for reform.

The one clear opportunity that the industry had to explain itself has been lost, not least because of Government's handling of the situation, its coyness in being open about some of its appointments to task-forces and focus groups, and, even more tellingly, its need for corporate money and goodwill in return for which some favours are allegedly being granted.

It does not help of course that as the decade closes reform of party funding is not yet really on the cards, although government pretends it is. Whatever is introduced will be useless without other controls. For example, the money sloshing around some 'Think Tanks', some lobbying companies, and some links with foreign governments need to be clearly identified, and MPs dissuaded from promoting them, or identifying their sponsors on all appropriate occasions. Idealists in the industry also point out that many commercial bodies which have links with the Think Tanks would, if the opportunity was there, like to share some of their research once confidentiality was no longer commercially necessary. However, there are very few formal ways in which altruism can be merged with the commercial world. Other Think Tanks, it should be said, rightly claim that they are ignored by government, despite the validity of the views they represent, when their conclusions do not reflect that which government wishes to hear – in other words, cronyism, ingrained culture and a desire to control, works against them.

Meanwhile, and despite 'Cronygate', the apolitical bias of earlier years appears to be returning as indeed is the demand for procedural and legislative knowledge. New Labour lobbyists who cannot offer these skills are as at sea on this one as are many of the Tories.

Those in Europe are specialising and extending into the United States. Straddle lobbyists are now the norm rather than the exception. Those in the UK are looking towards local and regional government.

The problem, however, is that far too few of the lobbying companies are any good at what they purport to do. They are unable to plan for tomorrow's market because they have not yet caught up with today's. In addition, some of those that are 'good' are unlikely to maintain their edge since they are so distanced from the ground.

Some companies are seeking to forge 'global' joint ventures in order to both stand still as well as stay in business tomorrow. It is easier for them to raise money to purchase new business, and new accounts, than to invest in what they have. In the meanwhile, their staff subsidise them and most salaries remain low.

The Future: Where is the industry going?

The market is likely to grow both in-house and in the commercial lobbying consultancies because government, world-wide, is a major customer of their clients and because the legislation that government enacts can give industry a headache. Detailed knowledge of tax and company law, economy and enforced familiarity with the minutiae of local politics across the globe will be expected as well as the need to get to know, and influence, 'personalities' from the local school teacher in remote villages, to the mayors of major towns.

The business community will not survive without lobbyists, who, increasingly, will be required to provide it with a mix of 'nous', the detection of new markets, and finding friends and influence to take advantage of those new markets. Increasingly, the market is public policy. In order to influence this, the actions of governments, locally, nationally, European, and further afield must be anticipated and lobbied. The biggest hold-up, in an industry which is changing rapidly however, is the reluctance to integrate core public affairs services with broader communications strategies.

As a result, those servicing the market are likely to divide into network specialists and generalists. All will need to build up a high degree of expertise in a basket of countries . Lobbying companies themselves will need to deepen their professional skills and get to grips with commercial, as well as political, aspects of their clients strategy, locking into organisations such as the World Trade Organisation, think-tanks, focus groups, pressure groups, charities and non-governmental organisations.

Both charities and non governmental organisations are providing lobbyists with lucrative accounts and useful contacts. Much of this work is provided on a pro-bono basis (in marked contrast to the 1980s) as the 'good' commercial lobbyists try to reinvent themselves as corporate citizens.

Back in the commercial world, clients of the commercial lobbyists are likely to retain them as they presently retain accountants and lawyers, and the status of political advice, whether in-house or provided by outside consultants, is likely to be elevated. As a result, those employing commercial lobbyists will no doubt chose one particular company and stick with them, not least because of client confidentiality, ending many insecurities in the industry. Inevitably, it will also favour the larger companies, and smaller ones will fall by the wayside.

That is not to say that newer insecurities will not emerge – they are already, not least in the lack of trained staff. This is particularly apparent in Brussels where lobbying companies do not have enough staff with industry and sector knowledge. Those with the best skills are usually lawyers who are used to working with the multinationals.

The job will become easier for outsiders to move into because of the opportunities created by the communication age. These will enable the lobbyist to position himself at the business hub as indispensable strategic adviser. Despite this, it is important to remember that technology is easily appropriated and does not displace traditional tactics such as knowing the right people. It is also important to point out that because of that same technology, bread and butter monitoring, which is still keeping a lot of lobbying companies in business, will disappear.

The market is threatened by those moving in. In a way, the commercial lobbyists are victims of their own success. They are also victims of the commercial pressures on other industries and professions (e.g. lawyers) who are always seeking new sources of income and are well placed to squeeze out the original commercial lobbyists. In the United States legal and other firms have provided lobbying activities for years and there is no reason why management consultants, accountants, and communications companies will not follow suit.

Government relations, market access advice, business development, strategic partnering, investment negotiations, media relations, corporate positioning, crisis management will all fall into lobbying company remits. Crisis management – e.g. disasters such as Exxon Valdez – and neutralising a threat, or gaining the support of key constituencies vital for company survival, is likely to involve the lobbyists with their clients ever more closely. It will also involve them with those who also influence their clients, for example, their insurers. These take political risk seriously – whether this be the potential kidnap of a senior executive and how this is communicated to the political and financial world; or the impact that legislation can have on the client's commercial environment.

In addition, it draws them closer to the legal world where lobbyists increasingly will find themselves handling a growing number of litigation mandates which embrace both public affairs and media attack management. That is not to say that the legal system in the UK is becoming more like America – it is to say that management of the media and political fallout during controversial legislation or court cases, is.

Another growth area for lobbyists is the fact that companies and organisations are being forced to demonstrate corporate responsibility and business ethics on an ever more urgent basis. The job of selling capitalism is trickier than it used to be, particularly if capitalism is not to go the way of communism and implode. The liberal trade agenda of the World Trade Organisation dictates this.

Today, and more so in the future, companies will need to appear ethical, in the same way that foreign governments, also employing lobbyists in order to compete, for, say, EU investment grants or other direct investment, need the appearance of respecting human rights to succeed. Like national government, many of the commercial lobbyists are not ready for ethical commerce, although they pretend otherwise. In the interim, they rely on spin (e.g. the defence industry does not manufacture weapons of warfare, but weapons that allow (some) citizens to defend themselves – presumably from the tyrant across the border also armed by the same defence manufacturers, but that's another story.)

There is a great deal of money in political spin, or public image building and manipulation. Increasingly working with foreign governments that do not conform to Western ideals, the lobbyists are seeking to change perceptions about them. Those working on tourism accounts are, for the moment, managing successfully to distance themselves from their client governments woeful records in civil rights, corruption, and other such issues.

Presenting themselves as educators of such countries, reformers of corporations, introducers of open dealing and curtailers of bad practice, the industry is beginning to assume a halo of hypocrisy a previous generation could only dream about.

It is understood, although it is only rumour at the moment, that the

Vatican (some would say, the ultimate Pontificators!) are the latest foreign government considering signing up with a global lobbying company. These are now acting, depending on your point of view, as window dressers and puff merchants, or corporate consciences.

Dealing with pressure groups and NGOs forms another growth area. Companies claim to operate within the law, and with the full support of their various host governments. However, the message of the pressure groups is that compliance with the law is not enough, particularly when vital human rights and environmental issues are at stake. The NGOs have to be taken seriously because, in addition to public support, they are major employers and educators, especially of women. However, it should also be said that many NGOs are coming in for some criticism these days. These range from anxieties in local communities in less developed countries that they are financed by foreigners and are accountable to no-one, to real problems with internal accounting and some corruption. In addition, NGOs challenge local status quo in these countries, eroding male dominated structures and placing, some would say, too much, pressure on women.

The multinational debate is about power, responsibility and accountability. It is about their social and political obligations. It is one that many of the pressure groups are winning – and one that the lobbyists are now having to defend on behalf of their clients. This they do by demanding that such pressure groups provide 'solutions' (the new jargon) and when they cannot, keep going in the same destructive direction.

In this, national government (which, along with industry, cannot afford for the pressure groups to be right, although they often are) colludes. What's more, it turns a blind eye as clandestine agencies (including state employed intelligence officers) seek to infiltrate the groups in order, at a later stage, to discredit them; while other organisations profile journalists who write about them favourably.

As the decade closes, commercial lobbying is back where it started – with spooks and big business. But then again, spooks and big business was always a large part of the industry anyway.

Meanwhile, the private security industry increasingly attracts attention, in much the same way as the commercial lobbying industry once did, as indeed do some of its connections with the lobbying industry.

In the UK

Until such time as the manifestly unfair political process is reformed and an effective public sector facility provided, lobbyists will remain in work but be blamed for many of the inadequacies in the political system. In addition, the public perception of lobbying will similarly remain low principally because of obvious and indefensible injustices and disadvantages.

This is likely to increase as the present Labour Government faces the inevitable problems ahead, and in consequence, loses some of its popularity. With predictions at the moment pointing to the wipe-out of Labour in Scotland once the Scots have their own Assembly, Blair then joins Hague as a party leader of England, not UK plc.

Any commercial lobbyist too identified with the governing Party is likely to suffer in consequence with the management consultants gleefully filling any gaps that arise. They will suffer even more if the country decides to back Mr Hague after all. However, the possible introduction of proportional representation is much more likely to determine the future of the Conservative Party than he is.

However, it also has to be acknowledged that such an electoral system is bound to encourage the trend towards single party government (proportional representation, favouring smaller parties, reinforces the political system) i.e. it is tantamount to a five year elected dictatorship. The present electoral system, of course, amounts to this already, and, as was said at the outset, the British public hardly seem to care. Those that do, appear conditioned/resigned to the long game i.e. elected dictatorship. This also favours the commercial lobbying industry.

The biggest catalyst for growth for commercial lobbying, however, is the fact that single issue politics cuts across traditional boundaries of race, class and gender, exploding the polarised categories of left and right and binding opposites with common cause. Commercial lobbyists, and the big communications companies will be right in the middle of it all. Despite the much discussed demise of ideology, the communicators and lobbyists know different i.e. new ideologies emerge to take the place of dead ones.

A further incentive will be the regional assemblies and the development of elected mayoral cities – London at the moment, with Birmingham and Manchester likely to follow suit. Local and regional lobbying companies, plugged directly into the EU and in future profiling all the new assemblymen and women, have already taken off. Their success will in due course diminish many of the London based agencies. Particularly vulnerable are the smaller and medium sized London firms.

This will lead to a shake up in the industry – many companies are heading straight for the bankruptcy courts – since the field is very crowded not only with established consultancies, global to specialist, but with ex-politicians all trying to become independent consultants, or Labour bag carriers who once worked for someone, anyone, in the Labour Party and are not tainted by 'Cronygate'. Those companies remaining in London will no doubt only be those with an international dimension except those specifically dealing with London as a local region.

Meanwhile, clients are suffering from sensory overload. There are too many to meet and too much to do. They flop out and then go back and do the same thing. The hardest drivers are those with American bosses or companies run along US corporate lines. Meanwhile politicians and Civil Servants will continue to complain about a stream of unwanted communications from lobbyists.

Now having to deal with youthful politicians the lobbyists will be employed as front men for old men still running the business community. Or, as a 'pigeon pair' to the slick, young generation of business leaders – who in fact are pretty identical to the middle aged and elderly generation that ran business in previous decades. Millions of pounds of public money continues to pour into lobbying companies from local authorities, government agencies and privatised organisations.

In Europe

In Brussels, consultancies are now specialising in the management of networks and application of consensus building resolutions across Europe to address EU policy issues and obtain grants and loans. Brussels remains an insiders town where operating effectively depends upon a dense network of interpersonal and inter-organisational links. The lobbyists offer both. Large public affairs companies have offices in virtually all EU Member States maximising the public affairs capability of their clients as the Presidency moves from country to country.

In Geneva (whether or not Switzerland dumps its neutrality and joins the EU or not) business is likely to grow as lobbying moves deeper into international organisations with their headquarters there. The link between firms working with the European Union and the growing influence of international organisations such as the UN Economic Commission, the World Trade Organisation, the World Health Organisation and the World Intellectual Property Organisation is awe inspiring as companies, hoping to influence on global issues, pay lobbyists megabucks to talk in a Switzerland that is trying to reinvent itself.   Of course the ethos of WTO liberalisation plays into multinational hands.

The EU faces political, trade and economic challenges with the accession to the EU of Central and Eastern European countries. Clients are focusing their corporate communications programmes on the regulatory problems and business opportunities which exist in the CEEC region and have fifteen different independent nations to move into. Their lobbyists will be ahead of them ensuring a favourable regulatory environment and tax structure. Meanwhile, others are assessing the implications of the EURO for them – as well as advising on Sterling's relative strength once most of the economies of Europe are painfully stitched together.

In Eastern Europe lobbyists are beginning to act like privatised outposts of national trade and industry departments and, were the EU not so petrified of Anglo-US lobbyists could well be employed by them to establish EU Embassies both in Eastern Europe and the Far East. What would HM Diplomatic Corps say if they lost their jobs to lobbyists!?

However, in case some of the above sounds too upbeat it is important to stress that lobbyists in Eastern Europe – along with all the lawyers moving out there – are very likely to catch a cold before too long, if they have not already. The financial returns are negligible unless one of the world funding organisations are paying for it (i.e. the tax-payer). And corruption is endemic.

Although the large public relations companies with lobbying arms are all now employing local staff in Prague, Moscow and Budapest in association with their public affairs companies, they still need time to prove themselves.

They are, it should be said, greatly assisted by those who have gone before such as experts in public administration, funded by organisations such as the IMF, World Bank or EBRD. Moreover, the same debate took place in the 1970s as companies weighed up the pros and cons of opening an office in Brussels. The return on these was also negligible, or ran at a loss for nearly a decade, if not longer. The difference however is that the 'pioneers' in Brussels were not faced with the endemic corruption and security problems so much in evidence in Eastern Europe, nor with the need to develop the administrative infrastructure.

In addition, many commentators interested in the ethics of lobbying have also pointed out that commercial lobbyists act undemocratically – when, ostensibly, the EU is wanting to apply the democratic model to countries of the former USSR – and are therefore teaching undemocratic practice.

The lobbyists are unfazed by such criticism. Eastern European countries seem to be developing their own brand of commu-capitalism none of which, the lobbyists argue, has anything to do with them. National and European government's message might have been to deliver Eastern Europe from communism, but business, including commercial lobbyists, have no such ambition and do not understand why they should.

Moreover, the message of national government has always been a phoney one anyway – following the collapse of Communism, it has become apparent that western antipathy to it was never based on delivering the people of those regions from it, but on ensuring that it never reached London or New York; and, equally, ensuring that, in due course, London or New York could access it as a new consumer pool. Since this was Government's mission, once the hypocrisies had been stripped from the arguments, why should the commercial lobbyists be different? No reason at all, which is perhaps another reason why there is growing empathy between government and commercial lobbying industry. Their position, however, sits awkwardly with their claims to act as 'corporate consciences' and is unlikely to be sustained indefinitely. Nonetheless, all accept that because of different histories and cultures, commerce is witnessing the evolution of a different indigenous form of capitalism around the world which the lobbyist is well positioned to take advantage of.

Such indigenous capitalism will eventually interact more responsibly with lobbying companies, the multinational clients for whom they are working, and the present manifestation of the globalisation of both.

Meanwhile, there is some talk of the need for a code of conduct for those commercial lobbyists operating in Eastern Europe. Since, however, the UK industry has not advanced too far in this direction it is a bit much to expect more elsewhere. Besides, a code for Eastern Europe would be almost impossible to police.

Global

American companies now own many of the UK companies (the Canadians own GPC). European based industries have been slow to develop but it is thought likely that the Germans will eventually emerge as the main challengers servicing Eastern Europe.

Those promoting industries such as aviation are developing an expertise with specialist teams in Washington, Brussels and London providing a global service for clients facing several regulatory authorities and differing business ethics, in different countries, and needing to co-ordinate the respective positions. Multinationals are having to lobby government to secure agreements with host countries.

The commercial lobbyists are there in force all assisting in the intense local, national and international consultations needed.

The potentially enormous China and Asia-Pacific public affairs and political consultancy market is currently beset with problems, not least because of it's the economic and financial collapse in the region, and because, like Eastern Europe, some of their political forums are corrupt.

Nonetheless, lobbying companies have acted as government relations and direct investment advisers for their clients, employing local staff in Beijing, Shanghai, Hong Kong and Hanoi.

Japan, and the Japanese multinationals, have recently dropped from view (including pulling out of projects in the United Kingdom with the attendant disappointments to local workforces), some Japanese nationals (rather wildly) blaming the CIA for the collapse of the Japanese economy (instead of corruption and dire leadership) which, they claim, was likely to invest in the EURO markets at the expense of the dollar. Those operating with the Middle East, mostly on armaments and construction projects, are kept similarly busy, despite the similar collapse of many Middle Eastern economies, admittedly bolstered by overseas investments made at the height of the oil boom.

Some believe that the American and British lobbying companies will be given a good run for their money by Australian lobbyists. These are slowly coming of age.

In Australia, lobbying has principally been an add-on offered by the largest national law firms and management consultancies. These have always seen their role as mediator between client and government and have concentrated on government administration, rather than party politics, politicians and their staff. Ideal training for dealing with the Far East, perhaps in conjunction with communications companies with important offices in Australia.

Opportunities for public affairs companies and political consultancies in China and the Asia region are seen as the major challenge to US and EU lobbying firms as global multinationals wrestle with the opportunities. Personnel however, sent out to supervise locally based staff, can have major adjustment problems when they get there – and do not always have a job to come back to – which may stunt the calibre of the supervisors.

The biggest problem, however in both Eastern Europe and the Far East is corruption. Such corruption attracts, and is fed by, Westerners. Not that this is a problem for all. Some so-called 'lobbyists' seem to relish the challenge.

Only a few years ago, the concept of lobbying was a very narrow one. Today, almost like barbarian invaders, some 'lobbying' companies are spilling out into new worlds in their desperation to make money. Their piratical standards damage those lobbyists legitimately operating in new markets and are unlikely to be curtailed unless the US/EU make a concerted stand, something which is equally unlikely.

It is to be hoped, therefore, that such companies will wither on the vine. This is not so far-fetched. Their current preoccupation with the global is likely to be characterised by risky judgements and the patternlessness of their large scale greed could well be their undoing as business ethics begin to penetrate public and media attention. Those lobbyists who confine themselves to local, regional, national, European and new market affairs via professional, publicly accountable companies are likely to sleep better at night and reap the benefits. Those moving into the corrupt could suffer the consequences. Corruption does not pay, although in the short term it enriches a clutch of the wicked.

Political Risk Consultancies: Do they threaten the commercial lobbying market?

Politics is one of the risk factors that is part of the investment checklist of any foreign investment. Political risk companies (the up-market end of the private security industry, sometimes owned by insurance companies which underwrite political risk all over the world) divide problems into three areas: high risk (e.g. kidnap and ransom, product tampering), medium risk (e.g. industrial action) financial risk (e.g. import restrictions, expropriation of assets by hostile government) and local risks (e.g. where things are agreed by national government but thrown out by local government).

As a result, some of them are trying to move into the commercial lobbying market. For example, on the basis of minimising political risk before their clients make investment decisions, they claim they are seeking to influence policy in the European Commission and Parliament. They are assisted in this task because many of them have well-established relationships with, for example, the Lloyd's of London market and other global insurers, and with the political world – their boards are often made up of politicians, Civil Servants, and ex service personnel, including the intelligence services. Their staff also include former public servants, as well as academics, economists and lawyers.

As a result, some political risk companies are claiming that they can challenge the lobbyists at their own game. This is certainly a possibility – many are moving in on the market – but it is unlikely that they will succeed, not least because what is needed is sector and product knowledge, which, unlike the new breed of lawyer-lobbyists, they do not have. (Nor, incidentally, do many of the commercial lobbyists – yet.) Moreover, the larger political risk companies, often working in tandem with public affairs companies, have no reason to be interested. Those who are, are those struggling to make a living as political risk consultants.

Nonetheless, it is believed that the industry as a whole will try to redouble its efforts to chip away at some of the commercial lobbying market, as their traditional markets in Eastern Europe and Latin America decline, and their clients, anxious about inadvertently becoming involved in corruption and criminal organisations, refuse to invest in those areas. Their success, however, is not guaranteed since, unlike the commercial lobbyists, they have no access to mass communications infrastructure.

Often small subsidiaries of insurance companies it is possible this could change if the insurers themselves sell them on to the large global public communications empires. Many of these know each other and have worked together, off and on, since the dirty mergers and take-over battles of the 1980s when private security companies – although it should be said that most political risk consultants believe it to be unfair that they are associated with this end of the market – were involved in hostile take-overs for the Predator or the Prey. Indeed, some of the skills of the political risk companies could be useful, such as their increasing reliance on forensic accountants, as well as their ability to 'eavesdrop' and 'investigate' – whether or not the latter activities are legitimate.

However, the provision of services does not make them a challenger. The provision of analysis, of course, does, particularly as many of them are 'hungry' . This is partly because many of their clients have an intelligence network to rival that of many countries and are, in addition, setting up in-house political risk teams, and their market is therefore diminishing. Much the same thing has happened to the commercial lobbyists' client base, as companies carry large public affairs teams as an overhead in the same way as they do their accountants and lawyers.

The thinking of many of the political risk companies mirrors that of many of the commercial lobbyists. The majority do not believe that their corporate clients are morally responsible for many of the problems found in their working environments.

'Companies have no responsibilities in areas such as human rights – their duty is to their shareholders, employees and clients. Competitive pressures have forced companies into these environments in the first place. Pressure groups often take a simplistic view of these issues and demand companies act outside their mandate.' (*PA Newsletter*, Steve John, March 1998).

Quite. And the evidence proves that public opinion is moving their way.

There are also other issues arising. For example, those offering business 'intelligence' appear to be ignorant of the widespread public disquiet about invasion of privacy, and have a cavalier attitude towards those demanding privacy legislation.

Moreover, were such legislation to be enacted it is not certain that they would respect the spirit of the law. It should be noted that, like commercial lobbying, the private security industry in the UK is unregulated. In addition, some aspects of insurance, such as kidnap and ransom policies, are barred on the Continent but legal in Britain. The private security industry can, of course, be cavalier, since it is so heavily involved with Government, as indeed is the lobbying market. The similarities between the two industries are often astonishing.

Many of the companies are seeking to disguise the fact that the risk analysis business is rarely profitable. As many are unaware that commercial lobbying is itself not always profitable and moreover is now, like political risk business itself, firmly in the hands of about six companies. Sophisticated analysis has been familiar to insurance companies and big financial institutions for decades. Whether they fall down in favour of the private security companies or the lobbyists has yet to be decided. It is probably wise to come down on the side of the lobbyists and communicators coming out as the winners.

The problem of course is that issues such as environmental concerns have not gone away. Both political risk consultancies and lobbyists will be assisted by the fact that Government does not want the business world to lose against the 'environmentalists'. Whatever the long term benefits, the short term would be far too expensive for them to address.

As a result it is likely they will assist companies fighting the greens, possibly using clandestine agencies. The environmentalists themselves have lost many of the arguments but will be able to make a comeback when they start putting forward solutions and positive alternatives, the new jargon to buy government a bit of time. Meanwhile, government appears to be saying that no change is an option.

The interests of the private security companies and political risk consultancies in the commercial lobbying industry, however it is resolved, reinforces the industry's links with the increasingly financially productive clandestine world.

As with commercial lobbying, people have been warning government of an 'accident waiting to happen' in the private security industry that could unravel into government, in much the same way as the 'Cash for Questions' affair did. Westminster refused to deal with commercial lobbying, sidelining it to a minor committee, ring-fencing arguments. It still exploded.

Westminster similarly refused to deal with private security, again sidelining it to a committee (Home Affairs, 1996) that ring-fenced the arguments, on that occasion looking at night-club bouncers employed in the industry. Two years later, the involvement of a private security/military consultancy company in Africa and its links with the Authorities is imploding the Foreign Affairs Select Committee, although at the moment containment seems to be working.

Those commercial lobbyists who warned that a refusal to study the private security market in all its manifestations would, as commercial lobbying did, unravel into the heart of government, including the soon-to-be-stood down and ineffectual Parliamentary Secret Intelligence Services Committee, watched in amazement.

As the legitimate private security industry tried to defend itself, government and public servant yet again tried to stand apart from the problem, refusing to admit its use to the public, let alone the legitimate need and role of the industry. Asking it to self-regulate, government proves yet again that it wants its cake, and wants to eat it too.

Bold legislation for both industries, strengthened by government's Autumn anti-corruption legislation, is what is needed. This would enable two legitimate industries to allow competitive trends to sort out the rest, despite the fact that much of their conduct has been, and no doubt will continue to be, disreputable.

Conclusion

In Britain, a generation of young lobbyists have watched those in public service, or formerly in public service, massage political systems with increasing regularity and skill. For many of them, the greatest shock was in knowing that those public servants put their own, rather than their country's, interests first. Everywhere they turned, whether nationally or in Europe, they saw the same story. Massive corruption in all but name.

The shock at what was witnessed remains, as does a knowledge of the collusion of some of their employers.

Those who sought to protect their customers from exploitation, and the citizen, both here and overseas, from the immoral; those who respected 'democracy' and all that it should mean, were crushed under a relentless avalanche of public servants' and commercial lobbying proprietors', misbehaviour. They drove the market, distanced themselves when aspects of it got out of hand, made fortunes – especially in defence, an industry of pirates, crooks and mavericks – and refused to take responsibility for their behaviour.

Because of their excesses, the product of democracy remained, without penalty, in the hands of those who could exploit, and did so, without scruple. Those employed in the industry watched the 'Christian' humbug and pieties of their public servants in amazement. They were accustomed to the pieties of their managements.

Additionally, a generation of lobbyists watched their employers, on whom they were beholden and from whence their own standards came, let down their staff, and the industry, by a diminution of their own standards or by closing their eyes to the conduct and standards of others.

Pretending to be oblivious to what was going on, they at first professed to disbelieve their staff and then pretended they could do nothing about the situation. Those few lone voices that tried to do something, including making their complaints known to the political authorities, were no match for their less distinguished colleagues.

These insisted on seeing 'lobbying' as a limited market – one man arms traders, Mr Fix-its, all of whom 'lobbied', were not 'lobbyists' at all, they claimed, although they floated in and out of all political forums. But, in confining themselves, to the limited market, i.e. traditional commercial lobbying, they still refused to throw out the cowboys, principally because the standards of most were compromised and the money was good.

In not supporting the staff who expressed their anxieties about the industry as a whole, or about the conduct of companies or individuals within it, they left their staff with nowhere to go. And most especially offered no home to whistle-blowers.

As a result, a healthy insolence in the industry has been lost (lobbyists sneaking legislation through in front of big business on behalf of small clients were insolent rebels) along with persistent innocence. There is no longer any impudent fearlessness, nor a home for those who were more successful at friendship, than politics, and all the better lobbyists for it. An industry that could be multi-faceted, marvellous and mischievous is now characterised by cynicism, cronyism, surface sophistication, lack of fun, and the corruption of hearts, minds and wallets.

Once dominated by the courageous and the independent minded, now it promotes only the reverse. Profit, poor standards, let alone ethical conduct, and a marked disinclination to promote enjoyment are its hallmarks. The various scandals, both transparent and invisible, have scarcely left their mark despite all the pieties.

Of course, there is some indication that some responsible bodies are genuinely tired of the appalling status and reputation of lobbyists and are committed to doing something about it. But not enough. Moreover, their efforts are likely to be concentrated in the UK and European Union but not beyond. In the long term thousands of pounds will be made by the giants, while toasting out the minnows. Meanwhile, any number claiming to be lobbyists will be swimming in ever murkier waters, sometimes as agents for not necessarily ethical businesses.

New ideas? Forget it. New romances? Forget it. New beginnings? Forget it. It is all about old ideas and old romances. And Money. Whether it is clean money is up to the industry, as is an unflinching commitment to the principles of integrity, financial probity and democracy.

With regret, it is easy to conclude, that despite individual effort, the industry has gone too global, and people are too crooked for such ideals to succeed. Therefore, it is up to a new generation to lead the way. Considering a career in commercial lobbying? Terrific. A luminous star is needed to turn lobbying, with all its potential for fun, magnificence and measurable achievement, into one of the leading professions of the next century.

It can be done, especially if, in much the same way as editors of respectable newspapers can distance themselves from their proprietors, the employees in the industry police the industry, and, if necessary, distance themselves from the conduct of some of their employers and/or proprietors or colleagues.

Regulation cannot be left to employers, any more than it can be left to public servants, until both employer and public servant merit trust. Employers argue that they are so busy running their own companies that they do not have the time to police the industry as well.

That is a bit like saying that the big legal or accountancy practices are too busy to support, and pay for, their regulating bodies. Commercial lobbyists cannot claim that their industry has gravitas, and earns the country megabucks, and needs to be taken seriously, unless they are prepared to pay for and establish a governing body with the authority to send in the 'hit squad' when it is necessary.

If they do not, then, despite the money sloshing around for some, they are what the public perceive them to be, namely – pirates.

The modern industry is still maturing. To reach full maturity, and, in due course, professional/chartered status with the appropriate educational/training infrastructure, commercial lobbyists must spend money on themselves. Arguments about where the money should come from is a phoney one. And not one that real professionals – e.g. lawyers and accountants – need to make. They value the profession and collective representation.

Why on earth do the commercial lobbyists feel that exceptions should be made in their case? Perhaps they want things both ways.

When the 'Cash for Questions' affair broke in the mid-1990s the perception in the newspapers was that paying cash for Parliamentary questions, offering sweeteners such as holidays, and commissions to politicians for introducing new business, was inherent. That was certainly the case for some, but, crucially, not for all.

The industry dismissed such conduct, claiming that it was a manifestation of the 'excesses' of the 1980s. It said nothing about the 'lobbying' going on and the 'commissions' paid to public servants to promote commercial contracts outside of Europe that adhered to no moral criteria. It said nothing about the conduct of some companies and individuals, including public servants, operating in the European Commission and Parliament (These are scandals waiting to happen); or the too cosy a relationship that can exist between any government of the day and the favours offered and accepted by it.

For 'excesses' read anarchy. Not the anarchy of rioters and mob rule. Not the so-called anarchy of protest marchers who are infiltrated by the secret state. But the anarchy of crooks and fat-cats endorsed by government and public servant.

May 1997 was meant to represent a new broom. Instead, cronyism and much more besides was established even before the keys to the Kingdom had been handed over.

The kids are not the problem. The grown ups are.

Get into the industry. And get yourself a potentially terrific career in an energising, ethical, commercial lobbying environment. A great deal is working in favour of new entrants now, from the fact that clients are more sophisticated, to the use made of communications' technology and the assistance of the media. This is slowly re-inventing both itself and its role as guardian of the people – a novel, exciting and thrilling time, and, as a by product, raising standards in the industry.

New entrants are no longer working in a vacuum. Even better, the anti-corruption legislation referred to above, is likely to address many of the problems in both the unregulated commercial lobbying and private security industry, most particularly their dealings with public servants. They are, and always were, at the root of the problem.

The debate, however, is not helped by, no doubt well-intentioned, Peers of the Realm who are not lobbyists but have lobbied on single issues, advancing naïve opinions on national media networks. One, more usually associated with the film industry, said that the way forward was for the industry to revert to its previous role as Parliamentary adviser.

Get with it. The train left the station years ago. Turning the clock back is both impossible and, more importantly, not the answer. What is, is to ensure that the train and its occupants are headed to a more ethical destination.

HOW TO BECOME A LOBBYIST

Introduction – A Career in Commercial Lobbying – Political
Techniques for Effective Lobbying – Salaries – Freelancing and
Consulting – Consultancy Cash Flow – Small Consultancies – Shares
– Large Consultancies – Mentors and Friendships -Relationships –
Chauvinism, Ageism and Racism – Clothes, Personal Presentation and
Business Pitches – Setting Your Work in Context – Training,
Education, Conferences, NUJ Membership, Policing – Some Things
to Remember : Employers: The Political POPPETS/the Political
BOGGLES – Political Activities and Civic Duties – Regional v
London Consultancies – Conclusions

Introduction

Everybody appears to worry these days about their children's
professional future. They, apparently, will not stop travelling so that they
can obtain a 'proper job', complete with mortgage and private pension,
with or without an employers' contribution. The fact that the same
thing was said by the anxious parents of those now doing the worrying
is all but forgotten.

Previous generations pushed off to toil on a Kibbutz, on
archaeological digs, conservation projects in the third world or to work
in the United States – usually illegally. The greyhound bus was chased
across America by a posse of anxious parents shouting 'if you get caught
you will be deported. You do not know how serious this will be for
your future.'

So let us offer reassurance about that future. If you force the kids to
hang up their rucksacks too soon they will miss out on things that are

far more important than immediate office life. Moreover, they won't make good lobbyists. A year or two, out of a lifetime, spent, for example, working as a VSO (an organisation which is having problems keeping its numbers up since so many kids want to work for money) broadens all horizons.

In addition, it keeps the soul going when professional life, characterised by hard graft and mundane chores, eventually intrudes. And intrude it does, principally because most young are sensible enough to realise that one day they will need a job, no matter how long they try to delay that day.

Meanwhile, who on earth wants twelve hour Mondays when the alternatives are travel in South America, teaching English as a foreign language in Nanking, or even – and this brings us to the point of this rather sentimental beginning – internships in the United States Senate or traineeships in the European Commission or Parliament.

If politics finds the kids young, they are usually hooked for life – which, given the Government's drive to encourage recent graduates and those with at least two years professional experience to apply for posts in the European Parliament, is just as well. Once they have 'done' that, one or two might consider taking a job in commercial lobbying – some knowledge of running the representational offices of, say, lower Chelsea in Brussels, or running the political office of an MEP, is always good on the CV

A Career in Commercial Lobbying

The working world offered by the commercial lobbyists is one of privilege. At a comparatively young age, you are required to exercise judgement and make responsible moral choices. Those unable to stomach the choices are usually forced out of the industry since the employer cannot be expected to carry their squeamishness.

If you remain, there are lots of opportunities to travel on your client's behalf and you can spend a lot of time in hotel rooms with a huge bed and luxurious bathroom the size of the Sahara. Usually entertained royally, teams of flunkies can spring into action in that absurd way, pandering to your every whim – including presenting you with a glass of water and an aspirin on a silver tray if you merely complain of a headache. Keeping your feet on the ground can be difficult unless you remember that any fool can be waited on hand and foot.

It will only suit those with an interest in politics or international relations. Opinions are mixed about whether practitioners should, additionally, be politically partisan. Some believe that you have to be and, in addition, that your convictions must chime with those of your client, or your clients objectives.

Others, however, disagree. Despite criticism of any number of New Labour Lobbyists for apparently having no socialist convictions, many do. These, many of whom are very young, moving into the commercial world, who wish to remain loyal to their political convictions are finding it awkward when their employers are demanding that they put their clients first.

As a commercial lobbyist, you set agendas; campaign on issues; build coalitions of, sometimes, unlikely supporters; and help draft intricate pieces of legislation. You provide specific services which benefit the clients of your employers. Because much of the time you are dealing with hard intelligence you are taken seriously as adviser and strategist and frequently act as a buffer between them and the press.

Competing with your clients' lawyers and accountants – and, increasingly, with their insurers too – you will need to be able to move across industries effortlessly. You will also come across professional hostility as those same lawyers and accountants try to move in on your territory, not to mention competition from those in PR such as financial and corporate relations.

You will collect, analyse and commission information and research. Issues move faster than ever before not just across geographic boundaries but across different types of political forums and media as well. You will have a thick press cuttings book, attend media planning meetings, as well as place amendments to statutory instruments (easier than instigating primary legislation). You will seek to influence EU drafting or try to influence tendering procedures at local and regional level.

Many young people are in senior jobs in the industry and have a vantage point that is second to none. They sit down with representatives from merchant banks, a couple of firms of brokers, DTI & Treasury officials, and senior executives from the organisation they are representing. They have to be discreet – leaking of information, deliberate or otherwise, is a very serious matter. (At the time of writing, the public relations industry is in discussion with the Financial Services Authority on this specific issue although for the most part the culprits appear to be those in financial and corporate public relations, as well as the press, rather than in lobbying.)

In addition, they attract the attention of senior players who may be sufficiently impressed to offer alternative employment either for a limited period, with the agreement of their employer who continues to pay their salary, or indefinitely with a new employer.

They have access to management consultants, lawyers, accountants, trade associations and in-house public affairs specialists.

The latter, many of whom operate out of Brussels, can be snide. Claiming that the standards maintained by the commercial lobbyists are not all they could be, many can seek to imply that their own are higher. This is a shame since in-house public affairs personnel often learned their trade in the lobbying companies that they now talk down.

Moreover, they are unlikely to have the broad knowledge of contacts they once had, which is the trade off if you specialise and leave the general lobbying world behind. There are real advantages working for a general lobbyist because of the spread of industries and issues covered. However, increasingly, specialist sector knowledge is a must – and is, incidentally, where most of the EU job vacancies lie. Commercial lobbying companies are also setting up specialist units. Here, however, there can be a long-term danger to your professional future if the industry you are required to specialise in is on the wane.

The industry is not usually kind to those with commitments. This is partly because of the numbers within the industry who have no commitments and partly because there has been a fundamental change in British culture in the past twenty years from social commitments and obligations to an emphasis on individual rights and freedom of choice. This is mirrored by legislative change where, in the formation of public policy, economic interests have become the key factor, rather than one among many. Present employment legislation, including minimum wage recommendations, does little to redress the balance.

Those seeking enlightened employers are not likely to find them. Some employers are exceedingly helpful to those with responsibilities but this is not the norm. Moreover, such employers tend to favour those with responsibilities who are at the top of the tree not the bottom when such 'responsibilities' are self-consciously paraded.

In addition, they can have double standards. For example, a senior (male) member of the Board who has a heart attack will be kept on at full pay until he has made a recovery. But a woman who has a baby, who is not on the Board, is more likely to paid the statutory minimum.

Selfish people with good interpersonal skills do best. It is a tough world for those with infirmity, small children, and sick, or elderly relatives.

The industry makes an ideal first career and provides a launch-pad for at least a second and third career. The contacts made as a lobbyist last a lifetime. You come across senior public servants, local, regional, Whitehall & EU bureaucrats, politicians, businessmen and journalists. Your clients range from the mighty to the not so mighty, including many small charities and caring professions. In fact, everybody should be a lobbyist at some stage or other in their professional lives, particularly those who want to make their own fortune, or become Chairman of the Board or Director-General of an international charity, let alone those who one day will find themselves fighting their local council about a planning application.

You acquire a practical knowledge of organisations such as EFTA (half of all UK trade is with the EU); and have a proper grounding in important issues such as the World Trade Organisation; UK/EU legislative procedure and those of other countries, such as the United States. You learn about other cultures and how your client translates into them; communications and technology, apart from law, public administration and people. You analyse the social and political environment and examine future public policy issues and how they impact on different publics.

Watching how legislation impacts on Member States or local bodies (many have failed to develop a parallel machine at local level) and how Ministers can pay more attention to quangos and task forces than to elected politicians is an education in itself. You work out where to pitch things e.g. the annual transport supplementary grant is applied locally but you are better off putting pressure on central government if you are trying to influence it.

You learn a great deal about how your, and other countries work. You end up with a good knowledge of marketing and media issues (the marketing men all want to be lobbyists these days!) and, in learning how to control your client, learn the value of knowing when to be quiet.

You can go on to set up your own company or become special adviser to a government ministe r, although the latter is increasingly under the spot-light. You can join pressure groups, Think Tanks, local authorities, trade associations, trade unions, businesses and charities.

While it is a fascinating career, much of the work is also very dull – collecting statistics and talking to local, national and European Civil Servants can be tedious in the extreme. This is not because the people are dull, although they often are, but because you are often dealing with technical issues which, while being of great importance to those you represent, are not guaranteed to keep the rest of the world awake.

The hours of work are very long, people work hard and the industry is fiercely competitive. New technology means information overload, accelerating the pace since you have to react quicker. In addition, there are fewer people at work – made redundant by new technology or the loss of a big account – which adds to the workload.

People put in the hours to achieve individual success and material rewards, although in lobbying you can have a long wait. 'Presenteeism', i.e. being at your desk so that people see you there out of hours, means nothing – people are not doing the long hours in order to impress but in order to be on top of the workload which is unstoppable.

On the other hand, individuals tend to be team-spirited, and it is an ideal environment for the enthusiastic and resourceful. The problem, however, about team working, is that the 'opposition' are not always the competition in the next consultancy but teams of colleagues in the next office. This, apparently, makes for creative tension although it more usually makes for bitchy and destructive office politics of which there is plenty.

It is a strange profession, with even stranger working hours.

At the moment, few employers offer staff sabbaticals, so burn-out can be a problem. Ambitious people without a solid domestic life have one obvious big advantage. They can devote every working hour to their ambitions. The dangers are for such men and women that with little or no private life they lose a sense of proportion, are not rounded and do not have the same cares as the rest of us – including many of their clients.

Family life or the support of nurtured friendships feeds resilience and provides ballast. It also makes for better commercial lobbyists since so many of those who oppose the practices of their clients do so because the latter have ignored society's social responsibilities.

Much of your time is spent advising your clients how much they should or should not pay an MP/MEP/Peer/Ambassador/Senior Civil Servant if, either pre or post retirement, they join the Board, although, again, this is one of the areas presently under scrutiny. As much goes into explaining the Honours system, and how to secure one, or offering sponsorship to ministers if they attend seminars and other events. More time again is spent in trying to find jobs for ex-politicians and Civil Servants who have been helpful to you in the past. This is sometimes embarrassing since ex-public servants seldom realise that their value was in the jobs they did, not in their own skills or personalities. At the moment, finders fees are not common. In addition, new guidelines are likely to be laid down in the new Parliamentary session.

Another favourite topic is how to access the many contracts offered by European countries and institutions (the process is not sufficiently consultative, and usually goes to insiders who know how to apply) or how to pick up lucrative EU grants. This can depend on having a crooked solicitor. Locking into some Think Tanks and Foundations, you are in a position to take a view on that which can be presented as independent information, when in reality it is often partisan, politically and other. Some academics you come across can be blatently biased and appear to relish the fact that they are compromised.

Working for a client on a pro-bono basis, such as for a small charity, gives you excellent access to politicians who, for obvious reasons, cannot be rude to you. On the other hand, working for commercial clients, gives you access to a different network. Ideally, the lobbyist should work for both at some stage in their careers. There are real opportunities for revenge – the MEP who has ignored you in your commercial work because your client was not offering him any money, chews the carpet when you pop up as the leading lobbyist for an environmental group or major charity whom he cannot ignore if he does not want to be rubbished on the Internet.

Travel is one of the real bonuses. However, travel is also exhausting, knocks hell out of a domestic life if you have one, and can get to be a bore. Those relocating to Brussels are often lonely since those they meet are often transients. In addition, there is little in the way of support mechanism so it can be a little awkward if you get sick, have family commitments that are not mobile, or have a nervous breakdown. Relationship breakdowns are frequent, particularly if you are working in different cities and countries. Cross-national relationships thrive but can come unstuck when one of you wants to go back to the country you came from.

Holidays are another bonus- which is to say you seldom have the time for them. As a result, your skiing suffers because the House is always sitting when the best snows are on the ground and you cannot take time off. This is in marked contrast to many of the public servants that you will meet both here and in the EU who can seem to be permanently on holiday.

Regrettably, most employers have not yet recognised that many graduates are not prepared to sacrifice their lives for their careers – they are prepared to work hard, but, quite rightly, want to clock off at an appropriate time. If that is you – don't even think about becoming a commercial lobbyist! As a rule, the working week is shapeless i.e. weekends are non-existent. Moreover, if you have an organised or perfectionist personality, you will not get to grips with the job. It is because you are not organised that you cope. Much has to be done on the hoof. Spontaneity is the key.

Practical Techniques for Effective Lobbying

There are any number of lobbying books on the market. One of the best is *Practical Techniques for Effective Lobbying* written by lobbyist Charles

Miller. Like any number of such books, Miller wisely stays clear of some issues, such as Parliamentary drafting. In addition, he is also coy about some of his 'tips'. For example, he mentions the excellence of the House of Commons librarians, gives good lobbying advice (no briefs submitted to the Library to be longer than ten pages) but you have to wade through an awful lot of the book to find such assistance.

Principal criticism of an exceptionally clear manual, however, is that Miller makes the system look too tidy, when, as everybody knows, it is not. For example, at an individual level, the citizen has to inter-relate with Civil Servants by being forced to run around lots of different departments to collect all the information he needs collectively, because co-ordination between departments and personnel is non-existent. It is the same for the corporate sector. To lobby, you have to be untidy. You have to put everything in a pot in a huge jumble, and try and work a way through the jumble since you will never be able to clear up the jumble. Miller gives the impression of order.

Another criticism, although an unfair one, is that Miller offers no solutions – your MP doesn't answer letters? Miller does not tell you what to do. The Select Committee will not call your Chief Executive Officer as a witness? Ditto. Miller is too intellectually self-aware, and discreet, to bring the spirit of public servants and political institutions alive.

For example, one of the golden rules of lobbying is never to go directly to the top. If you do, and get turned down, you have nowhere else to go. While Miller conveys this message, he does not do so, dare it be said, in 'people-speak'. So careful is he to avoid jargon, superficiality, exaggeration and anything crass, he has written a worthy manual that tells you how to breathe, and where the 'lungs' are situated, but nothing about the 'air' that is breathed, or how to 'filter' it, which is where the good lobbyist, including Miller, comes into his own.

For example, was the Government forced into giving way on issue X last week? Yes? Then the chances are that, in order to reassert authority or other political considerations, or out of sheer bloody-mindedness, it will not give way on issue Y, irrespective of the merits of Y's case. A good commercial lobbyist will tell Y to go away for six months, even if this means that Y will scorn such good advice and find a commercial lobbyist who will attack the problem now by pumping the 'wrong' air into the system with the result that the 'lungs' collapse.

If this happens, the result is a disaster, not least because political infrastructures, and those who service it, have memories like elephants. 'Breathe' at the wrong time, with the wrong 'air', collapse a 'lung' and you will not be forgiven. The 'good' commercial lobbyist, on the other hand, would have suggested that the client offers the 'lungs' a bit of help.

For example, the 'oxygen' provided by a local media campaign.

Miller's reasons for writing so concisely and circumspectly, of course, are understandable – he is anxious not to sound like a salesman, and equally anxious to avoid any suggestion that much of a lobbyist's work is unquantifiable or, as many have it, 'puff'.

His book is excellent. Next time around, we will forgive him for sounding like a salesman so that, along with the excellence, we can have some liveliness as well – and one or two anecdotes. After all, he knows quite a few of them.

Salaries

In your early years you will probably have to get used to living in almost permanent financial distress. Starting salaries in the UK range from £9,000 – £15,000 depending on whether the job consists of mostly monitoring or whether research work is also required.

Other salaries are:

Account Executive:	£15,000 – £25,000
Account Directors	£20,000 – £30,000
Director	£35,000 plus

Advertising in the *PA Newsletter* (April 1998), the Design Council were looking for International and Development Managers. Applicants needed 'a background of working internationally with experience of developing joint initiatives with government departments and other bodies'. For this, the salary band was £25 – £32,000 per annum.

On the other hand, if you are lucky, the work can be slightly better paid. Advertising in the same magazine, Peter Childs Associates, one of the leading public affairs jobfinders, recruiting PR and government relations personnel, was offering four jobs with the following salary bands:

Associate Director	£60,000 (30'ish)
Account Director	£45,000 (late 20's)
Junior Executive	£25,000 (mid 20's)
Parliamentary Monitor	£17,000 (early 20's)

Only you can work out whether you are prepared to put in the long hours, and sacrifice a private life, when there is not always even the ability to make a decent living!

The best place to look for jobs is in the public affairs magazines, as well as, of course, the national press, particularly the *Guardian* Media Section on Mondays. The Internet is also being used although it is hard to discover anyone who has actually found a job that way.

Some of the jobs advertised ask you to reply to a Box Number. These are worth writing to if you are new to the industry and have no history in it (although you should always be careful about your safety and, if a meeting is arranged with an unknown company, you should tell people where you are going) but are not always a good idea if you have been in the industry a while. You could end up applying to your existing employer!

Box numbers are often a chosen method of recruitment for cynical reasons and should not be applied to lightly. Incidentally, tell the truth on your CV since it is likely to circulate all over the place and can come back to haunt you.

Any number of companies can, and do, exploit the young by offering them so-called 'work experience'. This means an extra pair of hands, to whom some pay neither salary, nor, again in some cases, even expenses, until such time as they are no longer needed when they are ruthlessly dumped, incidentally reinforcing the arrogance of many of the permanent staff.

Apart from being immoral, the system also ensures that it is neither meritocratic nor representative of the workforce. Most people do not have the luxury of being privately funded and therefore cannot afford 'work experience'. Those who are employed therefore are usually on a government training scheme (again, free labour for the employer) which teaches them little if anything at all.

At the moment, there are not many from the ethnic minorities in the industry although ageism is an even greater problem.

Other companies take on unpaid, or poorly paid staff, on the basis that such 'work experience' could translate into a job in three months time. It rarely does. Such employers – from both large and small consultancies – are well-known, and could be named, and shamed, by their governing body (most are members of the Institute of Public Relations) if there was a will to do so which there is not.

The employers defend their conduct by repeating the mantra that:

– everyone (except, of course, their senior staff) has to get used to a disjointed work pattern;
– they, at least, are providing work experience;
– all companies are cutting down on their core workforces, using more and more temporary staff. (The latter have the commitment to the organisation of a permanent employee, of course.)

Well, yes. Except that real 'temporary staff' are highly paid; and real 'temporary staff' have already acquired their skills (e.g. those in the IT industry) which, in the flexi workforce of today, they can sell appropriately. This does not apply to the lowly in commercial lobbying.

Besides, the adventure of working hard for six months and then pushing off to foreign parts for six months eventually becomes less of an adventure unless you are at the end of your working life or have built up your nest-egg.

Freelancing and consulting

Once you have a skill to sell, you might chose to freelance. If you can dictate your price, and are highly skilled, you have no need to read this section.

For the more modest, it is worth remembering that 'freelancing' can mean that you end up servicing accounts that no-one else will touch, or working well below your capacity. Freelance work can be low grade, and people can steal your ideas. Contracts are often chaotic and not always paid.

In other words, freelancing is not all its cracked up to be except for the very skilled and the very rich. The word itself can be a euphemism for those who are more usually 'unemployed', a 'redundancy survivor', or the 'early retired'.

Many present freelance work (or self-employment as the government insists on calling it) as the answer to a thousand prayers. Anyone who insists on talking it down is a wimp since, apparently, freelancing frees the entrepreneurial spirit. This can be piffle. The vast majority of people want secure permanent full or part time employment within a commercial but people friendly environment, not freelance work which invariably works in the employers' favour since it cuts their overheads.

Freelancing is very useful, however, when you are genuinely between jobs and want to have a look at what is around. In the modern workforce, the contract of loyalty between employer and employee has broken down (with the best will in the world, the employer can no longer guarantee your job, training, or career direction) and therefore freelancing allows for mobility between jobs and employers i.e. you manage your own career. In doing so, however, life can be either feast or famine, and knowing when to say 'no', as well as prioritising your workload, can be a problem.

Also, the shrunken permanent staffs of your clients or the lobbying companies that want your skills on an ad hoc basis, tend to stay for years. Therefore, if, for whatever reason, you cannot work with them, the company is out of reach indefinitely. Another worry is the fact that organisations with small core or full-time permanent employees rely on gofers and juniors. (One wonders who is training up the next generation!) As a result they do not always know how to be polite, let alone decent employers.

Freelancing is a good idea if you have no interest in climbing the corporate management tree; if you find the changing corporate culture hard to live with and do not want the hassle of setting up your own company; if you do not feel that your skills are being adequately rewarded and are confident that you can both earn a living and top up your skills outside the work-place; if you believe that corporate reorganisation has hacked away at your values; or if you are too old for the top job.

That is to say, many freelancers come from the top of the heap, call themselves consultants, and have gone freelance because they do not want to manage companies, have been eased out, or merely want to keep the grey cells active. This makes it tough for other consultants who do not want to merely tick over.

Most consultants in other industries have MBAs (essentially a post graduate degree in general management) but a whole crop of specialist MBAs are hitting the scene. At the moment, this is not the case in lobbying and most consultants lack post graduate qualifications as well as appropriate knowledge of the new technologies realistically to be able to stay in the game indefinitely. However, they can offer the 'grey hairs' the industry so desperately needs i.e. wisdom, experience and shrewdness, a useful foil to the ridiculous culture of retirement which scraps people at sixty, if not considerably younger.

If you do go freelance, it is important not to get your charging wrong, although if you do, there are instances of clients, particularly ones who want you to do the work, helpfully nudging you in the right direction. Because of outsourcing, there are quite a few short term contracts around (including maternity leave cover) for people to do specific jobs or carry out specific projects. Short term contracts can give you control over your life, so long as you are money rich. If not, it can be a struggle.

However, there are several myths attached to freelance work. These include the fact that such work is family friendly. This is not always the case since while a project lasts, the freelancer is up to his eyes. In addition, although virtual organisations (with many working from home on a full time or ad hoc basis) appear to be the employers of the future it is difficult to see how people will be able to bond appropriately, essential in much of lobbying especially when servicing a big campaign. For such campaigns to succeed, it is essential that those servicing it do not work in a vacuum.

Cash Flow

Many companies, especially those that have grown out of the egos of individuals, have serious cash flow problems. Even those which have a comfortable income stream cannot always sustain the loss of a major account, let alone a run of them, as the collapse of Ian Greer Associates proved, principally because they have no realisable assets. Nor do many carry key man insurance or much in the way of professional indemnity insurance. It is hard to calculate the 'goodwill' of a client portfolio in this industry because sometimes there is none!

As a rule, consultancies with precarious cash-flow are unlikely to employ staff who can train you or offer you sufficient calibre of work to broaden your skills. Their clients are usually as out of date as the technology they are using. These companies can sometimes be spotted because of their staff turnover (massive staff turnover is often an indication of other problems too, although not necessarily cash flow, particularly when there is no staff turnover at board or consultants' level. Beware of the top heavy companies!)

When you are starting your working life, the problems above do not always matter since you could be employed on the one account, experience of which your next employer wants. This, if you jump ship quickly enough, can send your value sky-high. It is not a good idea to stay in these consultancies too long, however, since their poor reputation is likely to follow you around and, in the long run, will diminish your place in the market.

For the most part many of the companies specialising in commercial lobbying are as distinguished by their poor management structure as they are by some of the unpleasant, one-dimensional people in them. The majority suffer haemorrhage of high calibre personnel because they have no control over their career direction. Those that remain are trying to plug the gaps. These include greedy managers (who own equity); good managers who have too much to do and are therefore bad managers and those who are so bad that they have nowhere else to go.

In addition, many of the companies are trying to reposition themselves – they may have a rosy future but you will have to subsidise them in the short-term, sacrificing skills enhancement and salary – and find yourself dumped in the longer term. Short termism is in their interest - not yours. As many companies again, however, are training staff and have excellent management practices.

Small Consultancies

Start-up outfits, usually the result of an entrepreneurial youth culture, are usually fun to work in, with everybody pulling together. However, problems can emerge when the small company finds itself having to adapt to enlarged scale while wanting to retain the friendly atmosphere which has engendered a loyalty that is as much its driving force as anything else. Also, 'youth' grows up and therefore the entrepreneurial youth culture that once made it so attractive to the spunky diminishes.

As a result, the challenge of managing maturity is usually flunked. In addition, many small employers can be hurt by their staff who can take advantage of the friendly atmosphere, which is to say, take advantage of their employers. This can be a deeply wounding experience.

Small companies are people centred, and this usually goes out the window when they grow up simply because large organisations are still no good at supporting people friendly policies (which can be anything from an interest free loan to have an expensive holiday or time off for domestic responsibilities.)

The advantage of working in one of the smaller consultancies is that you know your superiors well, and are therefore usually learning from the top. In addition, your superiors are so busy that they are very good at delegating which gives you considerable autonomy. You end up liasing directly with client top-dogs, some of whom are very senior people. The advantage of working with these – many of whom are surprisingly loyal to the small consultancies – is that they broaden your knowledge of public affairs, which means you have a better knowledge of the market place.

This is particularly the case if the consultancy is a specialist unit – for example, in medical affairs or local government. Experience of such specialist work may make you very attractive to a larger employer although of course you will not necessarily acquire the general skills which you may also need one day.

The drawback of many of the smaller consultancies, however, is that they can give up the fight (for understandable reasons) of battling with the big companies and get gobbled up by them. As a result, you are no longer working in a small, intimate outfit but in a large anonymous one. That is if – and it is a big 'if' – you are not made redundant. Once you are sold on, you often find that on top of immediate bad management you end up with other poorly managed hierarchies. In addition, there will be a shortage of funds because of the pay-offs.

Shares

The belief is that if you are offered shares in a company you work for, you will work hard because you have an incentive so to do. Be careful, however, before you accept shares because it often means a lower salary. Shares can be fine – so long as you realise that in accepting a stake in the consultancy you may be locked in while never in a position to control the built-in rake-off.

Moreover, shares are paper money, can go up as well as down, and are no good to you if you want a mobile career. Shares are not, necessarily, a good investment and, certainly in your early years, what you need is salary not what could be phoney certificates pertaining to the paper economy.

You should also remember that all organisations are run by managements who naturally put their own interests first. Therefore, the argument that organisations are run in the interest of their shareholders and have naturally longer term horizons is a nonsense. There is usually a constant conflict between management, proprietors, staff who may be shareholders, and shareholders – and management always wins, particularly if they are responsive to the needs of their customer base.

Staff share schemes are an attempt to align interests but for the most part you are not given enough, or sufficient clout to make a difference. Moreover, the whole share debate has backfired principally because, for the most part, managers have thieved all the goodies.

The staff share debate is likely to be reviewed in due course not least because of the need to motivate the large army of part-timers, freelancers and consultants who are now in the industry. 'Self-employment' and virtual organisations smashes employee share-ownership on the head – and not before time.

The Pros and Cons of being bought by a larger Consultancy

Purchasers are usually, but not always, the big public relations companies (who are themselves often owned by advertising companies and communications giants). One of the first differences you notice when you go from working for a small company to a large one are the different client bases. Small companies usually work for fewer international companies and usually operate strict rules about working for foreign organisations.

The larger companies do not have the same scruples. (At one time the rule for most was never to work for foreign governments no matter how friendly. This included the Indian tea council. Now it seems that all the large companies are working for everybody. Including Serbia and Libya – watch out for the lucrative post-Saddam account!)

Therefore if you are anxious about promoting foreign governments or companies, because, for example you disapprove of their internal affairs, or because in so doing you could do your own community out of jobs, stick with the smaller agencies.

You may, of course, protect yourself by not having a view on the above. This may well serve your short term interests but not your long term ones since ethics, and professional morality, is increasingly

114

important. If you want to be a commercial lobbyist with a future you should always know where you stand. Even if your superiors do not.

On the other hand, the big public relations companies developing overseas markets for their clients, including their British ones, are promoting the country's prosperity. Many in the business community are grateful to them because hitherto they have had to rely on the services of the diplomatic corps. These may be polished and have brilliant plumage but are not communications specialists.

Or they may act for overseas pressure groups in London – a fast expanding and highly profitable sector of the PR and lobbying business. It is up to you to weigh these issues up before you make your decision as to whether or not you are prepared to work for them.

The main advantage of the larger organisations is that you are aware of other public relations activities such as financial public relations. The other advantage is that you come face to face with whether you are willing to develop the commercial edge necessary to make it in business. Not all employers are money-grasping – many, in fact, are both generous and gracious – but all are pragmatists. If you are unwilling to be commercial you cannot expect them to give you a job.

If you were part of a small organisation, now bought by a large one, your adjustment period is always awkward. Suddenly, you go from working in an environment where everybody knows you, to being part of an enormous one where nobody knows your boss, let alone you. This is even worse if the purchase (sometimes called a joint venture) entails an office move as well.

You will then have to accept the distractions of agency life and the fact that your previous management is now a very small cog fighting for recognition. In addition, many of the problems that you will have to face, will be the 'wrong' problems. These include:

– coming to terms with the conduct of your new parent company who may, for example, have represented Argentina in trade issues, while Argentinean soldiers were tipping 'dissidents' out of helicopters. However, it is important here not to have a double standard. The 'Troubles' in Northern Ireland, for example, produced their own version of the 'disappeared' particularly in the 1970s;

or

– losing time in corporate meetings, drawing up corporate plans that need to be rewritten the following week.

If you do not turn up to these corporate meetings you lose in-house political battles by default and become marginalised, as indeed do your colleagues. The meetings are the only way to control information flow, and therefore power.

Bogged down by administration problems when you should be out there doing the job that your clients pay you to do, your clients can get restless. They become even more restless, when, as a result of the 'merger' their fees double. This delights your new owners since your lower fee structure has been showing the rest of the company up. As a result, the pressure is on you to ensure that your clients remain 'profitable' which means that you have to start 'lying' by putting your time down to your subordinate's clients.

This makes the latter 'unprofitable' when the reality is that they are profitable, and results in the start of many an argument. The client lists of your now parent company command such high fees that your own client list looks, frankly, dispensable – which it is.

It is important however to note that many companies now are operating excellent time management programmes, especially those with focused units.

Back in the poorly managed environment, however, your old clients get even more fed up when you start marketing subsidiary parts of your parent company to them. These may be absolutely awful but have to be promoted on the basis that 'clients like a one-stop shop'.

Next, the parent company's accountants, not knowing the business, start throwing out loss leaders. An example of this were the Secretariats of twelve All Party Westminster Groups at one time run by one of the lobbying companies which pretty well gave them access to everyone in Westminster.

Others from your parent company do not understand the sensitivity of your work. To them, everything is the 'bottom line' and the skilled drafting that you may be doing, possibly at the request of a government department, means nothing to them. Or perhaps it does – but since they cannot enter into your world they would rather undermine it.

One moment you are dealing with an EU Commissioner or a Secretary of State, both of whom bracket you with the top-flight client you are representing, the next minute you are back in your own operating environment where personnel of your parent company do not recognise your value and are steadily emasculating you for their own self-interested reasons.

Big money comes by way of ad hoc fees and campaigns. This can often squeeze the service that is already being offered to the clients and, as importantly, squeeze your time. Because your fees are so reasonable, another department costs the account, so that you do not embarrass other parts of the organisation also making their pitch. The difference is then creamed off by the parent company which has only acquired the account by piggy-backing on your skills.

Meanwhile, you are having trouble reconciling your already heavy workload with the new demands. The parent company tells you to sort out your time management problem yourself. This you manage by telling your staff, who are already fully stretched, that they must 'learn to be flexible'. As a result they leave since they see no reason to maintain your obligations, which obligations are the result of poor time management being passed down the line.

Next you find out something that you would rather not have known about and feel you have to dish the dirt – here, you should remember that whistle-blowers legislation is now on the Statute Book to protect you. Alternatively, you could think in terms of tipping off Private Eye. They are brilliant to deal with – unless, of course, you are the one they are after!

Finally, the parent company accepts an account that, had your company still been a small independent one, you would never have accepted. You can either leave, or lump it.

Mentoring and Friendships

The idea of mentoring in the industry has not yet taken hold. This is a shame since mentors offer good support and help you without colluding. They can offer clarity, focus, honesty, challenge and respect, all of which are desperately needed in view of the fact that organisations have not been stripped of their bureaucracy and hierarchies, and are next to impossible to navigate.

In commercial lobbying it is especially important in view of the sensitivities surrounding the industry. These include anxieties about the democratic deficit, as well as the anti-democratic conduct of many associated with commercial lobbying, from individual lobbyists to public, or former public, servants, to the clients themselves. A good mentor offers a moral lead, as well as practical advice.

Advice can be taken from managers, but in lobbying's pressured work culture they can be pretty useless since they often do not have the time for their own concerns, let alone anyone else's. Following 'Draper-gate' of course, there may be some attempt to offer greater guidance and assistance but do not bank on it.

Immediate superiors tend to like the jargon while pretending not to. Many talk in terms of 'think positive' and 'deny the negative' which is a nonsense when one is not in control. It is also annoying when they deny the validity of the negative, believing that all negatives can be converted into a plus. Real life is not like that.

It's a war zone out there – and in a war, gentlemen move aside and the players take-over, which is to say that lobbying is a business where there are few gentlemen left. This is a shame because, for the most part, nice people, including those with pastoral skills, get passed over. Such people often have different criteria to their employers – i.e. loyalty, selflessness and creativity – all the skills that are desperately needed and employers say they want but are unwilling to nurture.

If you are very young with good skills, some employers and senior managers will act as patron. The point about 'Draper-gate' however, is that such patronage was not necessarily based on 'skill' but access to a network. They are unlikely to do so, however, with older employees since these are likely to push them out of jobs later on. This is replicated in countless other industries and is a national tragedy principally because we are a small country and need to make up for our lack of manpower though superior thinking. Most superior thinkers never make it into positions of authority. It is a gloomy fact that we produce dazzling talent but fail to capitalise on it.

Networking is vital, which is why lobbyists need to be socially skilled (particularly important when it comes to motivating virtual organisations). However, if you are very lowly, you have to get used to several bruising experiences. While networking, people rarely waste time with you unless they think it will be useful. Nonetheless, they can switch on a megawatt smile whenever a camera is pointed in their direction.

One of the best methods of spotting the extent of a network is keeping a close eye on the list of those attending some grandee or other's memorial service.

Chauvinism, Racism and Ageism

Here a word about 'isms'. Racism is a part of the lobbying culture if only because the political forums in which it operates can be racist. The worst aspects of racism, however, are usually more in evidence in financial and corporate PR than they are in the political consultancies. It is slowly being tackled, not least because the winning of some big American contracts can go against the consultancy if those from the ethnic minorities are not part of the team. It is still deeply entrenched however in political and administrative institutions.

Chauvinism, unless you have a title (parts of the industry are very snobbish) or a well-known relative, can also be a problem, but again, mostly in the financial PR sector. These have various entrenched problems, machismo being one of them, which machismo is shared by many in the financial press. The combination of chauvinistic press, PR and, for example, financial service clients, as well as political systems can be very destructive.

It is unpleasant, if not worse, if men, or women, come to that, behave like the Mujaheddin of Sidcup. Nonetheless, it is steadily being tackled. Along with chauvinism, sexual harassment can also be a problem. At one time there was a scoring book at the House of Commons, where the women scored every advance made with marks out of ten. Regrettably, data protection legislation knocked that one on the head.

If a light pass is made, it is silly to over-react unless it is deeply upsetting. Medium/serious harassment is another matter. It should always be acted on, and your employers' assistance sought if necessary (unless, of course, the employer is doing the harassing!). If such support is not forthcoming consult your Union (if you have one – see 'National Union of Journalists' – Press and PR Section) immediately. Assault, or attempted assault, should be reported to the police. Assailants can be politicians. Do not be in awe of their public positions.

For the most part, clients are anxious about the above and are usually on their best behaviour. Trade associations tend to be the worst and tokenism is often rampant.

In view of the youthfulness of the industry, ageism can be another problem although it is disguised by the fact that countless consultants in the industry are members of the 'grey' brigade. The lack of age spread, however, tends to make the industry insensitive to the life-cycles of their staff – from the birth of a first child (including the sleepless nights), to the changes that affect men and women as they mature, to the care of an elderly relative.

However, it is too easy to blame the employer for being ageist without reason. Many companies need mobile workforces – and older workers, or their partners, who have put down roots can refuse to relocate. On the other hand, older workers can be more loyal and want to nest more than younger ones.

You may encounter all the 'isms' above. On the other hand, you may be lucky and encounter none of them. If you are lucky, one of the worst things you can do is deny the distressing experience of many. However, it should also be kept in mind that some people do cry 'wolf', inflicting enormous grief on innocent accused.

Relationships

'Fun' sex in politics seems to be in decline although no doubt some lobbyists, politicians, clients, journalists et al are still going at it like rabbits. Libertines are to be avoided unless you are very grown-up since they take no hostages. Nor do those who prey on the young, naïve or vulnerable.

The sexual morals (as opposed to corporate ethics) of many involved in the commercial lobbying world do not necessarily conform to what others would call the upright and the decent. On the other hand, many do. As a rule, much goes on in political life that is, quite frankly, shocking. Not everybody lives in a moral vacuum, but some certainly do. Some are also amoral, lacking all respect for others.

Language is important – only the cheeky cheerful refer to 'slappers' and 'legovers'. Networking and political salons have knocked the elegant skill of flirtation on the head; and executive stress has ensured that charm is not in abundance.

Political correctness however has done the most damage – which is a shame since, as the cliché says, a little of what you fancy does you good. People are literally too frightened about being sued, to fraternise with their colleagues.

Those bold enough not to be frightened by political correctness are, for the most part, still having to look outside the office for a relationship. Happy hunting grounds for these are airports and long train journeys, although Westminster's Central Lobby is rapidly reclaiming its pre-eminence as the best pick up place in London.

Party Conferences too can offer interesting pursuits of a trivial nature since there is every possibility of lassooing in a macho type from one of the defence companies stalking the proceedings.

These are often fantasists claiming to have been in the SAS. Some are gay. Some are misogynists. Some are nutters/dangerous. A few are real charmers.

As a rule, and this has nothing to do with political correctness, it is not necessarily a good idea to dally with colleagues, employers, clients, journalists or politicians if you wish to earn your living in commercial lobbying indefinitely. Lovers can stack up.

Naturally, this rule is broken all the time. One commercial lobbyist ruefully admitted that if s/he had known s/he was going to remain in the industry so long s/he might have been more circumspect. The extent of sexual relationships however is nothing like as 'busy' as in the media.

If you do mix business with pleasure, good luck to you. Much happiness can result, and the office or professional romance, despite political correctness, is, thankfully, far from dead and can go on to other things. However, it is important to know the difference between courtship and a relationship.

Both can go wrong, and when they do, it is not always the case that people behave well. In so far as 'relationships' go, however, this can be detrimental for your career. For example, an affair with a politician that ends badly could mean that the politician will refuse to consider meeting one of your clients. The reverse is also true and equally wrong. In addition, there have been cases of alleged sexual assault which are usually not reported and are difficult to prove.

Heavy drinking can be a problem. As a result, any number of clients and politicians confide a thousand 'secrets', get very maudlin in the process and regard the lobbyist as a free counsellor. They also usually become emotionally dependent on you. Avoid this if you can unless you have a burning desire to be a counsellor.

Some would say that it was about time alcoholics anonymous and marriage guidance counsellors opened up branches in Westminster or at Waterloo Railway station ready for all those falling off the Eurostar.

Problems range from why the politician/client has been passed over for senior office, to whom they hate, as well as the problems in their personal/family lives. Many are forced to adapt to unwelcome changes leaving lonely and isolated spouses and the strain of the over bearing and unpredictable nature of commercial and political life can be unbearable.

At the same time, the cheerful, gossipy and buzzing socialising at Westminster or abroad can leave politicians and businessmen disinclined to go home – which can lead to a whole load of other trouble. They end up pretending their spouses do not exist, leaving them to sort out mundane chores and family commitments, which many then sacrifice on the altar of selfish ambition. All of this comes to a head, plus their guilt and loneliness, when alcohol frees the tongue and they wallow in their own unhappiness.

It is not fair to remember anything they say, far less to repeat it. Politicians and clients are very indiscreet about themselves and others. You, on the other hand, are paid to be discreet. It is always tempting to rush off to your nearest friendly journalist and tell him what has been said – resist it.

Betraying a confidence, usually means betraying a thousand other innocents, from elderly parents to distraught and loyal spouses.

In addition to alcohol you are likely to come across some drug-taking. Suffice it to say that, like getting smashed on a Friday evening, and emerging with a hangover on the following Monday morning, drugs are something most people grow out of. Tobacco, on the other hand, is going strong.

Clothes, Personal Presentation and Business Pitches

Regrettably, the industry can be very 'lookist' – the prettier or more handsome you are, the more likely you are to catch the eye in the early stages, unless, of course, you are offering something that has a commercial validity in a class of its own.

It is also very dress conscious, with, in some consultancies, everybody trying to look like a world class brand trying to get into the latest metropolitan bar. You have to convey the correct short-hand i.e. the right designer label or use of jargon to be taken seriously. Wearing a 'uniform' and speaking the 'language' is almost de rigueur.

This is a kind of tyranny but one you get used to. On occasions you yearn for the abaya (Arab women's dress which covers everything), which would dispense with all the nonsense – and, if your face is really looking puffy, the yashmak as well. In fact, an awful lot of men in lobbying should be permanently in yashmaks. As for the language – learn it. After all, learning languages is all the rage. It is an easy one – business jargon always is – and, what's more, you don't even have to understand it. Want to use the expression 'X' is part of the 'equation'? Don't. That's a definite no-no. After all, it's dated and everybody understands it. Use 'matrix' instead and pronounce it 'mate tricks' which is what its all about anyway.

Most men in the industry favour the dull, boring top end of the clothing market if they can afford it, perhaps with an original twist to convey humour and individuality. A few brave souls are favouring the equally expensive fashion end e.g. large baggy soft suits which, hopefully, will be out of date by the time this book is published. The mass market end for both men and women can define you as a non-player unless you have the appropriate and expensive accessories, although it is worth noting that one of the most successful British EU lobbyists used to tailor most of her own clothes.

Do not worry too much about the 'right' clothes and/or accessories if you cannot afford them because, quite frankly, in the commercial side of lobbying you will not be noticed until you have the funds to purchase them, and what people do not notice cannot hurt you. Or perhaps that is the point!

Often, however, the lobbyist is better dressed than his client or the public servant whom he meets. The exceptions are when the clients are multinationals, and EU public servants who are often very snappy dressers. If you are badly or shabbily dressed your employer might chose not to roll you in front of them again.

Regrettably, once you do have the funds to purchase expensive clothes and accessories, the tendency is to become a designer clone. It is worth remembering that wearing the clone uniform might impress some but is more a statement of your purchasing power than it is of your place in the business world. It can also be a reflection of your lack of self-esteem which can be a real no-no in the business world. Your identity is unique and should not be sacrificed on the altar of (expensive) consumer conformity.

Fashion is fun. Enjoy it. Meanwhile, when you do have some money your first two purchases should be a) decent glasses if you do not wear contact lens. The style of these should be constantly up-dated. And b) a decent hair-cut. If you do not move forward you are dead.

Continental or American dress is being seen all over London these days but, in the boardroom, traditional Savile Row dress can still predominate. Some mistake 'style' for flamboyance or wit when discretion with a little originality can be both safer and, sometimes, more courteous. Some form of casual dress is also creeping in, especially on Fridays. This does not mean scruffiness is acceptable.

Many Americans, however, judge by appearance. If you are not wearing the correct designer dress code they do not 'waste' their time with you. This, for example, was particularly in evidence when US writer Kitty Kelly, researching a book, attended a function in London where several British public affairs specialists were present. She seemed to give the appearance of 'dismissing' the one person she could have learned something from in favour of the designer dresser. It was hilarious, in view of the fact that the designer dresser was on the lowly side, whereas the person she seemingly 'dismissed' was the important one.

On the whole, Americans, especially if they are clients or proprietors, whatever they may think about all those ghastly Brits in their own country, still find traditional British dress and the British accent wildly attractive and reassuring. So do the continentals, who like nothing better than showing you off in smart restaurants in Paris if you are dressed like horse and have the figure of a hound.

Incidentally, when dealing with Americans do not carp on about America's moral decay. Its citizens are not all ninety year-old millionaires wearing designer shades and little else, trying to make it with a sixteen year old. We need America. One of the towering tragedies of the breakdown of the transatlantic alliance is that we appear to be saying that we do not – which is one reason (there are many others) why lobbying on their behalf can be difficult.

Presentation is about eye contact, gestures, smiling, tone of voice, and self-confidence. You can be dressed in a sack of potatoes and still win the job or account if you are very good. If not, it is better to look like a designer clone until you have the confidence to be more individualistic.

When making a business pitch, do not use gimmicks, they can come back to haunt you. On the other hand, they can be effective in quasi-social situations. For example, one commercial lobbyist always puts a clock on the table when being lavishly entertained in an expensive restaurant. Lawyers of course do this all the time – or they take unnerving peeps at their wristwatches. The difference is that the commercial lobbyist's clock is an antique and looks great with all the silver. The clock tells the client that you are conscious that his time is money. As importantly, it simultaneously conveys that your time is money too.

Some also favour subtle flirtation. This, especially if you have real commercial and political skill, can work – although subtle means subtle and should not be at the expense of your colleagues. Although it often is. However, be very careful about 'flirtation' because not everybody reads the same signals similarly. At its best, and in an appropriate context, it is glorious and charming. At its worst, it can be litigious and expensive.

Speaking of money, business pitches used to be a way of a client picking up ideas from half a dozen consultancies without paying for them. Make sure you charge for any business presentation you do – especially if you are freelance – the fee should be deducted if you win the business.

When pitching for the business, read the room right. The client does not always want slickness; nor does he always want chutzpah. You could lose a business pitch if the client believes your 'slickness' will frighten the horses; equally, you could lose a business pitch if the client wants you, and your work, to be invisible which is not usually synonymous with chutzpah.

Winning a business pitch or a new job (despite all this emphasis on psychometric testing) usually still boils down to first impressions and whether the client or employer likes you i.e. personalities, although who presents first, middle and last also plays a part. So that you are remembered, the soundbite can be useful. Three are advisable – beginning, middle and end.

A sense of humour is always in short supply in the business world these days, especially given political correctness and the thought police. So far as political correctness is concerned it is up to you whether to be politically correct or not. Let's face it, sometimes it does not make business sense to be politically correct. For example, it would not necessarily be a good idea to send a vegetarian to a butcher if you want to win the account, even though there is doubtless an equal opportunities directive from the European Commission saying that you should.

Setting your work in context

If you are considering working for one of the larger consultancies, you should insist on looking through their client lists and asking specifically what type of work is being done and whether this conforms to your personal ethics – if you still have any. Naturally, you should also bear in mind that if you ask too many questions the employer will not employ you anyway.

It is also useful to ask about what professional indemnity is carried and what confidentiality agreement you will have to sign. The latter, for example, could be so-embracing that they do not allow for matters of conscience or whistle-blowers. Bear in mind, however, that legal protection for whistle-blowers comes into force in January 1999.

Next, you should ask to have your work set in context, including any press hostility. For example, a trainee commercial lobbyist was drafted on to a baby milk account unaware that its parent company had once attracted controversy. When she eventually found out, she was incensed not to have been told the history.

In addition, it is as well to know whether you will be required to work for any of your clients' agents, such as briefing their insurers or private security consultants. If the answer is 'yes' it is well to remember that the latter, like commercial lobbying, is an unregulated industry and could mean that you end up mixing with those you would rather not.

You should also ask about the company's financial obligations to previous management/s since these could affect your payrises. Also about the company's previous campaigns, for example the promotion of what some might deem to be corrupt governments who want to boost their tourist industry, which may prejudice legislators here or abroad, and may, in consequence, prejudice your ability to meet those legislators in the future.

That is to say, ask if there is any history which the company is trying to live down. Ask what kind of clients are turned down and why. The answer could be because of a clash of interests or because the customer was not appropriately 'ethical'. Ask also if the company is likely to merge with another company in the near future, or if there is any gossip about the company's long term plans including any comment in the trade or national press. Many of these questions are obviously not appropriate to ask in a formal interview but due to the incestuous nature of the industry someone somewhere will be able to provide you with the answer.

Ask about political donations and pro-bono work. If the latter is for a charity, you may find this acceptable although this can affect your remuneration. In addition, it is well to remember that you may not support the objectives of all charities. For example, on which side of the abortion debate do you fall? There are charities on both but you may not wish to work for them. You may be even less keen if the pro-bono work is for a political party – especially one you do not support.

It is important for you to know about the political persuasions of the company and its senior management – and past associations – since this may actively prejudice those you are targeting. It is also, of course, necessary to tell your clients if X has accepted hospitality or money from Y.

If you are acquiring and evaluating information you could come under the jurisdiction of insider dealing legislation. As a result you may be stopped from making various investments, or advising your family and friends of those same investments. Make sure therefore that you are adequately compensated for giving up the right to make such investments. At all times you should be aware of your legal position, rights and obligations.

For example, staff working on privatisation legislation, such as the water companies, were expected to give up their rights to purchase shares in those companies, although the employer offered them no compensation for so doing. Some refused to waive such rights.

Needless to say, do not waste your time on companies with poor managements or management culture.

Training, Education, Conferences, Institute of Public Relations, NUJ Membership & Policing

Regrettably, the industry fails to develop young people through planned and structured education. Practitioners pay lip service to training and qualifications, although they make all the right noises. In addition, they have been known to advertise for staff with particular qualifications, when they have no job to offer but wish to show their clients and competitors what other disciplines they apparently cover. They claim this to be legitimate marketing.

Many employers are happy to exploit your skills today with no thought of tomorrow. There are no degree courses dealing specifically with political lobbying in the three legislatures you will encounter i.e. UK, USA and EU. Some public relations degrees however include political modules. The industry pretends not to respect PR graduates but since it is trying to establish an intellectual basis for its discipline this could change.

Those institutions offering public relations degrees include : Stirling University, Bournemouth, Central Lancashire, Leeds Metropolitan, Napier, Queen Margarets College and St Marks and St Johns.

Masters are offered by Stirling and Manchester Metropolitan. Post graduate diplomas can be obtained from Wales, Cardiff, Dublin Institute of Technology and Watford. MBAs now include PR and communication management within their curriculum and this can encompass government relations. In addition, the Institute of Public Relations (IPR) – aiming for Chartered status one day – is re-introducing its own diploma which may include a government relations dimension. The Chartered Institute of Marketing also offers some government affairs instruction.

The problem with some of these courses is that not only are they PR-minded (which is what, after all, they are supposed to be) but also some are rumoured to have any number of add-ons which the lobbyist finds ridiculous. These are said to include psychology courses (a lucrative side-line for the shrinks) which teach everybody how to fold their hands and look interested when a prospective client is meeting them – the problem being that everybody has been on these same courses, including the prospective client, so everybody is madly folding their hands in an identical way.

Other educational establishments include the European Centre for Public Affairs, based at Templeton College, Oxford; and the European Centre for Public Affairs Brussels (ECPAB), a training centre offering intensive courses.

More training is offered by a whole bunch of conference specialists. These can charge ridiculous sums of money for recycling the same old tired platform speakers and are not always well attended. One way of judging the calibre of these conferences is whether attendance certificates are offered and whether they qualify for inclusion in any recognised professional or academic qualification.

Competition to get into the consultancies is so tough that the larger companies take only the cream of graduates. This does not mean Oxbridge incidentally. Useful first degrees include languages, law and sciences. A Masters degree is increasingly a must.

Naturally, you must also be very technology-friendly. There is now a growing appetite for graduates, particularly those with sufficient software skills to handle the mind-boggling permutations of political address lists and databases. A broad range of skills are coming into the industry not least those of sophisticated logistical management. It must be added that despite all the technology there is still a need for people to stuff envelopes!

Once you join a company, your senior staff – usually in a disparaging manner – will most likely go through the motions of suggesting that you do the Institute of Public Relations exams, the latest to be launched in Autumn 1998. These could insult the intelligence of those with academic skills from other disciplines. Do them anyway. Although much of the content could be of a simplistic, common-sensical nature, some of it is likely to be useful and certainly worth knowing.

Find out how much of the office budget goes on training, and whether this training is done internally or externally. It is bad manners to dump an employer, especially a small employer, immediately after being trained if he has paid for your training when he is not going to get the benefit of it. Offer to pay the employer back, or ask your new employer to pay him back.

Those who do not train staff have two reasons for refusing to do so. One is that they are too poor. This does not always mean that they are bad employers (although in the lobbying industry it usually does). The other is because they want to limit your experience to the job they want you to do for them which is in their best interests but not yours. The answer is, once you have a foothold on the market, take control both of your own training and your career.

It is up to you to find out what you want to do and where you want your career to take you. For example, experts in sectoral fields are more important to the European Commission than anybody else so specialise if that's where you want to be. Remember, however, that if you specialise in yesterday's sector, you may find yourself out of a job when the sector disappears. If you specialise – pick something with a long future, not necessarily a long past.

Make sure that your employer does not overload you with mundane chores so that you do not have enough time to go on training courses – an old ploy. In addition, check out your employer's skills as well as those of your colleagues. Are scientists employed on pharmaceutical accounts?

Regrettably, training is so low down the priority list that most companies want recruits with several years experience so that they do not need to train them (one reason why there is so much talk at the moment about an industry training levy). As a result many are hiring entrants from Europe rather than the UK partially because of their language capability, partially because they have usually worked for the Commission and therefore know their way around, and partially because of their interpersonal skills. Regrettably, the British undergraduate can lack interpersonal skills – essential for all lobbyists – and, as a result, is losing out in the jobs race.

Sometimes, 'training' means attending various conferences and seminars. It is not recommended that you spend all your time attending these no matter how big the office budget. The likelihood is that they will provide very little information that you could not find out for yourself and did not know already and you could irritate your clients if you are constantly on them. After all, your clients are paying you because you are trained not so that you can get trained, which is your employers' responsibility. In fact, they are very likely to think that you are job hunting. If you are, conferences are not the best place to find your next employer, since so many going to them are also job-hunting.

Incidentally, look very carefully at any employer using the conference and seminar circuit as an excuse for not providing in-house training. The conferences are so expensive that they beg the question why the employer is wasting your pay rises on them instead of doing the job themselves. Employers training staff internally – so long as they really are doing so – are investing in their staff, company and clients. The perfect mix.

The conference documents, however, can be very useful which is why they are so expensively priced.

It is well to bear in mind that if your employer can spare you on a regular basis to go on these courses, you or your immediate superior, could well be marginalised or heading for the chop. Incidentally, if your superior is always going on courses himself – change job.

Those going to the conferences include people hoping to network and ex-public servants wanting to catch up with the knowledge their subordinates have.

On the other hand, the elite seminars that only the top are invited to are worth popping in on if you are invited which you most likely won't be. Console yourself that these for the most part are run by dated elites and even more dated or politically motivated Think Tanks and foundations.

If there is a particular conference that you wish to attend (and there are so many that you must be discriminating) see this as an investment in yourself. Pay for the conference personally so that your employer knows you mean business (if the employer offers to pay for it, accept) and, if the conference is a residential one, use up your holiday entitlement to go on it. Such conferences are usually more expensive than holidays – especially the European & Washington based ones – but can be a much better investment than heat-stroke. If, incidentally, you do pay for the conference yourself, make sure you tell the tax-man so that you can get some, albeit minor, tax relief.

Incidentally, a word about party conferences and hospitality. Good employers, with the appropriate budget, always 'work' a party conference so that while they are entertaining the 'big guns', their staff are entertaining those lower down the pecking order, for example, research assistants. Prior to such 'entertainment' questions are worked out in advance, so that the same questions are being fed in at different levels. The employer that does not know how to 'feed' the various levels is not worth considering. It should be noted, of course, that party conference itself is changing and links are now being developed with task forces and quangos.

Also, consider joining the **National Union of Journalists**. This offers the lowly more than, say, the **Institute of Public Relations** (IPR), now in its 50th year. The IPR, although at long last galvanised into some action including new training courses, and aiming towards chartered status, still has some way to go. Not everybody has a good opinion of it, however, and not all lobbyists are members.

The NUJ is slowly recovering from a few disastrous years and offers excellent, good value training courses to its members. It is also trying to boost its membership and raise awareness among lobbyists and public relations staff. Despite this, it has to be said that the mix is still a bit uncomfortable principally because most NUJ members do not even pretend not to look down upon PRs.

NUJ ideology and culture is such that it will probably take quite some time for attitudes to change. In fact, were the union not so short of money, it is arguable whether they would have you at all! That having been said, they are modernising like fury and are the only organisation offering employee support, which includes ethical guidance, something desperately needed in the industry.

NUJ benefits include the help of their legal department (all of which advice comes free), and advice and assistance on all workplace issues. If, as a condition of employment, you are not allowed to join a union make sure that the perks union membership offers are provided by the employer.

These include: pension schemes, car leasing agreements, Internet deals, training, and legal fees. The NUJ also offers discounts on holidays, insurance, and roadside rescue services. At the moment the union is offering far more than the IPR or the PRCA, the only other professional association that lobbyists can join, and at considerably less expense. In addition, they represent you, rather than the employer which makes a big difference if, for example, you have to go to Industrial Tribunal.

Some Things to remember

Good employers are **Political POPPETS**. Bad employers are **Political BOGGLES**.

The Political Poppets are **P**assionate about their staff and clients; **O**pen-minded about ideas and comment; **P**rompt in their attention; **P**recise in their execution; **E**thical in their manner; **T**rained in their disciplines; and financially **S**ecure.

The Political Boggles are the reverse of the above. They are run by Political Bogglers, who always look startled when they find out that you are unimpressed by them.

They tend to be **B**loodsucking **O**pportunists, or **B**rown-nosing **O**verchargers, who cheat their staff and/or clients. If they have the intelligence, which they usually do not, they excel at **G**amesmanship, which masks their lack of **G**roundwork, or manage to grasp only the rudiments of an argument in the belief that their gift of the gab will carry them through. They are **L**azy, frequently louche, but often have luck on their side. They see themselves as the **E**minence grises of the profession when really they are anything but. They are **R**apacious because they have to be – i.e. they know what many of us suspect – they, and/or their companies are built on **S**and.

When joining an employer, it is up to you to make your reputation and, as importantly, to hang on to it. Your employer may already have compromised his, not care about it because he wants to make a lot of money quickly, or, be at the end of his working life and therefore not necessarily as aware of the new ethics as he ought to be. Since you are starting your working life these factors matter as your lobbying past has the power to cloud your brightest hopes for the future.

For example, do not work for a defence client if, in the long term, you wish to work for a peace charity. It is sometimes possible to leave your past behind, indeed it can be an advantage to have an intimate knowledge of both sides of an issue, but not always. Reputations can never be clawed back – therefore it would be unwise for you to give yours away. And equally unwise to let an employer or superior to do it for you. Ethical accounts are all the rage now – if you have made a mistake in the past you won't get on them.

Try and hang on to real life, although this can be difficult. As a lobbyist you can spend your time in posh restaurants at somebody else's expense but this can be disorientating when the alternative is beans in Sidcup. When your working life is so different from your private life, real life can become make-believe and your professional life reality. Don't let it.

Your professional life can be amazingly privileged but it can also become so unbalanced that it is not life. Lobbying is addictive – and, unless you guard against this, you can have enormous adjustment problems when, for whatever reason, you leave the industry. You miss the perks, gossip, and being in the know.

Being 'in the know' is, of course, what a lobbyist's life is all about.

One way to short circuit this dependency is to make sure that you do not stay in the industry for much longer than a decade unless a) you take at least one year's leave from the business during that decade or b) you change forums e.g. from Europe to Washington. Unless you do so you will become stale and/or not top up your skills and contacts which you need to progress your career That is not to say you should not be loyal to your employer – it is to say that you should keep things in perspective.

Good lobbyists know how to step back from problems. To keep their distance. So must you. Let your client be emotionally engaged – not you. Being emotionally engaged is usually all-consuming when you are campaigning. Everybody is working all hours and you are all focused towards the same goal. When the campaign is over, the silence is deafening. Many do not know what to do with themselves when the drama is passed. You should. Incidentally, it is professional suicide to quit in the middle of a campaign unless you have very good reason.

Change employers as often as suits you because if you stay with one employer too long you may grow too used to your work-place friendships and the supporting atmosphere. You will therefore grow 'old' (become institutionalised?) without realising and may find it more difficult to find a new job or to fit into the culture of a new employer. And, when the employer wants some new blood, the new blood may be brought in over your head. Be aware, however, that this flexi-culture often works solely in the employers' favour i.e. by preserving the privileges of those at the top who do not move on.

Of course, you can be locked in by becoming 'management'. It is silly, however, to become 'management' if you want to be a lobbyist. Management is an entirely different discipline – although regrettably not in lobbying. This is one reason why the industry is so badly managed.

Needless to say, there is life after lobbying so never be too frightened to drop out of the industry altogether. The next shallow, burnt out executive you meet who does not know what to do with the rest of his life could be you. Get a life – lobbying can be all about buying in to the second hand. It's about other people's lives – not yours. Get your own life. That way you will never need proof that your identity is permanent. Lobbying is about balance and measurable achievement. If you want to be a good lobbyist you have to have an understanding of that balance.

Regrettably, far too many in the industry have never had a break from it and therefore suffer because of it. They spend their lives avoiding information overload but in so doing miss things from other's point of view. They see things in a vacuum, miss the agenda's of others and lose sight of the ability to think laterally.

When identifying your employer stay well clear of jobs that have no immediate or future benefit. Equally, stay well clear of those who have never done anything other than lobby. Lobbying is about networking. The problem however is that 'networking' often means talking to the same people, who often have identical mindsets, who have been in the industry too long. As a result information is recycled, including wrong information, or given inappropriate emphasis.

Therefore, try not to move within too small an orbit, otherwise you will end up group-thinking which is no good for you, your clients, or your employer. Old-style lobbyists were often able to avoid 'group think' because they, and their subordinates, had much wider exposure to a larger array of clients and client needs.

One way of avoiding 'group think' is by building up your own contacts and, in particular, meeting the 'Alternative Voices'. For example – working for a civil engineering contractor? Then meet the road protesters. Not sure which political line to take ? See whether the Monday Club would support it. Then try it out on a few members of the Fabian Society. Or, even more pertinently, on those who have no politics.

Another way of escaping the 'group think' trap is by avoiding current affairs programmes on the radio or editorials in major newspapers and periodicals. If you are working well, you should be able to write such editorials yourself and should not be having to rely on other people's comment and analysis to set the agenda. It is up to you to determine what are the main news and political stories of the day for your clients, not journalists or politicians.

Intimate reading of all reported speech in the Parliamentary documents is essential. This ensures that thinking for yourself becomes a habit. If you fail to think for yourself, you can be taken by surprise, which can disadvantage your clients. Always attend your client's press conferences – this may be the only way you find out what your clients are really up to, what they should be telling you but are not, and, more importantly, help you to spot their weaknesses.

Incidentally, if you find yourself embarrassed by something that a client, or your employer on your client's behalf, has withheld from you, disassociate yourself immediately. Journalists are usually very helpful when this happens – but not always for the best of motives. Be very careful, however, about your legal position. Until such time as you resign from a client, you are his paid agent, and, even when you have resigned you will probably be bound by confidentiality clauses in your contract.

Needless to say, do not knowingly lie to the Press. If you subsequently find out that you have inadvertently done so because of information supplied to you either by your client or employer, issue an immediate correction no matter how embarrassing this may be. If your client or employer refuse to allow such a correction to be made, consult the NUJ, whether or not you are a member.

Clients and employers do lie, although these days it is called being 'economical with the truth'. They are in very good company – the press themselves, public servants and all political forums can do the same. Do not join the lie-culture. It usually catches up with you.

In addition, never pass a story to the Press that has been told to you in confidence. Politicians are ridiculously indiscreet and are justifiably hurt when their confidences are exposed in the Press. They also have memories like elephants and, since politics is a long game, you may need the politician again.

Finally, if you have a complaint about the press – make it. If your employers refuse to support you, find out why. It could be that you are wrong, that you have a weak case, or that the error is so minor that it is not worth doing anything about it. On the other hand, it could be for more cynical reasons. That could tell you all you need to know about the press, the client, the employer or all three.

Political Activities and Civic Duties

It is usually a nuisance when you or your colleagues are called for jury service or if you or your colleagues sit as magistrates because the work still needs to be done. However, it should also be pointed out that the reason why, for example, juries are not necessarily made up of the best is because, given half a chance, many of us duck our civic responsibilities.

This does not set young people a suitable example. Nor, when subordinates are called upon to fulfil civic obligations do we regard this as anything other than an inconvenience to ourselves. While this is certainly the case, a more appropriate response is to encourage them to take their responsibilities seriously. Some employers, incidentally, actively encourage their staff to take on voluntary work and give them time off to do so.

It is even more of a nuisance when you, or your colleagues become, or assist, candidates in local, national and European elections because, again, the work in the office still needs to be done. The only rule worth knowing is to make sure that you are not the poor soul left doing it. Political ambitions are always a pain – and ones that takes far too long to work through.

Working for candidates is good for contacts but, remember, if your boss is a candidate his contacts are likely to be one-sided. This might work against your future. In addition, it is not likely to be in your clients best interests – although the jury is still out on this one (See 'Cronygate') – if those who advise them are identified with a political party since there is an increasing requirement here and abroad for work best suited to non-political or cross-party identification. The profession is reverting to its previously non-aligned position.

This is one reason why one commercial lobbyist always thought twice before accepting a Westminster Research Assistant's pass.

These gave kudos and access – i.e. prestige and convenience – but also meant that the lobbyist would have had to nail his political colours to the mast which he did not feel would be in his long-term professional interest.

When applying for a job in a commercial lobbying consultancy always ask about the past, present and future political activities of your colleagues because these can jeopardise your long term prospects. If any of them have, or have had, rather wacky politics – extreme right/left – be careful not to be sucked into their orbit unless you want to spend your life in the shadows.

In addition, always think twice if the company does not change its advertising literature – i.e. if they are still boasting about their one member of staff who once worked for the Labour Party but left last year they have a problem.

Picking your immediate superior

Try to avoid gofering for someone who has come into lobbying late, e.g. ex-public servants or apparatchiks since, although they have been brought in over you, they seldom know anything. They have been employed (at enormous salary, dwarfing your own) for their contacts (oh yes!) and prestige they offer, not the workload they assume. As a result, they become social lobbyists, unaccustomed to hard work without guidance. You, on the other hand, end up having to do all their work while they both learn on the job and take the credit. In addition, you are marginalised.

Those that are the 'bounced' e.g. former ambassadors, senior politicians, and, more recently, those who have worked for the Labour Party, have to accept that those who have been in a job longer than they, or feel they merited the job more than they, are bound to feel aggrieved. This is because they believe that given the chance they could do the job as well if not better. This is often true. It is up to you to convince them that you have the interests of them all at heart. Not of course that anyone reading this book will believe the above for one minute.

The market place is not meritocratic. It is ruthless, leaving many employees feeling violated by their employers. Your career can be blighted by popular new boys, those who are threatened by your talents, nepotism and favouritism, as well as by time-serving tyrants. Instead of getting bitter and twisted – bitter and twisted lobbyists are no good to anyone, least of all their clients – find another employer. Getting rid of your boss is easy. Leave.

In addition, do not be marginalised because your boss is marginalised. The latter can be corporately naive, unable to relate to superiors or colleagues and therefore unable to swim with the corporate tide. They give daily reminders of their need to live apart from the herd which is good for their mental health but can ruin yours as you see the less-deserving walk away with your pay rise or promotion. On the other hand, those not at the centre can end up challenging the centre. If this is what the boss is up to, it is sometimes worth taking a punt and sticking with it. Learn the company politics if you want to succeed in a large organisation.

Look out for the stars, the average and the mediocre. Never think that you're the star – unless you know what can happen to stars. They can shoot too brightly and disappear. Learn to become corporately mature, a corporate politician, by reading messages upwards and sideways. If there are no messages, you are going nowhere. Get out fast or re-position yourself.

Lobbying is about four things. Knowing the political world/s, how your clients fit into those worlds, the ethics, and how you fit in. If the working environment of any of these feel wrong, you are probably right. Leave.

Future Employers

At the moment there is very little challenge in the way firms think – it is not just about lobbying but about the fundamentals of running a business. Underpinning most management philosophy is a refusal to accept a fresh sort of corporate structure. The company that is completely employee owned, from the public affairs director to the switchboard operator, all receiving an equal share in the business, are few and far between. 'Hot desking' is all the rage when what is needed is root and branch reform of hierarchy and how such hierarchy rewards itself and its subordinates.

Virtual organisations are not yet the norm, which is just as well. Employers are not sufficiently up to speed in running traditional companies, let alone knowing how to motivate and recompense fairly those working from work-stations in their homes. And, as indicated earlier, the management function is not sufficiently separate to the senior lobbyists workload.

Most agencies are run with senior management taking the lion's share of the profits from the creativity and ideas of younger staff, while rewarding favourite new boys. There are a lot of greedy people in lobbying.

Regrettably, the industry is driven by ego, and, by and large, does not respect its employees although it pretends otherwise.

Problems are particularly acute when dealing with the egos of once sole proprietors of enlarged companies who can be almost impossible to work for. Until there is a radical change in thinking there are some questions to bear in mind when choosing an employer.

These include:

- How often do you have the opportunity to quiz senior management about where the company is going, ethics and so on?
- How many members of the Board do you meet regularly and, if they are new, how has their arrival been justified; ditto the arrival of new stars who may not be on the board but have been bounced in over your head at, usually, considerably higher salary?
- Will you be working directly with clients or kept at arms length?
- Will you be working on innovative projects for high profile clients and involved with the full project development cycle?
- Will you receive training on an on-going basis, once in a while, or be given a French lesson at a local authority evening class?
- Will your salary be linked directly to the quality of your performance or at annual review?
- Will you be told how much everyone earns in the company i.e. is talent recognised, or, will you at least know the details of the salary bands?
- Will you have the freedom to develop your skills or is this based solely on knowing and playing the corporate game?
- Are your employers prepared to be flexible e.g. if you have no

requirement for medical insurance but do require assistance in getting a mortgage/pension, will they help? What 'menu' are your employers offering in addition to salary?

It is bad policy to agree to the request of senior management that you parachute in to a 'poor' political unit unless you have a burning desire to train people up, particularly if the management are not prepared to invest. You should also play the numbers game. For example, if there is one commercial lobbyist, to ten ex-public servants or consultants, you have a problem. Pressure to work as a member of a team can mean spread yourself around our bad consultants who work part-time taking their salaries out of staff profits. It can also mean that they are out of the office for hours and hours while you similarly do all the work.

Too many chieftains come expensive and you're the one paying for them – especially if they have separate business activities, either private, or in subsidiaries of your employers, in which case you can end up subsidising the profit centres of others.

Find out about your employers' financial obligations to previous managements. You should also find out about 'investments' made by the parent group so that you do not unknowingly subsidise your employers responsibilities to his shareholders, which could prevent simultaneous investment in you; or his legal obligations to personnel too expensive to dislodge.

Above all, do not price yourself on the basis of the 'new business' you bring in because you may find that you are too overworked to bring in new business. You are a commercial lobbyist, not a salesman. You should also look carefully at the distribution of profit and share bonus. Many shares are no more than gimmicks. Be very careful about management buy-outs and the distribution of equity.

As for using your own money to purchase shares – be sensible. Are your employers investing in the company and its subsidiaries or merely desperate for liquidity? Have they cleared out the dead wood? How good are their supporting research facilities ? Incidentally, if you are required by your employer to sell some of your shares (perhaps because of insider dealing legislation) make sure that the employer pays the tax (if appropriate) and places you in a position to reinvest. Make sure that your employer does not compromise you financially.

Do not sign a blanket statement of 'confidentiality'. Deal with issues on a case by case basis because there may well be times when you come across information which is in the public's interest to disclose.

Do not draft legal documentation or discuss legal procedure unless you are qualified to do so; and do not refer to yourself as a 'consultant', or let your employer do so, unless you really are a consultant.

Do not be conned into thinking that you are management if you are not. Similarly, do not become management if management is not the management. More importantly, only become management if that is what you want to do – manage. Most lobbyists wish to remain lobbyists. If you do agree to become management make sure you are up to speed on directors responsibilities and liabilities.

Recognise that 'joint venture' means companies play family while being responsible for their own problems – which have even less chance of being sorted out. Recognise that 'take over' means companies play adultery without being responsible for the cuckolded. Recognise that 'management buy out' means divorce and you are part of the share-out of possessions. Merger means 'marriage' and a whole bunch of step-children who are either thrown out of home or neglected.

Look very carefully at contracts of employment. For example, you can be locked into a one year notice period, which would not allow the flexibility you require to move around the workforce. Also, 'gardening leave' provisions should always include adequate payment for the months/years of enforced idleness demanded by former employers.

Contracts given to freelancers are particularly harsh and need to be checked by outside lawyers before they are signed.

Regional v London Consultancies

Regional consultancies often offer their clients a better and cheaper deal than London based consultancies because their overheads are lower. Often staffed or set up by former executives from the London agencies, their skills are as good as any and they can offer better regional political and media contacts which can offer a quicker route into the European Commission. The issue of the local and regional press is also important since many London based clients, giving up, for one reason or another, on the national press, are favouring the latter to punch home either their message or products.

On the other hand, the very big accounts still go to London. London also has other advantages. These include the fact that it plays host to countless informal political networks and intelligence – casual meetings in wine-bars, pubs, hotel bars and cafes and the like. The acquisition of such information is vital for lobbyists. It is also appropriate to acknowledge that some regional consultancies are not always up to speed with the very latest developments, technology and best research.

Regional companies have not necessarily been quick to exploit developments in local government. For example, local government authorities and waste companies have enormous investment plans and procurement policies. Despite this many locally based lobbyists still tend to concentrate on officers rather than decision-makers, when the local authorities themselves are often looking to the lobbyists to apply pressure for increased expenditure on elected councillors, who are the decision makers at local level.

Nonetheless, given government plans to decentralise and hand government back to the regions the regional lobbyists are likely to improve rapidly. At the moment, however, some are concentrating too hard on positioning themselves for tomorrow, therefore ignoring today's existing market. The Scottish ones are the ones to watch.

Conclusion

Lobbying is a terrific industry to work in and a fascinating world to become involved with. However, because so many young people are in the industry, leadership of the industry as a whole has not been a priority. Young people usually want to succeed as individuals first.

The leadership that does exist can be compromised and many would therefore argue that it is not in a position to act as a role model for new entrants. Many industry leaders have pursued a strategy that is essentially in their own personal or company interest rather than those of the industry as a whole, and the young people learning from them. In addition, some have connived in the ambitions of public servants who themselves do not set the young an example. The young therefore learn from the morally bankrupt.

When the leadership of an industry is morally bankrupt, so indeed is the industry itself.

On the other hand, leadership cannot lead if there are no troops to lead. You – the troops – are desperately needed. Therefore it is up to you to inject the industry, and its leaders, with the appropriate mix of commercial acumen, ethics and decency.

It is a tribute to the interesting workload that so many put up with the industry's problems, most especially those created by its leadership and employers. That having been said, many employees are beginning the fight back. As an experiment, a former employee of a well-known consultancy sent out thirty-five invitations to other former employees, now well dispersed throughout the industry, to attend an after-work drink. Twenty-seven replied and all attended.

Instead of lasting one hour, the meeting lasted four and a half hours – the topic on the agenda being specific employers. Calling themselves the Colditz Club (i.e. escapees), the evening was such a success that it will now be extended and run on a regular basis.

Events such as these do not represent a sub-culture, and deserve to be taken seriously until such time as all in the industry have a shared agenda. Meanwhile, if the industry's large employers do not impress their present or former staff, what hope, in the long term, do they have of impressing the public?

Commercial lobbying is about politics and clients. It is also about loving political beasts and negotiating a way. At its best, it is about respect. That respect is not best illustrated by the employee/employer relationship.

THE LOBBYING WORLD

The Present Political Climate – The Boring B'strds and The 'Political
CUMMERBUND' – The Labour Lobbyists – Professional
Backgrounds – Lobbying Types: The 'Political Telly Tubbies', 'Political
Spice Girls' and 'Ghastly Gits' – The Lobbying Periphery: Public
Affairs Magazines, Watering Holes – A Tour of the Lobbying Industry
and some of the companies – What Company Do the Commercial
Lobbyists Keep?: The People – Politicians, Women, Gays, Civil
Service, European Union, Flashing Lights and Flared Nostrils Brigade,
Intelligence Services and Private Security Companies

The Present Political Climate

While commercial hype encourages us all to think in terms of the
global – those of us who do not are parochial, narrow-minded and
unsophisticated – no explanation has yet been offered as to why the
business world was so shell-shocked at the scale of the Labour victory
in May 1997. If business is indeed 'global', why should it have mattered?

The answer, of course, is that although business may be global, it, like
politics, is only perceived be active at local level. Business may use the
word 'global' in the French sense (i.e. to imply inclusiveness) but
communities are rightly reluctant to see themselves sacrificed for the
whole, when that whole, often foreign owned, does not have the
interests of their parts of the whole at heart.

Therefore, while individuals within communities may be
cosmopolitan in outlook, their aspirations are, unsurprisingly, selfish – as
indeed, are the aspirations of 'global' business. This clash is what makes
national government so important.

At local level, global business has need of national government, first of all to keep what it considers to be a proper check on the workforce; secondly, to pick up whatever favours it can; thirdly, to maintain a flexible regulatory environment (arms traders, for example, flourished in the UK because of such 'flexibility'); and fourthly, to smooth its way internationally, especially if some believe that, for example, they are wrecking the local environments of others. The importance of the political complexion of national government, therefore, cannot be underestimated.

Nor can it be underestimated for 'local business', by which we mean those who do not trade beyond their local area, region, country or the European continent. For example, business interests are an important category of interest in the European Union. However, Member States often have political objectives which may not be the same as business objectives. This can mean, therefore, that some businesses may want an interventionist policy, others the reverse.

This is good news for commercial lobbyists who are paid vast sums to nudge such objectives in their client's direction. However, it is bad news for global business since it is recognisably cheaper for shareholders if some national governments are already alongside, so that they can get on with oiling the wheels of other national governments. It is even worse for both local and global business, particularly in the post-BSE era, since the problems in the British Beef industry have led to enormous regulatory change and political realignment.

As a result, large numbers of products and materials are now at risk because of the precautionary principle. This is being applied in a conservative fashion – if there is a risk, no matter how small, the product has to be banned. The consequences for business are enormous and make it all the more reliant on influencing national government.

British government, however, has a rather novel problem. For the first time, and for its own survival, it has to view the electorate as a customer. To put it bluntly, it recognises that while business may have a lot of money, it does not have as many votes as the customer. Therefore, business does not have the power to see Government re-elected.

Of course business collectively could, were it so minded, put forward quite a convincing case for having just that power on the basis that there should be no taxation without representation. Bearing in mind the proportion of tax income accruing both to the Treasury and local authorities from businesses it is astonishing that organisations such as the CBI and the Chambers of Commerce do not kick up more of a fuss. Perhaps they are too concerned about their members continuing to be offered the sop of a seat in the House of Lords from time to time.

Indeed, the new 'Blairified' House of Lords might be quite an opportunity for business to increase its representation in the Upper Chamber if it plays its cards (or lobbies) right.

A further problem for government arises because an awful lot of the 'customers' are not buying. As a result, governments talks of things like 'Cool Britannia' or Ministers get themselves photographed with pop stars to attract younger people, only to find those same pop stars rubbishing them in the *New Musical Express*, one of the few papers really read by young people who will vote in the next General Election.

This is presumably why previous government took little notice of young people, favouring commerce instead, and encouraging it to think globally, while it secured the appropriate regulatory environment. However, some would argue that it was brought down by those who refused to think continental, let alone global, thus allowing Mr Blair to run off with the cookie-jar.

And what a cookie jar it was! National government has massive resources and statutory powers if it cares to use them which it usually does – providing commercial lobbyists with a great deal of work in the process.

'New' Labour

While sinister political undercurrents – from rancid right to the remaining loony left – tried to write the script for both political parties at the time of the last General Election, Tony Blair managed to bash Labour into blandness while being clever enough to get himself elected on his shiny newness. The country welcomed him as a breath of fresh air.

Unaware that the 'new' politics patronised it, as much as the 'old' politics ignored it, it welcomed as its new MPs financial statesmen? Political visionaries ? Er, no.

Labour's ranks contain a mixture of social workers, polytechnic lecturers, trades union officials, school teachers and local government officers, all of whose professions have collectively failed the country. As a result, the government has set up dozens of focus groups and taskforces, all of which have attracted the attention of the anti-democrats, but which it believes more accurately reflect the citizen's wishes or needs than those, selected by dated party hacks, elected to Parliament. This is not to imply, of course, that Parliamentarians of yesterday were any better. They were not.

As the new regime moved in, the commercial lobbyists only just managed to hide their self-satisfied smirks. If ever their clients, needed them, they reasoned, now was that time. And indeed for some they were right – until 'Cronygate' went and ruined some of the fun.

Those, of course, not involved in 'Cronygate', adamant that they were different to the others, spoke of long term political trends – consensual rather than confrontational – while still employing any number of Labour Party members.

Speaking in hushed voices, they warned solemnly that the present Government ignored its backbenchers (suffering anxiety, fatigue and insomnia) at its peril, since it ignores the strength and depth of their convictions, while equally solemnly similarly ignoring them, in order to pursue the centre.

Operating in non-touching worlds, the gulf ever widening between government and business, the commercial lobbyists presented themselves as a bridge between the two. And indeed, a couple of firms for a while had some notable success. The trend towards youthful politicians assisted, first of all because many of the lobbyists, especially new arrivals, were themselves young, and secondly because many politicians acknowledged that they were largely ignorant of anything outside of politics and hoped that some of the lobbyists would bridge the gap.

To put it bluntly, Labour needed the commercial lobbyist to meet the business world. As a result, it offered policy documents to lobbyists in return for a hefty four figure annual subscription and seats at the breakfast table. The extra good news for lobbyists was that in so doing it left their clients, any number of whom were big corporate players, as the outsiders and therefore impressed by and reliant on the insiders – the lobbyists! Simple isn't it?

Not only was business the outsider, but an outsider that was now expected to listen to government, even though it had some leverage by offering sponsorships, and ignored it when considering its own pay rises. The business world that respected no-one other than its competitors, least of all the national governments of democratic countries, was in alien territory.

Gone was the friendly government that held the hand of business while the threat of the demon 'Vredeling' directive (the EU directive supporting worker directors) dominated the late 1970s and early 1980s. Gone too was the government that told its Civil Servants not to ask too many questions.

In its place was Labour Government which called the voter a 'consumer', and the workers 'employees' with employee rights, challenging the McJobs mentality so beloved in the United States and, to the self-interested delight of the business community, swallowed whole by previous UK government. Gone too was government that fought Europe's social chapter tooth-and-nail, in consequence giving new energy to pro-European British unions.

And, finally, gone was the familiarity. While, today, Secretaries of State make mistakes, such mistakes appear to be ones of naiveté – the one thing the business world finds hard to forgive. It longs for the old days when 'naiveté' was non-existent, and Conservative government worshipped on the altar of commerce irrespective of the price the country, and other countries, paid for such worship.

The country was not what it used to be.

Out had gone the young men who adored Mrs Thatcher (although an argument could be made that many of them, irrespective of 'Cronygate', are advising Tony Blair!) and the ostentatious grandeur epitomised by the 1980s. Out had gone the rancid right who believed they could do a better job than John Major.

Out too had gone the old men who worked down the mines before being elected to Parliament, and who, once there, were denounced as raving reds or depicted in terms of patronising sentimentality. And finally, out had gone a generation of tabbies who had devoted their lives to political Party or MP, becoming, in the process, key targets of the commercial lobbyists.

In had come Formula One, self-made millionaires that voted Labour, other businessmen with 'trendy' workforces who, courtesy of Mrs Thatcher, did not expect a pension from their employer (although it would be nice) but did expect parental leave, courtesy of the European Union. In, too, had come the over-simplification of politics and, worse, the denial that that which was difficult to understand had any relevance. After all, it was easier to cry over a sick animal than it was to figure out how to pay the farmer. In, finally, had come the exciting radical right – with the radical left yet to emerge.

In too had come the New Labour Lobbyists.

Business was terrified. The Labour Party had slotted in so easily – even the cock-ups had a familiar ring to them – that the corporate world could not even comfort itself that Labour's stay would be of short duration. After all, the country now seemed conditioned to the long game – eighteen years of the Tories had done that – and the electorate was just as likely to give Mr Blair a decent run as they had the Conservatives. The planned reform of the voting system could well see to that. And, what's more, he was so popular and squeaky clean. His government the same...

Business remained stunned. If the kids could do the job, it muttered, what hope of the Tories ever making a comeback? In their panic they could not see that voting changes do not necessarily work in Labour's favour; nor could they see that images tarnish swiftly; nor did they appreciate the Conservative Party's historical ability to reinvent itself quickly. Best get alongside the Labour Party fast, it panicked. And how best to do that?

Why, the commercial lobbyists. Especially the New Labour ones. But surely, these are not really necessary. After all, business has massive links with the Executive – i.e. the Civil Service, doesn't it?

The Civil Service

Bad mouthing the servants of the State is almost an art form these days. This is not strictly fair. It is not the Civil Service's fault that business, instructed by its commercial lobbyists, has had to learn to present its needs by showing the servants of self-interested Government what is in it for them.

Nor is it the Civil Service's fault if business has hired reams of ex-Tory ministers to deal with their former underlings, only to find to its cost that Civil Servants hate dealing with their previous masters. Nor is it the Civil Service's fault that individual Civil Servants do not know whether they will still be in a job tomorrow and are therefore disinclined to be as efficient as they might have been had morale been higher. Surely the business community, as well as the citizen, can understand that?

Up to a point, yes. But the business community and citizen can also empathise with Prime Minister Blair, who went out of his way to thank the Civil Service for the smooth transition it offered when Labour came to power, before dumping it as quickly as he was able. The Prime Minister's colleagues appear to be following suit pointing towards a wholly politicised Civil Service along American lines – witness the wholesale sacking of Whitehall departmental press secretaries and their replacement by a group of Millbank politicised robots or tired old media hacks.

At the time of writing, the latest to set up his own Think Tank is Foreign Secretary Robin Cook. Chancellor Gordon Brown has done the same. The implications for business are enormous since Mr Cook's apparent anxiety about 'ethical' foreign policy is not something that business is known to welcome. Nor Civil Servants come to that.

As a result, business depends on its commercial lobbyists even more than it has done in the past. These slip into local, regional, national, European and international government at will, representing as they do not worlds within worlds but several unrelated worlds.

So who are the commercial lobbyists who bridge these worlds, what sort of people are they, and do you want to work with them?

The Boring B'stards and the Political CUMMERBUND

The commercial lobbying world, nationally or in Europe, can be summarised by the term the **'Political CUMMERBUND'**. This can be rich, exotic and discreetly tasteful, or equally, garish. It adorns the commercial lobbyist's ample stomach and contains:

The **C**ourtesans, of both sexes, who seek out the wealthy. These can be lobbyists looking for rich clients; politicians and other public servants, local, national and European, looking for equally rich clients; and those seeking sponsorship, usually, although not always, for good causes.

The **U**nbalanced who believe that no world exists other than the political one.

The **M**achiavellian who flourish in deceit and perfidy.

The **M**ystique of political forums, especially political centres such as The Treasury, which is impressive to the layman, and without which the commercial lobbyist, politician and public servant, would all be out of jobs.

The **E**spionage – political, commercial and industrial – which riddles political forums. There are so many spies running around London and Europe that they really ought to set up an All Party Group
　and

The **R**acketeers who believe that local, national and European governments are there to be collectively screwed. While political infrastructure/s concern themselves with arriving at common positions so **B**land as to be useless, the racketeers enjoy themselves racketeering.

Regrettably, for those who wanted a pro-commercial lobbying book, the conclusion reached is that the vast majority within the 'Political CUMMERBUND' are the **U**ngodly and the **N**arcissistic. There are also, of course, one or two **D**iamonds. These however, are sadly too few in number to make the difference but when they do, shine transparently with brilliance, fire and decency.

Labour Lobbyists

Back in Britain, Tony Blair's victory spawned a load of new kids on the block and a brace of fresh Labour appointments in the industry. Like any number before them, and no doubt those after them, their ideology seemed to be principally about serving themselves – a somewhat harsh judgement in view of the fact that New Labour hardly invented opportunism.

Besides, where else do junior Labour research assistants go other than to the Think Tanks, lobbying and PR companies, no matter how tenuous their links with Labour, how immature they are, how poor their skills, or the fact that some of them do not know the first thing about humility?

Not that they can be blamed for moving into industry, commerce, charities or public affairs. A political party is no fun to work for when it has won office – it is the fight that is important; and, like all political parties, they are lousy employers. Moreover, there were no jobs for them in-house any way, so dozens had to be off-loaded, even though very little thought, from the centre, went into the off-loading.

Presumably today there is some angst as to why there was not more thought given to where the Party's apparatchiks would find a home – not least because 'Cronygate' drew attention to the deep divisions in the Labour Party, especially the centre and centre left's loathing for 'New Labour'.

Labour Lobbying had arrived. And, in the case of some, been and gone as the lobbying companies, discovering their Labour duds, frantically tried to off-load them. The commercial lobbying industry's appointment of Labour arrivals was not necessarily to access Labour (although this was very useful – in some cases, apparently, too useful) but a marketing tool to retain clients and take on new ones.

Those that remain in the industry manage to swallow any apparent anxiety they might have had about their anti-lobbyist past in their desperation to share in the spoils. They join those Labour lobbyists already established in the industry – employed as an insurance policy against incoming Labour government – and long ignored, now enjoying a field day.

Some possess what appears to be a superficial understanding of the product 'democracy', and nod in its direction while trying to make money out of their political friendships. These have adapted quickly to an environment of Labour/Conservative division and irreconcilable jealousies, where literally everyone with a political past hates each other.

Such hatreds are reinforced since, with only a few exceptions, Tory political advisers have no hope of breaking into the lobbying world – which they have derided for so long – at the moment, because they no longer have the appropriate contacts. Feelings are trampled on, or at least they would be if there were any feelings to trample.

Conservative and Labour lobbyists eye each other up wondering what on earth each other does in real life. And those are the reasonable ones! Some go home, with tainted memories, leaving London behind. Some of those who survive behave like spivs everywhere – what's in it for me, how much will I make and how quickly can I make it?

There are however some common characteristics. These include:

– a refusal to respect the antiquated ways of Westminster (e.g. the time consuming Speaker's Procession that turns Parliament into an extension of the tourist industry and the Speaker into an international television star)
– a desire to mount the European gravy train
– a recognition of the on-going debate about whether 'cab rank rule' would be more appropriate to the industry, than political identification with the client. ('Cab rank rule' would require commercial lobbyists to undertake work for all who can afford to pay them without regard to private views in much the same way as lawyers and barristers are required to conduct their professional lives.

Not, of course, that barristers themselves adhere to strict cab-rank principles i.e. never picking cases – although they pretend to.)

So, other than the Labour entrants, who have many of the characteristics of their Tory predecessors, who are the other commercial lobbyists and where did they come from?

Professional Backgrounds

The commercial lobbyists can be former political 'apparatchiks' once appointed by and answerable only to their political masters. Others came into the industry merely because they had been made redundant from other professions – politics offers something to everybody.

Out of work? Then put on a suit and tie (although you do not have to), head for the House of Commons, avoid the tourist queue, and go listen to a Select Committee. If you attend enough meetings, and become a face, the likelihood is that you will come across a potential employer eventually.

Commercial lobbyists can also be MPs – some claim it was considered normal for MPs to take on 'consultancies' to make ends meet – former legislators, sole practitioners (small commercial lobbyists live precariously with the big boys) or partners and associat es in the international accounting partnerships – (who also have lobbying arms), the management consultancies, and large law firms.

For the most part, however, mainstream lawyers do not understand the profession and only take an interest in it, both in the UK and on the Continent, to follow or extend their client base. (There is a long debate as to whether the lobbyist or the lawyer got to Europe first.) As a rule, they are unable to set their service within a political context.

The commercial lobbyists do not believe that they have benefited financially from their affiliations with lawyers, although in a highly competitive business, such affiliation gives credibility to both sides. As a result, both sides tend to use each other as a marketing tool. However, because political consultancy developed out of a marketing ploy much of what lawyers offer is no better than a 'contacts' programme, on a grand scale, or reports on legislative trends.

Because of the problematic partnership structure, any number of lawyers are having trouble remunerating their commercial lobbyists (as well as keeping their own lawyers who are not partners and ought to be), a problem which will not be resolved until they all become plcs and manage to off-load their dead wood. Such dead wood includes Peers who once impressed clients with the dining facilities in the House of Lords.

Another group moving in on the lobbying scene are the Parliamentary Agents who once occupied themselves exclusively in the drafting of private legislation. These, historically, have been scathing about the viability of the commercial lobbying industry, most particularly when commercial lobbyist Commander Powell was drafting legislation, including private legislation, more efficiently and at substantially lower fees than they were. In some ways it is therefore rather gratifying to watch them trying to punch their way in.

Given the narrowness of their client base and experience, it is possible that some of the Parliamentary Agents will go through something of an identity crisis as they lose out on business in Europe. However, one or two have had some notable lobbying successes. Dyson Bell have even appointed their own Head of Public Affairs. Rees & Freres on the other hand utilise the political antennae of their senior partners and devote a lot of resources to providing a specialised Parliamentary monitoring service.

Individuals, who are not lobbyists, but who have impacted on the industry include three remarkable brothers, i.e. Charles Powell who served Mrs Thatcher, and his two younger brothers, Christopher and Jonathan, both Labour spin-doctors; as well as, of course, the two Saatchi brothers who dominated the political world in the 1980s, along with Tim Bell (see below) when advertising was king.

Lobbying individuals also include ex-journalists. If PR is the bone-yard of former scribblers, then lobbying is its heaven – or rather it would be were they not forever wishing they were still chasing the big story. The sandy-haired pace-setter of the 1970s and 1980s, Arthur

Butler, is the most distinguished of these. Those ex-journalists employed by American outfits have more problems than their colleagues (which is saying something) as they try to come to terms with both their American masters, whom they loathe, and their lost journalist status.

Working with them can be sheer hell as they disappear for hours without telling anyone where they are going. As a rule, they make lousy managers, and even worse employers (or employees come to that) since they loathe internal office politics, believing it to be poor game compared to real politics. As a result, they, and their staff, can lose out. On the other hand, many offer a network that is second to none, a loyalty that makes them the guardian of a thousand secrets, and a clarity of mind that takes some beating.

Others are from the world of advertising, PR and spin-doctoring. These, as a rule, know nothing about political infrastructures. Not that this matters since big money lobbying is still, it would appear, all about popping into Downing Street. No doubt that is why Rupert Murdoch has recruited Tim Allan, one of the Millbank whizzkids and for the first year of the Labour Government, Deputy Press Secretary in Downing Street. Mr Allan will (and indeed has) denied that access to Downing Street played any role in his appointment. And the Pope's a Catholic...

Others again are ex-soldiers, that is to say the ones who have not found a home in financial or corporate PR and made fortunes in the process. Some of these have good organisational skills which often compensates for their lack of education. Their careers are tortured however by agonising adjustment problems as they move out of the armed services and into civvy street, where such adjustment problems can include an inability to deal with ethnic minorities, gays, and women.

They are fine with the ex-debutantes and public school-girls in the industry (although these have had their day, some are soldiering on, proving that a little bit of class is still rather quaint) but come apart with those women, who would be classed as 'other ranks' in the real world, which is to say the one they came from. Their attitude to ethnic minorities and gays can be off the scale.

It is easy to tell when an ex-soldier is speaking to someone he respects on the telephone because he stands up. Conversely you can tell when he is speaking to a 'tart' (that is to say his wife, girlfriend or secretary) because he lounges around, undoes the top button of his shirt and puts his feet on the desk while squirting an unpleasant spray in his mouth to hide the stench of the lunchtime snifter.

Other commercial lobbyists include a clutch of recycled executives from the public affairs departments of heavy industries or professionals such as barristers and accountants. These have great intellectual pretensions yet cannot come to terms with the fact that they are in lobbying because they failed at their chosen vocation.

The former public servants – politician or Civil Servant – in the industry are a mixed bunch. Senior ones allegedly have two assets – they give credibility and they are useful introducers of new business. Since, however, big business tends to flatter their vanity rather than teach them any new, worthwhile skill, they suffer from insecurities which they usually hide in egos the size of the business they have joined. Acting as glorified PRs, they dream of their former employment years while pretending not to.

For their own survival they encourage the belief that without 'contacts' (but not those provided by New Labour!) the client is denied access to the political system. This maintains their fee and perpetuates the myth that 'contacts' imply access to the citadel. The fact that this is not – except in the case of New Labour – true is immaterial. Their principal role is to impress gullible (usually non-British) clients – a role in which they are remarkably successful.

The downside for them is that over a period of time they become financial drains, as their contacts drop off their perches, and they try to invent contacts they never had in China. By this time they have irritated more able subordinates, who have had to spoon-feed them while they learned on the job and swallow their pay-rises, and been unable to train up the next generation of lobbyists since they were never trained themselves.

Nor have they offered the next generation any help as they try to make daily decisions on a good or moral basis since, protected by fat tax-free pensions, but feeling hard done by, they omit to bring the ethos of public service with them, therefore, in their unseemly scramble for money, fail at the one job they could have done.

Too bleak a picture? Perhaps. It is cruel to those public servants who have served their country with the utmost probity and vigour. Even these, however, some would argue, have let the country down not least because of their naiveté. What is more, for the most part, they make poor lobbyists although some succeed in serving themselves with unflagging self-interest.

Ex-diplomats have a worse time than most, suffering as they do from ex-pat syndrome and domestic drama as their wives try to cope with life back in 'Blighty' without servants. The taxpayer has provided many with a lifestyle beyond that which they would have achieved had they not gone into the public sector. They therefore hope the private sector will maintain that lifestyle for them when they retire. And who can blame them?

In the commercial world they become very good at introducing their clients, for vast fee, to foreigners who speak English. However, this usually means that the client is therefore presented to a school-teacher (who speaks English) whom he does not want to meet, rather than the dodgy politician (who does not speak English) whom he does want to meet.

The biggest problem the ex-diplomat has, however, is in not knowing how to deal with modern life. To him, those running pressure groups are the 'kids' (a good example is Labour Minister Peter Hain) who went on student marches in the 1970s when he left the country. He has no idea that the 'kids' are grown up today and are the ones who matter. And even less idea as to why they are relevant to business.

They are relieved, however, to have got out of diplomatic service just in time. The Foreign Office now expects so much – such as cost effectiveness and competence – and the urbane skills of yesterday when the (male) diplomat was the equivalent to the thinking woman's crumpet with looks to die for, are gone. Thank God for the public affairs industry!

A Bit of Class

In general commercial lobbying is home to the not so hot shots of the upper middle classes who were even rejected by the Army or the City. Not quite up-market enough for the grander estate agencies, wine trade or antiques businesses, they measure the events and achievements of their grown-up life against the hallowed memory of the past. Employers like these impeccably turned out products of various public schools and are proud of their poshness since this is suggestive of old school honour and integrity. Nice but dim, they help old ladies across the street. Tosh!

The real reason why the upper middles have dominated the industry is that at one time rich people all knew each other, and since only rich people used lobbyists, lobbying had no social stigma. Those days have long since gone, however, and employers are keen to point out that large numbers of their staff are not from the expected background.

Nodding in the direction of egalitarianism, they imply that their staff are accentless and educated at anonymous comprehensives. Many, they say, are East-end born and bred. Actually, many of their staff are from Essex, deservedly driving a coach and horses through indefensible snobbery and the social army. Admitting to a few straight-forward toffs, employers also claim that a cut glass accent can be a disadvantage. Such a disadvantage that it becomes 'cool'.

Seeking to out-do the toffs, many non-toffs try to give the

impression that their background was tough, dangerously on the edge – in short cool and metropolitan. Both are exaggerating. The truth is that the industry is littered by those purporting to be 'gentlemen', when their conduct is frequently unbecoming to real gentlemen, and very few in the industry have made it up from the inner-city sink comprehensives where survival is the priority and actually learning anything at all is a significant achievement.

Similarly, however, the industry is known for long friendships. An example of this are the thriving 'Commander Powell Ladies' Nights' which, as their title suggest, are open to all those who once worked for the old buzzard. Unashamedly sexist and not open to employers, these meet a couple of times a year for chinwagging, food and sophisticated 'news' (!) analysis [Editor's Note: she means gossip].

And so to the lobbying personalities.

The 'Political WOMBLES', 'Political TELLY TUBBIES', 'Political MR MEN', 'Political SPICE GIRLS' and 'GHASTLY GITS'.

Before getting down to some of the individuals in the industry it is important to explain the commercial lobbying 'type'. There are five. All of them are androgynous.

The **'Political Wombles'** were once past their sell by date but have now made a comeback. At the moment, the Womble Lobbyists are cosseting Tories, who themselves dream of making a comeback, marooned on Planet Opposition. Watch out for Ian Greer who may yet prove himself to be the Chief Wombler of them all.

'Political Telly Tubbies' i.e. the **'Political Dipsies, Political Laa Laas, Political Poes**, and **Political Tinky Winkies'** are the prickly independents – some of whom go bust, but who can make great TV.

The 'Political Poes' are red (politically speaking); The 'Political Dipsies are green (environmentalists who cannot understand why everybody is demanding that they come up with 'solutions'); the 'Political Laa Laas are yellow (too terrified to be truthful about their politics be they Monday Club or lefties); and the 'Political Tinky Winkies' are those who thought that just because they were gay, the world was their oyster.

Some of the 'Political Tinky Winkies' (many of whom are rumoured to have been no more than boys, not yet passed the age of consent) have come to terrible grief. Encouraged in various excesses in a bitchy, backbiting and competitive world, some have paid the penalty of many on the fringes of power i.e. some have been dumped by the powerful that toyed with them.

The **'Political Mr Men'** are the 'Luvvies' of the industry. These include Mr/Ms Slimeball, as well as Mr/Ms One-Dimensional. The latter are a bit like their cooking. Great on presentation but a little bland. Favourites are the **'Political Spice Girls'** (the 'Political All Saints' have yet to make an appearance!) These are the public school boys/girls ('Political Posh Spice') who believe that 'ethics' is the English language version of et al, that is to say et hic(k)s.

The Et hic(k)s are:

'Baby Political Spice' – the New Labour Lobbyists

'Ginger Political Spice' – the old Labour wallahs trying to jump ship

'Sporty Political Spice' – the ones trying to re-position themselves including ex-Tory MPs.

The best of the bunch are 'Scary Political Spice'. The 'Political Scaries include a whole lot of professionals, such as barristers, who bring probity and decorum into the industry and expect to be respected because they are professionals. Commercial lobbyists are all frightened of them – so frightened, in fact, that when one of the Scaries set up the Association of Professional Political Consultants (APPC) to clean up the industry and establish a register of lobbyists and their clients, not everybody joined. Since 'Cronygate', all those signed up with the APPC could collectively be called 'The Political Scaries since they are all running around all over the place, frightening the life out of each other, recriminations flying...

The **Ghastly Gits** in the industry used to be noticeable by the number of times they went to the opera. Since, however, Pavarotti made it common by singing in the rain to the hoi-poloi, they have stopped. Another reason they have stopped is because clients would much rather go to football matches than watch an elderly dumpling perform Salome in the Dance of the Seven Veils. As a result, corporate hospitality is constantly evolving. Many Ghastly Gits leave lobbying in order to join public affairs departments of major industries.

All the above have two things in common. The first of these is that despite all the talk about non-intervention and the market economy, they all make their living because business and politics are inextricably linked. The second is their knowledge that the corporate consultant cannot function to the full without a political associate. And, as that political associate, they make rather a decent living.

So who are these political associates, what are their props and where do they hang out?

The Lobbying Periphery: Public Affairs Magazines and Watering Holes

On a monthly basis the best way to keep abreast with who is who in the lobbying world is by subscribing to journals such as *Public Affairs Newsletter*, which is edited by Steve Atack. Atack started *PA Newsletter* in 1992. It quickly established itself as the industry 'bible' and before long he was on the lobbyists lunch circuit himself. A former Liberal Democrat Parliamentary candidate, he gravitated into the world of lobbying before spotting the gap in the market that is now his esteemed 'organ'.

Since its first issue, the *Newsletter* has grown in size and importance. Apart from subscription income it is also supported by advertising. The *Newsletter* is a mixture of newsy items, mainly about who has moved to which consultancy, and interviews, supplemented by features. Atack also published a *Survey* of the lobbying companies (July 1998) with the London School of Economics.

Struggling to keep abreast with lobbying industry news is *PR Week*, which, as its name suggests, is the house journal of the public relations industry. Being free to PR executives, it has a much wider circulation than the *PA Newsletter* yet it suffers from the fact that from an editorial viewpoint it has yet to decide if lobbying is part of the PR industry or not. It also suffers from the fact that it has failed to hang on to the two reporters who actually knew something about lobbying. Most lobbyists read *PR Week* purely to see what their competitors are up to and to see if they themselves have made it into the gossip column.

Most lobbyists also read the *House Magazine*, Parliament's in house journal, which appears weekly while Parliament is in session. The bigger consultancies also have regular adverts at the back of the magazine and often advertise any job vacancies in it. *PA Newsletter* tends to advertise the bigger jobs. Other political/Parliamentary journals read regularly by lobbyists include *Parliamentary Brief* and *Manifesto*.

Apart from reading about themselves, most lobbyists enjoy a good lunch. Although the more sanctimonious in the industry deny they 'do' lunch any more, the truth is that good business can be done over lunch. Any self respecting journalist knows that a politician is bound to leak some juicy morsel over a lunch and lobbyists are no different. Conversation over chicken liver pate is likely to be far more rewarding than a stiff, formal chat over the ministerial desk.

The more ostentatious (i.e. rich) who like to impress their clients, or their political prey, may well decide that nothing less than Claridges or The Ritz will do (after all, its rechargeable, isn't it?) although the Savoy

Grill is also popular. However, those with a modicum of common sense will look for more suitable eateries around the environs of Parliament Square. Unfortunately, there is not a lot of choice.

Shepherds (formerly Greens, and, even before that, Lockets) in Marsham Street is where one is likely to happen upon older lobbyists and even older politicians. If it's roast beef and yorkshire pudding that gets the juices flowing, Shepherds is the place to be. However, expect to be noticed and even eavesdropped. The tables are very close together.

The Atrium has become the doyen of lobbying restaurants. Located in the cavernous centre of 4 Millbank, the home of all broadcasting political journalists, it is probably the most convenient restaurant for MPs to head for if they need to get back to the Commons quickly. At least, it would be if the service was not so painfully slow.

L'Amico is an eccentric Italian restaurant on Horseferry Road, which has a good selection of signed photos of politicians who have eaten there adorning their walls. Another Italian restaurant can be found in the basement of Church House on Great Smith Street, although the words 'cheap' and 'cheerful' come to mind. Good for a quick bite, but little else.

Lobbyists tend not to be fans of clubs, although a few can be seen in the hallowed portals of the Garrick, Carlton or Reform. Frankly, they only go there to impress their clients. More surprisingly, it works every time.

Another place which lobbyists frequent is the Westminster political bookstore and coffee house, Politico's. (The publisher should declare an interest here and admit to being the majority shareholder of Politico's, whose sister company has published this book!) The balcony coffee house regularly plays host to cosy lobbyist chats and the bookshop is the only one in the country to devote a whole shelf to books on lobbying!

An unsolicited compliment was paid to Politico's by a senior Civil Servant who said that he used the coffee-house for meetings, especially with trades unions, because the non-confrontational environment was ideal for resolving problems.

A Tour of the Lobbying Industry and some of the Companies

It is a measure of the industry's lack of self-esteem — yes, really! — that to date there is no public affairs 'Who's Who' or Directory of Companies and their clients. The latter is an omission that is currently being corrected by the publishers of this book, who will be publishing the *Directory of Political Lobbying* in Autumn 1998.

The five big British public relations companies are **Brunswick, Bell**

Pottinger Communications, Financial Dynamics, Dewe Rogerson and the **Maitland Consultancy**.

These are not specifically commercial lobbyists although they are closely involved in political spin. They are joined by the big PR multinationals which include **Shandwick, Hill & Knowlton, Edelman**, and **Charles Barker**.

Many of the directors of these companies have made personal fortunes, although lobbying fortunes are generally not in the same league as financial and corporate PRs, or commission-agent Mr. Fix-its. Some of these companies are circumspect, never talk to the Press, and market themselves on the basis that they have no profile – unless the flash car can be considered profile. Conspicuous consumption does appear to work for them, and their business comes by referral.

The specialised commercial lobbying field is very crowded with new companies, often set up by executives of old companies, coming on stream all the time. These have either high or low visibility, although most would prefer the former if they were able to attract the attention of the Press.

The majority of the companies are shockingly badly managed and organised. All of them spend their time cosseting other people, from client to politician to European bureaucrat, and being macho about the fact that nobody cossets them. Since most of the good ex-Labour functionaries have already been picked up, those companies without any, talk in terms of being more interested in hiring 'people with experience of business and the Civil Service' which gets around the problem that there are simply not enough good Labour people about.

All the companies claim to be the 'largest', the 'leading', 'the best'. They have real problems when it comes to skilled staff – almost non-existent. The good companies, on the other hand, have done themselves proud with, seemingly, employing a clutch of Oxford graduates, or the equivalent from foreign universities, with an equal clutch of foreign languages at their command, that make them sound like the League of Nations. European Affairs companies similarly have high calibre and multilingual staff – the problem there is that they have very few at middle or senior executive level with sector knowledge – a boon for lawyers wanting to enter the profession who do.

Some of the companies are as follows:

Adamson Associates, specialising in Europe, seems to be going from strength to strength. Still dominated by its founder, the seductive Paul Adamson, there are some who believe it could become over-extended. On the other hand, the opening of a Geneva office proves the company is positioning itself for the long game in order to pick up the leading international quangos.

The only thing that could upset the apple cart is if the Swiss, the dourest people on earth, do not manage to re-invent themselves and therefore lose out on their quangos, which is very unlikely. Watch Adamsom Associates soar. The company is privately owned and, were it to be sold, would command a high price.

Adele Biss & Co, at the other end of the spectrum, has entered the market by limiting her new venture to British regulatory, local or central government affairs. Having first made her name, and her first company, in the PR field, it remains to be seen whether she can repeat her earlier success. Those in the game believe that she can. Watch out as she grows in strength and starts moving into Europe.

Ms Biss took over the ashes of the Ian Greer empire but has been quick to reposition the outfit. Having moved into new premises and retained a core client base, Biss & Co have survived what must have been an extremely difficult first two years. Ian Moss, who used to work with Labour Minister Alun Michael is now on the staff, as is Alex Cole who used to work for Jack Straw.

APCO are one of the new boys in the industry, backed by big American money. Infinitely superior to their sister, GCI London, they are picking up some well-heeled accounts. Personnel are highly educated firsts among equals, and include ex-Fabian Simon Crine and excellent former Treasury Civil Servant Martin Sawer, who can always be relied upon to get his priorities right. (A decade ago, he and his fiancée, took off around the world for a year before they got married on the basis that they could both get another job – but not another life).

Top man at APCO is the highly likeable Simon Milton, an ex Tory candidate and Deputy Leader of Westminster City Council. Milton has built a high calibre albeit very young team in a very short time. Unusually for a lobbying company, APCO also retains the delightful and often outspoken Angie Bray as its in house press spin doctor. Bray's contacts among the lobby journalists are legendary. APCO's main disadvantage is its location, just off Oxford Street, in the building of its parent company. Rumours abound of a move closer to Parliament. Both she and Milton, along with John Fraser, came from Ian Greer Associates.

However, on occasions, APCO does seem to lack 'the grey hairs' whose experience might have restrained it from picking up every single piece of American jargon in the book. In addition, the sophisticated American product it offers might not so easily translate as it suggests, since unlike America, business practice varies from one country to another in the rest of the world.

The company's interest in new markets in Eastern Europe and the

Far East is exciting, and it has the cash to play the long game. The pioneering role suits its style. It has recently formed a practice dedicated to applying technology to the management issues faced by clients on a daily basis, one of the few companies to do so.

Small beer at the moment is **Advance Communications** although the knowledge of its youthful and ambitious proprietor, Berkeley Greenwood, is sound. Greenwood, previously on the staff of CSM and the Public Policy Unit before setting up his own company, is an intensely political animal and, if there was any justice in the world, which there isn't, would be swiftly recognised as an ideal representative of the new breed of Tory politician. That is to say a young man with genuine business experience, decent manners and a sincere moral code. In the 'Tory wilderness years' he is slowly developing a company that is distancing itself from the flotsam and is said to no longer have any political ambitions himself.

Beaumark fields as one of its directors what must be the only lobbyist to have once wanted to be both a vicar and a Tory politician (Michael Windridge). Rory Scanlon who worked at Millbank is now a member of staff.

A new arrival is **Brown Lloyd James**, a public relations company set up by former BBC man and, afterwards, political secretary to John Major, Howell James, and Sir Nicholas Lloyd, former editor of the *Daily Express* and presenter on the London radio station GLR.

Brunswick (one of the 'big five' – see above) personnel are very grand. They offer their clients an island of integrity, industry, intellectualism... This does not, of course, stop the rest of the pack giggling like mad at them since, just like everybody else, they are interested in 'income' and the only thing that really distinguishes them is the size of that income. The company is one of the few still welcoming ex-Tories into the profession and has successfully made a name for itself by being secretive – an effective marketing ploy.

Jeremy Galbraith's career (**Burson Marsteller**) has rocketed – some would say far too swiftly. He leads a mixed team of youths and oldies of varying skills. Richard Aylard, formerly Private Secretary to HRH The Prince of Wales is now Director, Public Affairs. Committed European and ex-TV personality Alan Watson, formerly with Charles Barker, is Chairman.

CSM remains independent, its proprietor Christine Stewart Munro having first learned her skills with Commander Powell. She has been known to belly ache about training people up only to find them going on to bigger organisations. A member of the IPR's Government Affairs Group (which, like the Association of Professional Political Consultants, is unlikely to go anywhere in its present form despite the presence of its adorable president, Stephen Twigg MP), she gets brownie points for her heroic struggle to remain independent. It would be a shame if the high standards for which she is rightly known eventually fall victim to commercial pressures.

Arthur Butler, a legend in the industry, sits on her board. Previously associated with **Charles Barker Watney & Powell**, and before that John Addey Associates and Partnerplan, Butler was, for some years, running mate to Evie Soames. Regrettably, although individually excellent, they were, in combination, a gruesome twosome.

Always witty, Soames did a splendid impression of Butler, and his then sidekick Frank Richardson (ex-Shandwick and now running his own modest but successful company), as Mainwaring and Seargeant Wilson of Dad's Army fame.

Butler, on the other hand likened Soames' office to a Debs Tea Party.

Neither were fair to each other and many an opportunity was lost as the company that once blazed the trail both in the UK and on the Continent imploded. Today, Soames remains at **Charles Barker** (risen from the ashes, leaving small creditors behind while its Chairman sat on the Citizens Charter looking at late payment). Deserted by the excellent if dizzy European Lobbyist Maria Laptev, (now gone to GPC Market Access), Soames is cleverly rebuilding her team. Her knowledge and contacts are second to none.

Many in the industry watch the rise of Gill Morris (**Connect**) with pleasure. Daughter of a former Labour MP and former business partner of Nick Raynsford MP she is less arrogant than many of her colleagues, and has succeeded without compromising the social convictions she started with. Now independent of Market Access, she comes across as being substantially more focussed than during her Market Access days. Located in the notorious Millbank Tower, Connect is very New Labour and specialises in public sector and charity causes. It also runs a small conference organising sideline. Labour MP Rosie Winterton used to be Managing Director.

GPC Market Access has recently been in the news at the heart of 'Cronygate', as Derek Draper's erstwhile employer. As a result of this it has been reprimanded by the Association of Professional and Political Consultants. This appears to be a minor hiccough and the company is thought likely to recover, although morale at the moment is rumoured to be low.

It was for many years the industry's dynamo. At one time, its personnel operated as a young, fiercely competitive family under the benign but right-wing paternalism of ex-journalist Peter Simmonds. As a result of a boardroom coup, Simmonds (now a consultant to Burton Marstellar, headed by ex-Market Access man Jeremy Galbraith) was ousted. The company eventually settled down again, in good measure due to the excellence of Mike Craven. Interminable boardroom decisions later, Craven resigned and is now on 'gardening leave', although rumours abound that he may be considering setting up a new lobbying company himself. If this is true, the industry will have regained one of its stars. Craven's departure was followed by several excellent members of staff (mostly to APCO's gain!). Many would argue that the arrival of Prima Europe in the group, which is said to have precipitated some of the changes, was scarcely equal to the talent that was lost.

Today, the company is repositioning with its parent company, GPC International hoping to become the first global brand. Caroline Wunnerlich heads up Brussels, John Dickie – one time adviser to Paddy Ashdown, and now a Blairite – London, and Scottish Parliament candidate Jane Saren, Edinburgh. The Chairman is the rather pompous but clever Sir Ian Wrigglesworth, a former SDP MP, who, in 1990, became the first Libdem President.

Along with Derek Draper, it picked up its Labour strength from Dan Fox, a former junior in Tony Blair's office and Prima Europe's arrival in the group.

Among others, **Prima Europe** was set up by SDP founders Roger Liddle and Dick Taverne. Following the May 1997 Election, Derek Draper also joined the staff, moving to Market Access after the merger. The position of Liddle, co-author with Peter Mandelson of *The Blair Revolution*, and, after severing his connections with the company, a member of Mr Blair's Policy Unit, was publicised by *The Observer* at the time of 'Cronygate'. All politicians associated with the company have a strong commitment to the EU and many remain close to Libdem leader Paddy Ashdown. Some believe that this explains his links with Tony Blair, which could lead to problems for both of them in their respective parties. Prima Europe was previously a subsidiary of Burson Marstellar.

Nearly everyone looks tiny compared to the ridiculously titled but enormous (American) **Hill and Knowlton** Public Affairs World-wide Co. This offers seamless public affairs services, managing public policy issues in the Americas, Europe, Asia, Middle East and Africa. Anthony Snow, the UK Chairman, is the PR Chieftain who, when top-dog at Charles Barker, was big enough not to sack his entire staff as they fell out of their chairs laughing when he praised an American advertisement which proved too sentimental for British tastes.

Rather too dazzled by the Big Apple, he heads a company capable of running a centralised press office across fourteen European countries, locked into the attendant political infrastructures, which is second to none. Bernard Ingham is one of his non-executive directors. The problem for Ingham and Snow, however, is that the age of the chieftain is dead.

Hill & Knowlton's UK public affairs director is former Foreign Office Special Advisor Edward Bickham. He is one of the few commercial lobbyists to have acquitted himself well when defending the industry in the media. He runs a professional outfit which very rarely loses clients. His senior directors include the excellent Simon Pearce whose talents will surely lead him to a top job before long.

Political Context Chairman Leighton Andrews, meanwhile, has built up an impressive business in a relatively short time following stints as Public Affairs Director at the BBC and prior to that as managing director of Rowland Sallingbury Casey. His company has an impressive list of consultants including polling supremo Peter Kellner. Tim Clement Jones, Chairman of Environmental Context, now sits as a Lib Dem in the Lords. Associate Director of Political Context Glenys Thornton has also become a Labour Peer.

Charles Miller of the **Public Policy Unit** has inherited the mantle 'doyen' of the lobbying industry. He has been involved in lobbying since the early 1980s, and was one of four original staff to follow Ian Greer following the Russell-Greer break-up. He is also Secretary of the Association of Professional Political Consultants, which over the summer of 1998 cannot have been a happy experience!

He is a consummate professional both in terms of how he looks and what he says, yet people in the industry do not seem to warm to him. Not that he cares. His company is best known for its work in Whitehall rather than in Parliament and has done particularly well in the defence sector. Miller is the author of several excellent and well thought out books on lobbying techniques. Like many lobby outfits the PPU has suffered from a high staff turnover of both consultants and employees which leads one to the conclusion that Miller and his senior managers are hard taskmasters and may not be particularly easy to work with – but that is not unusual in the industry. Greg Rosen, formerly at Millbank, is now a member of staff, as is Rex Osborne who used to work with Peter Mandelson.

EPPA (**European Public Policy Advisers**) is one of the few companies to have recognised the value of the ludicrously tiny band of genuine, British European specialists. Specialising in electronic commerce and trade – two areas which are presenting a range of global regulatory opportunities and threats – they could forge ahead.

Fishburn Hedges are not lobbyists but have been shrewd in acquiring political friends should their clients need them. This has partly been achieved through their pro-bono work, as well as their public relations work for organisations such as the National Health Service Equal Opportunities Unit. They are growing increasingly skilled at blurring the line between public relations and public affairs, and, capitalising on their media relations strengths, are good at drawing together a number of separate arguments behind one case.

And so to **GJW**, one-time enfants terribles of the industry, now very much part of the lobbying establishment. At the time of writing, the company, like Market Access, has been reprimanded by the Association of Professional and Political Consultants for the part played by a member of its staff in 'Cronygate'. This is not exactly a comfortable position to be in since Andrew Gifford, one of GJW's big-wigs, is Chairman of the Association of Professional Political Consultants.

Founded at the beginning of the 1980s by Andrew Gifford (David Steel's assistant), the late Jenny Jeger (Callaghan's), and Wilf Weeks (Ted Heath's), the trio exploded on to the scene as the Young Turks of their day. Talking in terms of cross-party representation (making the political identity of a lobbyist an issue for the first time); taking on fewer clients, some of which were American, therefore allowing themselves time to give their clients a better service, and sock up the fees; they altered the industry forever.

In addition, by deliberately courting the Press at the time of their high profile press launch, some would argue that they changed the industry's traditional low visibility, and, arguably, humility, into an active pursuit of high voltage media attention forever. Traditionalists had apoplexy.

Today, GJW have come full circle. Fighting shy of profile – not recommended when you are working for the Libyans and have a whole bunch of defence clients besides – Weeks and Gifford are also desperately trying to shake off both recent exposés and their 'Elder Statesmen' tag, the latter, the result both of getting older (although in Gifford's case not looking it) and of having been in the business a long time. They have moved to new offices close to Parliament and have also restructured into focused units, a trend which Market Access started. Karl Milner, exposed by 'Cronygate', a former adviser to Gordon Brown is now a member of their staff, as are David Leam, Melissa Robinson and Richard Sharp (Millbank). They have one of the best qualified teams in the business, academically and professionally, although it is not yet known how they will recover from recent media coverage.

Maureen Smith, once of Good Relations, now of the

Communications Group, appears to be going from strength to strength. Peter Bingle, who saw two of his contemporaries (Chris Chope and Paul Beresford) make their names on Wandsworth Council before getting themselves elected to Parliament and rising through the ranks at Westminster, has been pragmatic enough to sing (convincingly) Labour's praises, and has employed four Labour apparatchiks. The company is apparently the only PR consultancy in London offering consumer, financial, corporate and political affairs teams under one roof.

Maureen Tomison (**DecisionMakers**) has the singular pleasure of disturbing many a transatlantic-crossing commercial lobbyist's good night's sleep because they opened their in-flight magazines to find her face beaming out at them and her skills lauded. She will never live down her appearance in front of the Nolan Committee when she proposed that lobbyists should all have fully accredited passes to the Palace of Westminster.

With a talent for self publicity, this former European Woman of the Year will always find a way of keeping her smallish company in our consciousness. Dame Angela Rumbold used to sit on her board.

Laura Sandys (**LSA**) is offering an interesting mix of expertise. Her modesty is steadily paying off and, quietly going about her business, she is going from strength to strength. She offers a sound, ethical, and well priced service and a highly respected team of New Labour young turks – most of them female.

Lawson, Lucas and Mendelsohn (**LLM**) the real new boys on the scene, were doing well until the 'Cronygate' difficulties, challenging the lobbying world in much the same way as GJW, Market Access and Ian Greer Associates once did. They have come badly unstuck, however, (much to the delight of any number of commercial lobbyists, journalists and Conservative and Labour politician alike). At the time of 'Cronygate' they had not been in the business long enough to become a member of the Association of Professional Political Consultants – not that they would necessarily have joined even if they had.

Founded by Neal Lawson, Ben Lucas and Jon Mendelsohn, who all advised Tony Blair before the May '97 election, their company is believed to have a fairly complicated share holding structure. To survive, they are talking in terms of 'quieter' lobbying but it will be interesting to see if their clients stay loyal after recent media profile. Ilan Jacobs, who used to work for Philip Gould is also a member of staff.

They were well financed when they set up so they could well tough it out successfully. However, in the future, large money is still dependent on a European presence and it is not yet known whether they will be able to pick up the big (American) clients to form such a presence, nor whether they have the skills to service them.

Tim Bell gave them their first break in the industry but the trio behaved a little prissily as they loftily disdained the culture that they hoped would make them a great deal of money. They rushed around all over the place implying that these days, hard work was the name of the game, as if it wasn't before. In addition, in their early days, they are said to have claimed that the parties were fewer, and wining and dining was out because people, apparently, were into quality time, and any free time available was spent with families.

Giving the impression that they were going home to a can of beans, while the vast majority of their commercial lobbying colleagues were actually still out there networking (although they insisted on calling this socialising!) in the hope that they might be invited to one of the new Political Salons, this all changed pretty smartly when they set up on their own. Champagne and canapé parties – subsequently to attract a great deal of media attention – attended by special advisers, lobbyists, researchers, MPs, journalists and policy specialists all became the order of the day.

Although they have for the moment come unstuck because of a mix of arrogance, naiveté and lack of subtlety, it is worth noting that such a combination is hardly unique in commercial lobbying. It is also worth noting that the industry is short of talent, therefore the arrival of the LLM team, despite their early troubles, is a welcome breath of fresh air.

Following the departure of the Likely Labour Lads, Lowe Bell, (now **Bell Pottinger Communications**, with Piers Pottinger temporarily picking up the Al Fayed account), the former employers of the LLM team, have David Hill, one of Tony Blair's former spin doctors, on board. Also with them is Amanda Clow, who worked in Tony Blair's office; Nicholas Williams, former adviser to David Clark, who is a consultant; as is Amanda Francis who used to advise Mo Mowlam.

The feeling however is that agencies have only one life and the former Lowe Bell might well have had its. It is ridiculously overloaded with ex high flying Tories (including ex Parkinson aide Mark Pendlington, Kevin Bell, Stephen Sherbourne and the fragrant Elizabeth Buchanan) and originally found it hard to cope with the loss of the LLM Threesome and replace them. Tim Bell's thoughts of recent events would be worth knowing – but at a rumoured £750 per hour, these would not come cheap! Meanwhile, purchases and mergers abound – the latest to come on board being John Russell (once the other half of Russell-Greer before both principals went their separate ways) and his team.

Rowland (owned by Saatchi) is fronted by ex Prescott staffer Jonathan Hopkins, who, it is to be hoped, treats his staff better than one or two of his predecessors. Here, it is worth mentioning **Sallingbury**, legendary for two reasons. The first because so many in the industry, at one time or other, have been employed by the company – a not entirely complimentary comment. The second, for the once looming shadow of General Gribbon who was associated with the company in the 1970s and 1980s. Now in his 80s, the General had a distinguished military record. He entered public affairs went he retired, and, before joining Sallingbury was managing director of Partnerplan.

Shandwick was founded by its now Executive Chairman Lord Chadlington, brother of former Tory Cabinet Minister John Gummer. Some have commented that one advantage of setting up your own company is the benefit of over-promotion.

Shandwick's Public Affairs Division is headed by (Lord) Tom McNally, a former Labour MP and assistant to Jim Callaghan, now a Libdem. He is assisted by Colin Byrne, a former Labour Chief Press Officer, now head of lobbying. Byrne is separated from Julie Hall, former press secretary to Neil Kinnock, and used to share a house with Peter Mandelson. With him is Andy Corrigan, former aide to Ron Davies, and Rachel Blackmore who worked with Mike O'Brien.

The company has recently been taken over by Interpublic, in an agreed all share bid – which came as a relief to shareholders since Shandwick's fortunes have been mixed. The combined group, including PR agencies Golin/Harris and Weber, becomes the world's second largest PR combine behind Omnicom of America.

The **Waterfront Partnership**, headed by Nick Finney, specialises in transport public affairs, although it is trying to branch out. Finney's Number Two is ex Civil Servant Steve Bramall who has previously worked for both GJW and Market Access. Former Department of Transport Head of Information Martin Helm is also on the staff, while John Gansler, formerly with the European Commission and Department of Environment, Transport and the Regions heads up the office in Brussels.

There are so many '"Westminster" this' and '"Westminster" that', companies, that people are always getting them muddled up. The problem for all is that 'Westminster' no longer sums up the business now that local government, Whitehall and Europe offers the major share of all new work. They are, of course, reluctant to change their names because of the real possibility of losing visibility.

Doug Smith (**Westminster Advisers**) followed Partnerplan's lead by moving into local government years before it became fashionable and from which he, with former Tory MP Peter Fry, made a decent living.

Westminster Citigate took a hammering when, following Ian Greer Associates problems and wide public disapproval of politicians being involved in public affairs companies, Ann Taylor (Lab), Menzies Campbell (Libdem) and Keith Speed (Con) all resigned as directors (1994). Also to go was Marcus Fox, who, along with Keith Speed, founded the company in 1982. Marcus Fox was Chairman of the 1922 Committee, and, until 1992, Chairman of the Commons Committee of Selection. The latter position had always had its critics since some were concerned about the perception of a possible clash of interests when Fox had to choose which MP to place on which committee.

Westminster Strategy's Mike Lee's day has come, with a Labour background now worth money in the piggy-bank. He used to work with David Blunkett. Jo Moore, also at Westminster Strategy, was deputy to the Party's Chief Media Spokesman David Hill (who has now joined forces with Tim Bell).

What Company Do the Commercial Lobbyists Keep?

In presenting a picture of some of the people that one meets in lobbying, it is easy to overlook the stars. And stars there certainly are. However, a knowledge of them does not necessarily help the lobbyist steer his way through some of the stereotypes. These include:

The Politicians

The influence of the gifted and qualified does not predominate in local, national or European public affairs. This is unlikely to change because 'selection' of our politicians is controlled by those who, often for self-interested reasons or spite, deny opportunity to the competent and gifted.

This, plus the demands of working or family life, renders it impossible for most people to contemplate standing in winnable seats. As a result, excellent candidates who would make first class public servants never get the chance to stand or are blocked by obscure local worthies or talentless party hacks. Both the major parties say they are doing something about the problem but the truth is somewhat different.

The lack of high calibre politicians is particularly noticeable in Westminster because of all the rookie backbenchers and ministers. However, it is unfair to imply that the present crop are worse than the last lot. They are not. It is many years since politics has been in the hands of the competent and bold.

Part of the problem is inexperience – the sight of MPs checking the Yellow Pages in order to assist a constituent is not reassuring; as well as education – the idea that MPs should drop their constituency surgeries because 'they are not social workers' in order to concentrate on, say, foreign affairs, is laughable. So laughable, in fact, that it is hardly surprising that Think Tanks, task forces and focus groups are springing up all over the place even though, for a variety of reasons, including the cynical, not everyone likes them.

To be fair, some politicians have a very tough time. They speak in terms of stress, aching loneliness and relationship problems. In addition their lives often comprise no more than late hours and punishing schedules of busy but meaningless idleness. Others take to the job like a duck to water. In constant need of adulation and praise they are usually dropped by those unprepared to play the minion role around their greatness. As a commercial lobbyist, you will probably have to play this role on numerous occasions.

The lack of calibre is similarly in evidence in town halls where many councillors (like MPs and MEPs) lack education, vision, financial skill (let alone probity), commercial acumen or a knowledge of sophisticated social justice. This is a scandal when one considers the fact that they control millions of pounds worth of public expenditure. Lobbying councillors is a mix of shutting your eyes to the fraud and hiding your disgust.

As for those in the European Parliament? Join the gravy train here. The authorities are hamstrung in dealing with any MEPs caught cheating, or failing to abide by disclosure rules, because the Parliament has been allowed virtually no disciplinary procedure. It is also hamstrung because the bureaucrats in the Commission are not above a little – all right, let's face it, a lot – of corruption themselves. Mr Blair is understood to be contemplating changes to combat some of these problems prior to the 1999 European Elections. Good luck to him.

MEPs love lobbyists – once they've signed on for their daily expenses they're quickly off meeting them – a bit like members of the House of Lords. At the moment the European Parliament is trying to improve the reputation of MEPs by instituting a Register of Members' Interests. This initiative however has been undermined because the Parliament has had to admit that fewer than half the MEPs have declared their outside payments.

Women

Some women in lobbying and political forums behave like fluffy bunnies and try to steal a march on their colleagues who do not. These can give every indication of being happy to prosper in a man's world at the expense of their sisters.

This is especially hard on those who have multi-faceted lives, rather than the single focused lives of many involved in commerce or politics. Some are cruelly accused of being moaning minnies when all that they are doing is looking for solutions; others are cruelly ridiculed for being over-promoted. Like men, women can be both.

The suggestion that 'politics' is improved by women because they are fundamentally disposed to get on with each other is patronising. Politics is an arena of clashing cultures and terrible hatreds. Emotion, selfishness and ambition is not confined to one sex or another. Cross party friendships do exist, among men and women, but there is a tendency to over-sentimentalise these. In a world of competitiveness, malice, and envy, the only survival buoyancy aid is a close inner circle of friends.

An older generation of women were able to take advantage of the old Masonic or old boy's Mafia if they were the wives or daughters of freemasons. Other women, like men, have succeeded through other types of patronage. A few lone women, like a few lone men, have made personal and heroic stands for various issues and been vilified in both politics and the press as a result.

In dealing with those women who have been in politics a long time, there is a tendency to forget how hard it has been for them. Few can remember the days when a woman MP, visiting, say, a factory, with her male colleagues, in order to go to the loo, had to arrange for her office to telephone her so that she had an excuse to leave the tour. Even fewer can remember the days when a woman MP, elected for the first time and able to buy her own clothes, saying wistfully 'it is so lovely to have my own money. I wish I had had some before but my husband never gave me any'

These women can be useful to commercial lobbyists if only because, as a rule, they are very happy to be noticed and are always prepared to meet your clients – especially if they are Tory.

The women to watch are those with 'attitude'. These are unafraid to admit that they are leaving other women behind, and, while retaining old loyalties, are forging ahead as modernisers. Watch out when you introduce them to your commercial clients. They know how to read a balance sheet and can spot humbug from a mile away.

The steepest learning curve is for women in the Commission and European Parliament. They tend, as a result, to be very tough. However, a few also give the impression of belonging to no real world, fixed in attitudes they held before they were elected, attitudes which they have now globalised without realising that such attitudes were dated when they first held them, let alone now.

In Westminster some of the 'old girls' have been given their comeuppance. When Speaker Betty Boothroyd tried to tell new women MPs to learn the ropes and put up, they retaliated. It was Betty Boothroyd that had to learn.

Gays in Lobbying

'Gayness' is both a political movement and a way of defining oneself either to one's intimates or to the wider world. It is impossible to write a book about politics or lobbying without considering gays separately, even though this insults some gays and non-gays alike who do not believe their sexuality should be an issue.

Politically, gays have made considerable headway in national politics but none at all in Europe (where many still have to conduct themselves furtively). Locally, and in the workforce, things are patchy. Gays are well represented at local activist level and in local government.

Because of some of their excesses, and indeed successes, there is a real danger that they could provoke – some would say encourage – a vicious backlash just for the hell of it. Those, whether gay or non-gay, who find it awkward to smile at some of their cruel excesses, are accused of homophobia, narrow mindedness and under-sophistication. This is an insult to both the straight and gay community.

One MP, too anxious about upsetting the gay lobby to be named, said: 'They (the gays) have done a good job at raising awareness about gay issues at Westminster. But they have deliberately ignored some of their public/s (including their own) who wish them well but do not want any sexuality, gay or hetro, to be an issue. It is difficult to say this however because they will accept no criticism of themselves as a group or of individuals that form a part of that group. I think that that is one reason why poor old Ian Greer copped it so badly in the media. The Press could indulge their virulent homophobia under the title of "good causes". It was a tragedy for Greer. And cruelly unfair.'

A few women are reporting trouble with the gays. Said one commercial lobbyist who, for similar reasons, also did not want to be named "Some of the Parliamentary clerks are gay and, like all networks, this can work against others. I find it particularly tough because the clerks who are not gay are pretty mysognistic anyway. The women Parliamentary servants, incidentally, are sniffy intellectuals. The arrogance of all of them is almost beyond belief.

'As for your question "is lobbying a gay industry?" because someone suggested it to you. The answer is I have never thought about it. And no, I don't think it is. To say otherwise would be to insult both gays and non-gays alike. If it was a gay industry, the kind of macho men who would not be seen dead with over the top queens, would not be employing any of us, gay or non-gay.'

It could perhaps be noted that gays and bisexuals do have a long history in the industry.

The Civil Service

Civil Servants have had a rough couple of decades. After all, they have had to put up with all those dreadful Conservative Ministers – while those same Ministers have had to put up with all those dreadful Civil Servants – and now, horrors of horrors, they are having to put up with all those dreadful Labour ministers as well.

The rot set in under the Conservatives when Ministers refused to protect them in the law courts (arms to Iraq inquiry) and made Civil Servants carry the can for what they had been doing. Civil Servants are not used to carrying the can for what they have been doing, as Labour is finding out today. The net result is that each one is for himself, the system is in free fall, individualism has crept in, and the conventions have all changed.

How did we get to this state of affairs? That's an easy one. The vast majority of Civil Servants are lazy intellectual anarchists. Those, that is, who have an intellect as opposed to an Oxbridge degree. These have joined with their various publics in despising their masters, the Oxbridge contingent, some of whom have been promoted on the basis of freemasonry, and some of whom have done incalculable harm to the country, not least by blocking or refusing to promote, those from without their elitist circle, with talent, vision, and an overwhelming loyalty to the country rather than the status quo, while maintaining in jobs both the corrupt and the incompetent. Civil Servants, whose faces might not fit, but who have provided the public with excellence are sent on 'gardening leave'.

While the Tories were in Government, lobbying the Civil Service was easy because so many members of the business world were on secondment to it. These busily accepted hospitality, and much else, from all over the place, apparently wholly unaware that hospitality, and much else, should not have been accepted were corruption considered to be an issue which it is not. Some career Civil Servants meanwhile got on with the arduous business of feathering their own nests because scrutiny and audit procedures in the public sector are almost as non-existent as they are unsophisticated.

Both have wholly undermined decent Civil Servants who cannot even consider reporting a culture of corruption, let alone narrowing it down to individuals, without massive penalty to themselves. Enormous internal changes and modernisation are (again) said to be on the cards although it is too early to say whether these will succeed or indeed whether the modernisers will have any assistance from the bulk of Civil Servants who are adept blockers when their interests are threatened.

Such changes meanwhile slow the rate of improvement and promotion. Morale is exceptionally low, many are having to work very long hours, as many do not know if they will have a job tomorrow, as many again complain that the extent of their learning process has not been appreciated. As many again, especially younger ones, some in senior departments of state, say that they are working in a vacuum with no career direction.

An equal number, however, simply do not understand the extent to which they have been cosseted and only find out when they enter the private sector. Here, regrettably they do not always take their culture/codes of public service with them so great is their desire to make some 'real' money out of the 'barrow boys' from whom they once tried to protect the public.

One of the publics to have suffered most at the hands of the Civil Service is the business community. These, sometimes with the assistance of commercial lobbyists, have, with little success tried to make the Civil Service both here and in Europe more responsive to their needs. As a result of their failure, as many again have tried to short-circuit the Civil Service and, with the help of commercial lobbyists (resulting in 'Cronygate') tried to access the centre.

Many of those stuck with Civil Servants, have, for the most part, found themselves stonewalled, the Civil Servants resenting the fact they have to act as unpaid management consultants and preferring to deal with those they know, who know the traditional rituals and Civil Servants' language.

This involves the businessman saying what he wants in terms that fit into the Civil Servants remit i.e. problem solving and problem prevention expressed in political, rather than commercial, terms, when the businessman has no political objective. This of course is not the fault of the Civil Servant. Elected Government demands that things are seen in political terms. What is the fault of the Civil Servant is the response time – if a Civil Servant catches a cold he takes an entire month off to recuperate.

It should be made clear that many Civil Servants are at pains to point out that they consult the business community widely.

Those businessmen who suffer most are those who try to go it alone.

An example is businessman Richard Moir, who set up and personally funded the European Film Finance and Insurers Association (EFFIA). From a standing start, he got the EFFIA in the door at Secretary of State, Departmental and European level. In addition, he was the only member of the film community trumpeting the UK's then Presidency of EUREKA.

So what happened?

Says Moir "Nothing. Absolutely nothing. While individual Civil Servants were exceptionally kind and constructive allies, the system only knew how to deal with insiders, or those the insiders found it politically correct to promote. As a result, it busily chucks taxpayers money in the direction of those who do not deserve it, while the rest of us have our fingers on the pulse and are taking all the risks.

'The system then sets up advisory committees and God knows what else besides with all the tired old names on – or a few new ones who are hardly always the talent – while still availing themselves of your information and squeezing you dry in the process. In the end I saw no reason why I should further the careers of other people without getting any of the benefits so I stopped assisting them.'

The worst culprits, says Moir, are the Civil Servants of Europe. A member of the Round Table discussion on the film industry, on one occasion he found himself in Brussels where the European Commission, including British Civil Servants, were discussing a film guarantee bond.

'They had talked to everybody' says Moir 'and everybody was present or represented. Everybody, that is, with one exception. The insurance industry. The lapse was incredible since it would be the insurance industry who would be underwriting the risk.'

Moir, pointing out the omission, briefed the Commission and, in addition, was asked to arrange for the bureaucrats to meet the insurance industry. He did so, setting up and laying on a series of meetings with the London Insurance Market at Lloyd's of London. Continues Moir: 'I didn't even receive a thank you, let alone payment for my work. The next thing I knew were the reports in the Press about what had been decided. It was all as a result of my work.

'I found it infuriating not only because I should have been declared as the author of the work but also because the Civil Servants concerned had paid enormous amounts to "consultants" who were busily absorbing the kudos for what they had not done while I was left not only out of pocket but feeling utterly used as well. It is immoral what happened, completely immoral. It is bad enough launching a business as it is without public servants coming along and thieving your ideas. No small businessman should be left out of pocket for helping. The problem is that they are so well paid, and so many of them are on gravy trains – countless outsiders are being employed from academics to consultants – that they will not pay up for information they should pay for. I found their arrogance, detachment and financial manners beggared belief. It's all so wrong.'

Europe

Immorality and the European Union go hand in hand. Its Civil Servants, including British ones, consider themselves so superior it is hardly worth saying. There are apparently 15,000 of these arrogant overpaid inepts. Because of the extent of their rudeness and inefficiency, along with their freebies, it will never be possible to obliterate their predominant culture of greed and arrogance. It must be said however that the cream of Civil Servants go to Europe, which some say diminishes the calibre back in the UK.

Some of the Eurocrats apparently, with their large salaries, allowances and expensive lunches are going through an identity crisis. This is because the Commissioners for whom they work – who are meant to set an example instead of enjoying the gravy train and long holidays as well – are loathsome creatures. Most aides working for Commissioners are sick of them, as well as being sick of having to trumpet the Commission's line which is always twaddle. They are nearly all desperate to get back into policy making but cannot dump their respective Commissioners until their replacement has been found which makes life even more difficult since nobody actually wants to replace them.

Broadly speaking the commercial lobbyist has an easier time in Brussels than he does in Westminster or Whitehall (although new rules have been laid down) principally because Europeans underrate the practice of PR let alone lobbying. Lest there be any piety, it should be said that continentals underrate PR and lobbying because greasing palms is all that is necessary in some places. Indeed it could be argued that commercial lobbyists protect the citizen from that sort of fraud.

Because clients are more knowledgeable, however, know how Brussels works and have a good understanding of the complex multi-layered nature of the decision making process, the demands made of commercial lobbyists are much greater than they used to be. As a result, sectoral knowledge is desperately needed. The policy making process has slowed down and there are many more green papers and discussion documents around, as well as long term thinking.

Those lobbyists thinking about moving to Brussels should not take the decision lightly unless it is viewed as a fast way of paying off a mortgage. Some say it beats going to Saudi! This is because as fat consultants pack into exclusive restaurants and cackle in an impressive array of different languages, lonely hearts abound. Attractive Eurocrats who speak four languages and have a job for life in one of Europe's best paid Civil Services are socially lost souls.

What should be a melting pot of the best of life is not. The community is transient, therefore it is not worth the effort of making an effort. Brussels has two separate communities whose inhabitants rarely mingle unless telephoning one of the various escort agencies advertising in the Bulletin, the Brussels weekly guide to expatriate life, counts.

In the end, all these sophisticates become as parochial as ex-pats everywhere. While complimenting themselves on their cosmopolitanism, and their ability to think globally, their non-touching worlds allow them to sentimentalise their roots to which they are seldom happy to return. However, while looking at the big picture (or in commercial lobbying speak 'the broad canvass') they are always astonished when they are foiled by 'provincialism'.

All find it awkward forging and sustaining relationships with 'real' people and none make any contribution to civic life. The latter is the final irony of all those involved in public affairs, be they elected politician, public servant or commercial lobbyist. Meanwhile, hundreds of millions of pounds of taxpayers money is lost through fraud and incompetence.

The Flashing Lights and Flared Nostril Brigade

Commercial lobbyists also come up against the zealots, either by representing them or because their views and conduct can impact on the commercial world of their clients. The relationship can be difficult for both sides particularly because the passions and arguments that some commercial lobbyists have to confront are often culturally alien to them.

This is especially the case with a younger generation of lobbyists – Thatcher's children – who were not brought up on, or inherited, the student marches and protest movements of previous generations. Encouraged to prosper as individuals, the new generation can find themselves both detached and adrift from the modern equivalents.

This detachment tends to enflame passions, rather than the reverse, as the commercial lobbyist looks in wonder at those who sacrifice the ability to prosper individually for the sake of a wider community; while those who do so see only materialism and lack of vision.

Both sides are often characterised by selfish attitudes and an ignorance of each other's societies. Both sides often go down the easiest route i.e. condemnation, insult and a refusal to accept that all valid arguments need to be addressed civilly and, if possible, compromises reached. And both sides need to sort their relationships out.

To put things in perspective, the protester is not always 'good', any more than the commercial lobbyist or his client is always 'bad'. For example, some commercial lobbyists have represented clients whose staff have had razor blades stitched into their gloves and lost the tops of their fingers because 'road protesters' have not liked what they were lawfully contracted to do; others have represented pharmaceutical clients whose directors' families have been terrified by aggressive animal rights groups.

As a result, some commercial lobbyists fall into the trap of not being able to distinguish between those who act lawfully, but have strong passions, and those who do not. This unfortunately can leave them disinclined to sympathise with the many legitimate protest movements who can have the odds stacked against them because they do not always have the same access to the system as the commercial lobbyists' wealthy clients.

Lobbyist Commander Powell got around this problem admirably by getting his 'cat' to level the playing field. On one occasion, the 'cat' wrote anonymously to both a Select Committee Clerk and those politicians opposing a particular clause Powell was working on, because information had come his way which he believed offered him, and therefore his clients, unfair advantage.

However, the protester does not want to have to rely on the integrity of his opponent. He wants access to the system as of right. And that is a matter for government.

Religion can be another problem. Commercial lobbyists representing the food industry, for example, may come up against the religious slaughter brigade; others working for the pharmaceutical industry, Roman Catholics against an abortion pill. All religions have enormous influence, and the lobbyist ignores them at his peril.

Finally, the commercial lobbyist can come up against extremist political groups that cover a whole spectrum from the loony left to the rancid right, as well as foreign political affiliations. A distinction here should be made between the legitimate left and the equally legitimate radical right. A great deal can be learned from extremists, most especially that neither represent extreme forms of patriotism although they try and play it that way.

Both groups are all over politics. They are notable for their inadequacy, fear and envy and have absurd notions of their own greatness. Most of all they are remarkable for their dangerous stupidity. None are profound thinkers nor have they any understanding of economics. All have strong organised groups across the UK and the continent.

Regrettably, some, including commercial lobbyists, have been sucked into their worlds. Exposed by accident, they swallow unquestioningly the poison of those who have no existence beyond the margins. A few escape by being lucky enough to be spat out, a few more merely by growing up. The rest live in cloud cuckoo land and worse.

The Intelligence Services and Private Security Companies

Another bunch who live in cloud cuckoo land are those who spend their lives in the frequently corrupt, nasty and dangerous world of the cloak-and-dagger. Nothing, incidentally, will infuriate organisations such as MI5 and SIS (British Secret Services), the CIA (American), the KGB – or whatever they call themselves these days (Russian) and Mossad (Israeli), more than to be bunched together with private security companies and 'other' clandestine organisations. Some of these, including the private companies, conduct themselves with dignity and courage; others are out of control.

All swirl around political forums, and lobbying, for a variety of reasons. Some of these are political – which many would claim are a legitimate activity of the clandestine servants of the nation states; others are commercial – not always legitimate since this can mean the theft of commercial secrets; others are crime prevention. It is regrettable that the latter is not the sole preserve of an accountable, corruption-free, and skilled police force.

The commercial lobbyist, as an information source, can be the target for any of the above. One was approached when running an All Party Group at Westminster in the 1980s by those interested in the Group's Labour members. In addition, the lobbyist was asked to supply names of commercial lobbyists specialising in European Affairs. Both requests were refused.

Today, given the number of lobbying companies opening branch offices in the countries of the former Soviet Union, as well as the Far East, it is very likely that other commercial lobbyists will similarly attract attention. Commercial life is stuffed full of former public servants maintaining their own and/or other countries' status quo to sustain the commercial ambitions of the international business community – even though this may not be in the best interests of the people of those countries – and the commercial lobbyist is right in there too.

Because lobbyists are commercially aware with the appropriate business and political/administrative contacts, they can be a more attractive source of information than journalists, a traditional (although often rebuffed) alternative; and more commercially aware than the private security companies with whom some of them, as well as the intelligence services, have links.

Advice for Outsiders considering acting as an Intelligence Source

Those commercial lobbyists considering clandestine work could consider the following before committing themselves. The advice could also be useful to those who are not lobbyists, but who may be considering acting as an intelligence source.

The intelligence services are not necessarily up to speed on how the British political system works and do not always display a knowledge of the Constitution. This is particularly the case if you are dealing with 'No Names' i.e. those whose identity you are not allowed to know, although they may be your only line of communication.

Intelligence work can often appear seductive and, as a result, can appeal to the gullible. It can also attract those who are desperate. Relationships can be a mixed bag. Those agreeing to assist the intelligence services can do so because service to their country or community is a noble duty and/or because of the excitement that such work sometimes entails. As a result, there is some scope for exploitation.

The work can seem like an intoxicating prospect. However, those who go in with ideas, especially good altruistic ones, will not always see them implemented. Nor is it always the case that those who recruit outside sources will have the same value system or motives.

The resulting relationship can reek of unreality and there is some probability that it could end unhappily.

There are some obvious cautions to be made. For example, there can be problems if you meet client representatives who have separate relationships to yours, with private or national clandestine agencies, and/or other commercial clients such as arms dealers. There can also be problems if you are recruited by a named Civil Servant and are then passed on to a 'No Name' i.e. those whose true identity you do not know. There can also be problems if your case officer changes – your new case officer, for example, might have a different attitude to payments made and the paperwork may have gone 'astray' making explanation difficult.

Other pitfalls include the moral one i.e. you are usually spying on those who trust you, and consider you to be their friend; and you can end up furthering solely the material objectives of your individual employer who can couch his demands in patriotic terms. Spying is a serious profit maker and a market leader. As a result, motives are not always the best and 'intelligence' employers and colleagues may not always be the finest example of humanity – although many indeed are.

The latter are distinguished by their modesty, courage, skill and disinterested service to the country.

Your 'secret' work can involve enormous personal sacrifice which is out of all proportion or merit to the job demanded. Jealousy can also be a problem, not least because as an outside intelligence source you frequently have all the contacts, and therefore all the fun. Without doing anything 'wrong', you can be put into systematic run-down. This is not always for disinterested reasons – i.e. it can be done in order to prepare the careers of others who wish to monopolise a small but lucrative market. Spying can be very big business. It can also be very well paid and there are often other perks, such as commercial assistance.

Other issues that an Information Source could consider before taking the decision to assist are the following: You could lose your life, or endanger the lives of others, particularly foreign nationals. 'Intelligence' work can be emotionally and intellectually draining. This, on top of the demands of a stressful job, may mean that you make mistakes which are dangerous for you and/or others. In addition, once passed your usefulness – often when your assistance has been exposed, you are likely to be dropped ruthlessly. You may also lose your original career, for which there is no compensation.

The Security Services do not, necessarily, have a good record in protecting 'outsiders', no matter what they pretend, if things go wrong – and they often do. Senior people can look after themselves, although not always. The lowly cannot, not least because they are always working in a vacuum. When things go wrong, and they frequently do, no-one exists.

In addition, you can inadvertently involve your family and friends in your activities. Working as an intelligence source you do not always have protection in law and you may be dealing with those who believe that unquestioning obedience to them, teaches respect for the law.

'Sources' are just that – sources. They are outsiders. Therefore, other things you could consider before becoming one is that if, for example, you come across fraud or discrimination – social, racist, and so on – there will be very little that you can do about it. You will be in even more trouble if you fall out with the intelligence services. If this happens you could be up against an amazingly powerful spite machine. You will also be up against the arrogance of those who never move out from behind their desks, while you have taken all the risks.

Bearing in mind the Intelligence Services' current campaign to recruit outsiders as Information Sources those considering assisting could think in terms of: written terms and conditions, details of remuneration (unless the work agreed is pro-bono), such terms and conditions to be agreed with verifiable personnel representing the sponsoring Department of State (e.g. Foreign or Home Office), on Government stationary. Most Information Sources are asked to sign the Official Secrets Act. Those who do so should be aware that signing the Act can work against the citizen, especially if he has a complaint, grievance or public interest matter he wishes to raise.

Other things you could be aware of is the fact that in signing up to the Intelligence Services, you are signing up for life. You are never at liberty to cease being a source. As a result, you can, inadvertently, sign up partners and/or children who have no choice in the matter. Other problems arising could include not having access to appropriate medical attention (mental health is often an issue); and poor accounting procedures which can lead to problems, for you, or those associated with you. Paperwork is especially incompetent at the time of bereavement, leaving untold burdens to sort out for loved ones. Clarifying issues can involve enormous insult and much worse.

There is a two-tier system operating. One for career Civil Servants, and one for 'Sources'. As a result of this two-tier system, appropriate salaries, career improvements, direction, pensions, complaints systems, even decorations, are scarcely available to you. Things are even more problematic if you are only dealing with No Names since you will be given nothing in writing, and, moreover, will have to deal with No Name contacts of the No Names, which can involve you in unauthorised work.

Outsiders still determined to act as Sources for the intelligence services should in particular remember the 'Seven Deadly Nevers'. These are:

– Never allow the intelligence services to force you to travel on false documents
– Never allow the intelligence services to force you into signing a 'blank' sheet of paper
– Never trust intelligence services verbal agreements – keep everything in writing, including copies of your reports
– Never have an intelligence service bank account, secret pension, or agree to a false identity

- Never deal with intelligence service PO Box Numbers or No Names
- Never allow a member of your family, friends, or associates to be drawn in
- Never switch from working abroad to local work.

Needless to say, working for another country's security service is treason, even if that country is an ally. However, some Information Sources are said to work for several countries. This can be because of greed, the money on offer is reported to be very good, or in order to access other types of information. This can be with the tacit agreement of the original intelligence employer.

In European political forums literally every spy imaginable is running around. The European Commission attracts them as did, at one time, the United Nations. (It is easy to forget that in the fifties and sixties the UN attracted the cream of the nation states' Civil Servants. To a certain extent, that cream is now servicing the European bureaucracy.)

Substantial money is available and every national under the sun is running around. As always, where there is money, there can also be coercion, intimidation, bribery and corruption. There can also be farce.

Spies running around the European Commission range from bureaucratic Brits to fanciful Frenchmen, dodgy ex-Soviets, to Israelis desperately trying to seduce those whom they believe could be useful. The former, while claiming they do not work for Mossad, are constantly asking the latter about pro-Arab activities in the Commission or Parliament, saying things like:

'Hmmn, you are so beautiful, darling...' lighting cigarette, eyes flickering seductively 'tell me about this intergroup the European Parliament has just established. You know the one, darling. The one promoting the Arabs...'

American clandestine activity both in the UK and the EU is legendary. In fact, Brussels is likely to tackle the US over certain allegations when the EU Council of Ministers publicly debates national security and surveillance issues in September '98. (This follows a European Parliament study that confirmed the existence in Britain of US spy bases targeting the EU). It seems however a little churlish to single out the Americans for censure since everybody seems to be doing it!

Contrary to public perception, the US did not only use the UK as a base but also undertook many internal operations in Britain. For this reason, the long-standing joke in the 1970s and 1980s about the number of American research assistants piling into Westminster and working free of charge for anyone who would employ them has worn a little thin.

Activities are said to have included donations to various organisations including political front companies acting for political parties.

The 'donations' issue is, of course, not necessarily a 'CIA' one and, as the decade closes, reform of party funding is at long last on the cards. Reforms, of course, will be useless without other controls, for example, checks on money flowing into some "Think Tanks" and Foundations, backing specific political lines and promoting those politicians and public servants who follow them. Also needing to be checked out will be those lobbying companies from abroad, including foreign governments.

Throughout the 1980s and 1990s the Conservative Party was always on the look-out for wealthy funders. A regional network of front organisations raising money for the Party was well established. A loyal Tory fundraiser, David Hart, is alleged to have split the Party as, from the Conservative conference, he launched the Committee for a Free Britain. While many agreed with the Committee's aims some were said to be uncertain of its funding.

Labour Party funding is also an issue, although not yet fully investigated. In August 1998 Labour revealed its list of supporters who had given more than £5,000 to the Party during the previous twelve months. Nearly one third of the individuals listed had since been given honours, appointed to the House of Lords or appointed to a government quango. Two lobbying firms, GJW and Citigate Westminster featured on the list.

There is one school of thought that believes that front companies did not become necessary until CIA money, for whatever reason, dried up. As a result, the political parties had to look elsewhere. This, in due course, also meant that they looked abroad, opening up a new era and a whole new can of worms.

Many believe that the only answer is for the tax-payer to fund the political parties. The tax-payer, on the other hand, would probably rather not.

Private Security Companies

The business world works closely with national intelligence agencies but also has a use for the private sector companies as well. This is where things could come unstuck given business' preference for employing politicians, public servants, commercial lobbyists and private security companies. The latter, when they are not working for big business operations, are rumoured to spend an increasing amount of time running around government looking out for security contracts. The private security industry, therefore, is both customer and supplier.

As with lobbying, unpicking the private security industry poses problems for government . This is because, like lobbying, it reaches to the heart of the British political system. It is no coincidence that, again like the lobbying industry, the private security consultants have been asked to self-regulate so that government, as is expedient, can get away with doing nothing.

Doing something would mean a journey through British foreign policy including the activities of mercenaries and the hire of the SAS; London Insurance Market and Lloyd's, including confidentiality, the banks; the SIS, MI5, the police; Department of Social Services (who employ private investigators) and so on.

The little that Parliament has done is ring fence issues in the hope that the bigger problems will go away e.g. the Home Affairs Select Committee's inquiry (1996) which took a cursory look at the lower end of the market i.e. night club bouncers employed by some of the private security companies. In addition, it also set up another ineffectual committee, (1994) the Parliamentary Secret Intelligence Services Committee, to assist in the 'going away' process. Both committees have shown they have an aptitude for isolating what they consider 'maverick' questions and questioners which is short-termist and ultimately dangerous. The explosion will come as suddenly as the lobbying one. When it does it will do nothing for Parliament's catastrophic image problem.

Those who agree to work for the private security industry, or have formal and/or informal links with them, should think very carefully about their relationship. It can damage professional careers and is not without other dangers.

Conclusion

Despite having access to fascinating information and assisting in the creation of legislation that impacts and improves the lives of thousands, many in the **Political CUMMERBUND** appear to be swimming in a shallow pond. Much of what they do and say is vacuous and they can have minimal attention spans.

There is some original and creative political thinking going on but this is in short supply, and most that does exist is outside the system, and therefore, like lobbies, is having to punch a way through. Regrettably, it is impossible to escape the conclusion that until such time as there is a transformation, the commercial lobbyist is surrounded by the:

Privileged. Some of these are gracious enough to recognise exactly how privileged their life is and are both modest and humble about their good fortune. Others believe privilege to be their right – indeed believe that they are not privileged enough.

Anoraks. These are the political junkies. Often brilliant and witty enthusiasts, they are always embarrassed by the number of bores in their number. Others can be marginalised extremists (ultra right or ultra left) or, in France, anarchists with cigarettes hanging out of their mouths unprepared to recognise that (socialist) government has to make hard choices.

A better class of Anorak is available in Spain and Italy, in that they dress better. German Anoraks come in two types – the really well dressed and the ones wearing combat boots.

Nationalists. These have been accused of everything from racism to fascism, sometimes correctly. Many however form an honourable group of people who believe in the sovereignty of the citizen (not government) and do not favour closer links with the EU, preferring that it be wider rather than deeper, because it undermines sovereignty. Except in the case of France, the Nationalists are usually pro-NATO and get uptight when the latter is described as a 'sacred cow'. More naive Nationalists have been caught up with the 'nasties' – see anoraks above – and the narrow minded.

Think Tanks. Some of these across Europe, especially the supra-national bodies, have had their day. Those that remain are pretty tortured, their once talented visionaries, who were prepared to break the taboos, having pushed off to more lucrative pastures. Staffed by timeservers who think that teamwork is sitting down to an expensive meal in a Brussels restaurant or taunting pressure groups in unison, many are now as desperate as their tactics. They believe in conspiracies, are seldom democrats and some have rather dubious connections with political, financial and other worlds.

The Infectious – that is to say, the few who can illuminate ideas and do not know the meaning of idleness. Their ability to identify with the arguments of others, and therefore negotiate, on the basis that the whole is inter-related make them the real gems. They eschew those who offer instant gratification (e.g. government controlled by spin-doctors), dated ideology and offer instead the brilliance of independent minds. This independence includes a willingness to deal with commercial lobbyists without compromising such independence.

The **Elites of Europe**. No, not the Aristocrats but, for example, the 'Oxbridges' and their latest equivalents that run Britain or the ENA that perform the same function in France. Representatives of the Ecole Nationale D'Administration (ENA) are blamed for everything from the arrogance of Parisians to the anarchy of the French workman.

The **Scramblers** and **sociopaths** that litter the political world. These are cramming themselves on to gravy trains, struggling over the rough ground to spy out new markets and clients.

Too cynical and depressing ? If you want to be a commercial lobbyist you have to arm yourself for all that is cynical and all that is depressing. The people that you will meet in commercial lobbying include the brightest and the best. Most of the time however it does not.

That is the citizen's tragedy as much as it is yours.

Those who conduct themselves with dignity and discretion, albeit untainted by pretence, are the ones to cherish. In the interim, for your own survival, you must learn to recognise those with whom, given a choice, you would rather not spend any time.

In being in favour of the commercial lobbying industry, it would be wrong to present the industry to the newcomer as anything other than an accurate reflection of the political infrastructures and personnel with whom you will have to deal. The Political CUMMERBUND is not for the fainthearted. Neither is a career in commercial lobbying.

However, not withstanding all the above, commercial lobbying can offer an excellent career to the young with the added bonus that other careers can become available. Delight in politics, and the rare chance to discuss and progress altruism and public service, alongside glorious hearts and minds, keep you going. These bursts of brilliance see you through the cynicism and worse.

NOTE

The Law Commission published its recommendations and draft bill to modernise the law of corruption in March '98. This updates the Prevention of Corruption Acts 1889–1916 and the common law offence of bribery. It now includes provisions to tighten up the law on corporate hospitality which hospitality can, in some circumstances, imply bribery.

The Law Commission report also highlighted two other areas where the present laws are out of touch with modern society – in making a distinction between public and private sector corruption, and in tackling international corruption, for example the corruption of foreign officials by UK companies or their agents to win contracts overseas.

The Home Office is now considering the report. Anti corruption legislation, including the position of politicians, is likely to be included in the November 1998–99 Session of Parliament. This is likely to bear in mind the OECD's attempts to ban bribery of foreign politicians and officials, due to be ratified in December 1998. One of the OECD's aims is to curb the standard practice in some countries of secret bribes and commissions. The DTI may put a memorandum ratifying the OECD Convention before Parliament in November 1998.

Other initiatives include legislation and employment protection for whistle-blowers which comes into force in January 1999.

THE CLIENTS

Some of the Industries You Will Represent – Client Tours – Fees and Tendering – Johnny Foreigner – Trade Associations and Chambers of Commerce – All Party Groups

Some of the Industries You Will Represent

Clients are like **Political Pilgrims**. They believe in themselves and/or their industries. They often have a burning desire and sense of mission to bring about change. And hope to find a St Paul who will see the light and undergo a massive conversion. In their favour.

Their only problem is all the other Political Pilgrims ploughing the same road and also heading for St Paul. No wonder the latter was a terrible bully. Their route is strewn with those wanting to throw them to the lions; or, for thirty pieces of silver, are willing to sacrifice them to others. The Political Pilgrims cannot complain because, given the chance, they would do the same. They are always concerned about the 'religion' of those they deal with and those with whom they come in contact.

All businesses these days try to claim to be 'good' corporate citizens i.e. they have their own 'faith' but say that they are also responsive to and respect the 'faiths' of others. Certainly all those wanting a bone fide commercial lobbyist to act for them ascribe to this. These businesses are increasingly aware of the fact that they need to appear to demonstrate their corporate responsibilities and ethical conduct to political forums principally because if such forums are to assist them it is easier if there is minimal public hostility to them. This need to interact with political forums is additional to their desire to influence legislation. Because of the size of Labour's majority in Britain, this also means targeting the tabloid press, which appears to be having a much larger say in influencing the Labour Party than their own backbenchers.

There is real excellence in the public affairs departments of some industries. As a result, a few big, politically sophisticated companies only employ outside commercial lobbyists because they have some basic information needs, or on an ad hoc basis to obtain a 'second opinion'. This can mean bringing in a lobbyist to judge other outside advisers such as a corporate PR.

Those with the financial muscle to develop their own in-house departments say that one reason why they do so is because any number of lobbying companies identify with the governing party which, ultimately, is no good to their long term relationship building programme. Certainly, the fight to bring into the commercial lobbying industry all the Labour apparatchiks supports this view. Other clients approach a commercial lobbyist to prove they mean business; because they are in big trouble in either the media and/or politics and therefore need to gear up their lobbying/PR response; or because they don't want their opposition to hire them.

Some top managements remain structurally and dispositionally removed from the political fray – they hire expensive ex-public servants to bridge the gap – and, usually when it is too late, find that they need commercial lobbyists to reach the parts ex-public servants cannot reach. This is sometimes knowing who to access, sometimes how best to attract their attention, and sometimes how to draft legislative input with, or, as frequently, without, attracting attention. That is to say, their employment of ex-public servants is part of their machismo (bluff strategy) which does not always pay off.

Bankers, company directors, and establishment figures all have an entree into various 'top' worlds but are always shocked when they find out that those worlds are not always the ones that matter and the commercial lobbyists can point them in the direction of the ones that do. They also have problems in coming to terms with the non-deferential world. The commercial lobbyist, on the other hand, thrives in the non-deferential world, not least because he is, himself, non-deferential.

Public affairs, once a part-time function, is now in the hands of professionals. However, many of these professionals are themselves having trouble coming to terms with non-deferential society particularly because most society believes that the status quo can only be relied upon to do what is best for itself. They therefore find it difficult to defend their own position, if they are part of the status quo, or the status quo if they are not part of it. More lucrative funds for commercial lobbyists.

Newly arrived foreign corporate invaders have also provided the commercial lobbyists with work. They have very little time for deference or any of the trimmings such as expensive and time-consuming hospitality – but are uncertain as to how to present themselves to what is to them 'foreign' government.

Representing huge global interests, the foreign corporates have no sophistication at all when, for example, they are called to address a Select Committee at Westminster. And why, indeed, should they? After all, these Committees are hardly forensic, nor are they the equivalent of Congressional inquiries – although they may yet evolve in that direction – and have buttressed the status quo since they were established in 1979. Minor improvements appear to be on the way, not least a greater willingness to investigate that which should have been investigated years ago. After all, what on earth do backbenchers, trying to cut a dash, do otherwise – particularly now that private commercial interests are rather frowned upon – and journalists are at long last beginning to take an interest in them?

Any number of clients do not know how to put their case to local, national or Euro government. Other clients want consultancy expertise which they then pass off to the rest of the Board as their idea. When they retire they set up as consultants themselves only to find that since they can no longer rely on the real consultants, they go under.

Other clients do not know why they are hiring a lobbyist! One lobbyist reported that a client had said that 'we've reached a certain size so feel we ought to have one – we might pick up some publicity that way. Although the fees are pricey it is cheaper than advertising.' Others do – which has problems in itself if what the client wants only (just) borders on the legal.

Yet others again do not always tell the lobbyist the truth; others run down their trade associations, membership of which can be expensive. They pay the latter as a mark of their respectability but also to sit next to the one person that matters at the trades association annual dinner. When this does not happen – usually because they have been rude to the poor sod who has to organise the seating plan or because the trade association deems them to be too lowly – they bring in the commercial lobbyists.

Campaigns are the real high spot – mergers, acquisitions, take-overs – because they are so dirty, neurotic, moneyed and paranoid. Other campaigns run themselves (e.g. Sunday Trading) and an awful lot of money changes hands for what is a very easy, but timing consuming job.

Others (e.g. the campaign to save the Greater London Council) come from nowhere, have everything stacked against them and exert spectacular influence even though in the end they usually fail.

Huge sums of money come from privatised utilities, local authorities and some government agencies. Some money comes from Think Tanks and foundations. However, legislative drafting, which is time consuming, is often poorly rewarded.

Client Tours

Today, most commercial lobbyists have restructured and now have focused units. As a result, individuals starting in the industry do not necessarily have the opportunity to gain a picture of the clients of the industry as a whole, before specialising. This is a disadvantage because specialising too soon can make for a rather blinkered approach, and information and network vacuums.

Some clients, especially in certain sectors, still do not know how to relate to lobbyists, especially if they are women. One, for example, was once given the task of ringing up a **government agency**, which took a small cuttings service from her employers, and was interested in any mention of 'radiation' in all political documents.

Every time she rang the contact it was like ringing Fort Knox. Every time she eventually got through to the contact, having identified herself to layer upon layer of hierarchy, her contact apparently knew everything anyway, only had contempt for the service being offered, didn't know why the service was being taken and 'felt it inappropriate that a young girl (as she then was) should be bothering him'.

He also always claimed to have 'already been in touch with the Member'. This, actually, was not true since the fledgling lobbyist was in regular contact with the particular Member on another issue, and was therefore able to check . European information was never of interest to the client 'because we are a government agency protected by government.' (Those who used to have to sign the Official Secrets Act were full of laughable airs and graces, and even more laughable assumptions.)

Other clients send people in for their lobbyists to meet without telling the lobbyist exactly whom they are meeting. The author was given a very good lunch by a 'consultant' from a **pharmaceutical company** who, it appeared, was a private security man working for an insurance company employed by the pharmaceutical company.

However, it proved nearly impossible to ascertain exactly what he wanted. This could have been because, as a precaution, she had taken her then employer, Commander Christopher Powell, with her. She had been told that the 'consultant' wanted to discuss 'competitive threats'. As a result she prepared the information she had been working on – namely the then threat posed by the Japanese given that at that time any number of pharmaceutical patents were running out; and hence, the company's anxiety about finding new lines of profit; and anticipating the regulatory environment in the European Union.

Needless to say the man did not know what she was talking about. The discussion then moved on to 'blackmail'. The author agreed that the pharmaceutical industry as a whole could be accused of blackmailing the then government since, at the time, many in the industry were threatening to shift their operations to the Continent if Government came down hard against animal testing.

That, apparently, was not the 'blackmail' the 'consultant' had in mind. Looking furtively from right to left, he removed a brown A4 envelope from inside his briefcase. It contained – wait for it – a copy of *Labour Research*! Shock, horror.

The discussion then moved on to the Labour Party. At that time and along with many other industries, the pharmaceutical companies were paranoid about the Labour Party's threat to nationalise them if they secured office. In this matter, it is understood, the American Intelligence Agency (CIA) might have had a watching brief. However, both the author and Commander Powell were surprised when the pharmaceutical company's 'consultant' asked whether, in their view, 'any additional funding would…er…assist to smooth the way.' The Commander looked up from his cutlets, raised an eyebrow, and replied succinctly: 'No'. The rest of the meal was eaten in silence.

In those days, the pharmaceuticals came under the heading '**Animal**' client, as did food manufacturers (all that dye in green peas tested on animals), government agencies (all that radiation used on the poor beasts), cosmetics industry, chemical companies, defence and insurers. They all claimed that they 'seldom' used animals to test products because it was not cost effective to do so.

Other clients would get odd-balls to ring up their lobbyists. One came through on behalf of a large industry beset with union problems. The information that the man wanted was distinctly unsavoury and the commercial lobbyist put the 'phone down.

Some clients were in a lot of trouble. Often, the amount of trouble they were in corresponded directly with the revoltingness of their staff. Other clients, however, also with problems, had wonderful staff. For example, the public affairs team of Turner & Newall behaved impeccably when the author, then working for a company providing

T&N with a small Parliamentary cuttings service, refused their legitimate request to provide them with particular information. They were fielding a barrage of hostile press inquiries at the time, and the press often seemed to hold subordinates personally responsible for past events. (Staff might not like the conduct of National Westminster Bank in Serbia. That does not mean that they all resign from NatWest.)

Other clients had double standards. For instance an **insurance** client telephoned the author for a note on 'asbestos' issues. When the author replied that she had just compiled such a note for another client (not T&N above), the insurer replied 'Let me have it.' The author responded that she would have to ask the commissioning client's permission since 'they had paid for it'.

The insurer refused on the basis that his company might be named, went out of his way to find out who the author was working for thus demanding that she break her client's confidentiality while maintaining his, and aggressively tried to remind her of the heavy legal penalties she would incur if she breached his confidentiality. To be fair to the insurance industry in general, it would be correct to say that the author's contact had problems when dealing with a woman which, at that time, was not uncommon. Some would say that the insurance industry still has problems when dealing with women.

The author has always declined to work for the **tobacco companies**. That is not to say that, as many would have it, that the tobacco industry's personnel have forked tails, cloven hoofs, or horns on their heads. As a rule, the industry have been good employers in this country (although it may be different overseas), and respectful of their outside consultants. Relationships with their unions have also, for the most part, been good.

These days those working for the tobacco companies live rather less well than they used to and the industry itself may soon be as extinct as the empire it once flourished in. Having once employed the executive cream, today it seems to be employing an awful lot of spivs. It is regrettable that the industry has always maintained that it was not medically qualified to say whether tobacco was bad for you – unlike, for example, the alcohol industry who never pretended that alcohol was good for you, although it often is.

It is assumed that it will live again once it has found a more modern product – the legalisation of cannabis could do it. After all, if snuff has given way to ciggies, why shouldn't ciggies give way to marijuana? Just think of all that lovely tax income!

Because the industry is in so much trouble, dozens of new consultants, who do not necessarily have the legendary skills of leading tobacco lobbyist Arthur Butler, are bleeding the industry dry. Gorgeous Clive Turner has now retired from the industry body, the Tobacco Manufacturers Association, his place taken by John Carlisle, a former Tory MP from the right of the Party.

Rumour has it that Carlisle is doing a very good job in an impossible situation but the industry could have done better to bring on vigorous new faces to update its image.

Three things are likely to work in the industry's favour – tobacco is not 'illegal', therefore why can't it advertise? The pragmatic response of many – some people enjoy a cigar, cigarette or pipe – and, to allow them to light up, without disobliging others, makes good business sense. And thirdly, increasing numbers dislike both the Nanny State and those with jackboots on who imply that they are Nanny. Nanny is not always right.

Nonetheless, it is impossible to deny that a once mighty industry may well be past its sell-by date. Or is it? Anyone with any interest in fashion could do well to hide their ciggies at the back of their wardrobe, since, a bit like the mini-skirt, they are bound to come back into fashion one day. Particularly if society continues to move along liberal lines, which it gives every indication of doing, and the industry manages to come up with a 'healthier' product.

People in the **Film Industry** are even more spivvy than those in the tobacco industry. When Christopher Powell drafted a private members' bill for an industry body in the early 1980s, which made it to Statute, some of the trade association's subscribers could not understand why they could not 'buy' tickets to attend Westminster, and had even less idea about what had been achieved for them. The only saving grace of the entire industry was the excellent man who ran the trade association.

The publisher of this book has recurring nightmares of a reception he organised in a House of Commons dining room to help in the campaign for tax breaks for the British film industry. They were all there – Jeremy Irons, Helena Bonham Carter, Michael Winner – and what did they do? Talk to each other about their latest films, rather than talk to the star-struck MPs who had given up their time to come along to meet them and hear what they had to say. It was Jeffrey Archer who came to the rescue and got them to sing from the prepared hymnsheet.

The **opticians** were another group whom Christopher Powell assisted. These had every understanding of Powell's work (another private members' bill on the Statute Book) and, despite their wealth, always conducted themselves modestly. As a profession, however, they could bore for England, Scotland and Wales.

Vets are gorgeously indiscreet particularly when they know you are working for all the animal welfare groups. As a result you usually have a lively picture of what is going on in the charities you are representing, as well as having an even livelier picture of those associations representing the vets, or with touching interests e.g. the Meat and Livestock Commission. They are exceptionally clued up about the European Union.

Were the vets not so commercially minded they would all be anarchists. They are very disrespectful of government, most particularly when they are asked to respect the Official Secrets Act requiring them to keep quiet about all this radiation on the hillsides, animal victims of which they are treating. They are instantly recognisable in restaurants in this country or on the Continent as they always pay cash.

Personnel of big **chemical** companies are sinister because they are so ordinary. All of them go into denial when confronted with the effects of human intrusion on nature, and simply do not seem to understand that they need to have an instinctive respect for nature and human life. They have no respect for the EU, although they throw a lot of money at it, and believe in conspiracies. As a result they employ dozens of public or former public servants to keep them informed about what is going on. The agro-chemical industry, and the pharmaceuticals, come to that, have recently scored quite a hit with the EU Directive on Biotechnology Patenting. Monopoly profits down and patents running out all over the place, they now have a new directive which allows them new monopolies. Pity the medical institutions who lose as a result (i.e. pity ourselves) and pity the farmer in the Third World.

Those from the **defence** industry are surprisingly cackhanded given how many urbane personnel float around in their astonishing world. They are absolutely neurotic about 'confidentiality' – and then go and employ lobbyists who are using freelancers who have not been told that the client is a defence company, find out anyway, (its not difficult) and are not signatory to any confidentiality clause.

Aware of the sensitivities, it is astonishing that they can take it on trust that outsiders are vetted and have no moral objection to working for them; and do not appear to mind about the enormous staff turnover in some of the companies they employ which diminishes confidentiality. It is equally astonishing that they do not always check other elementary details such as how confidential information is to be transferred, or whether those politicians to whom they are being introduced will do them any good. The answer, incidentally, is often negative. Neither the industry nor their lobbyists have yet understood the extent of public antipathy to much of their conduct. Or, perhaps they have, and do not care. Either way, they are both bad performers when forced out of the dark to confront their publics.

Years ago, **financial clients**, from banks to insurance companies, to others, were lumped together under the innocuous sounding Seven Secretariat. This was a secretive umbrella group established to address attitudes, and organise a response, in the then Labour Party, which threatened to nationalise them.

There were any number of such groups – the shipping and ports authorities had another; the construction industry another, brewers, tobacco companies, pharmaceuticals and oil another. Some of them got together under one roof for overseeing meetings organised by equally innocuous sounding names such as the Lunch Club or the Discussion Group.

These groups believed they were defending free enterprise rather than the Conservative Party i.e. they believed that their support for the Tories, and their anti-Labour position, was in the wider, not political, interest. There are any number of rumours about the conduct of some of the groups, or of individuals attached to them.

Some representatives from the above industries still attend some such groups, and the dozens of new ones that have taken their place. These often meet in rather swanky hotels – but for the most part all they do is 'shoot the breeze'. Of the older groups, which lack the funds they used to have, they seem to be pretty much old hat, stuffed full of conspiracy theorists (who still believe the EU is a Communist or Papist plot) and marginalised right-wing, tired old MI5 officers and cast-aside CIA men. (As indicated in 'The Overview' the secret service supported the right wing business lobbies and many had roving agents.)

To a large extent, the game has moved on to some of the foundations and Think Tanks backing specific political lines, and politicians promoting them, with moneys from, say, the European Union.

Financial organisations still act as retirement homes for former public servants, of both the clandestine and non-clandestine variety, which is one reason why such financial organisations have been out of sync. with modern political ethics for so long. MI5 and MI6 personnel think that their command of international relations is second to none. Actually, their knowledge is very dated: one reason why the City itself is dated. And why hostility to a democratically elected Labour Government still remains, if somewhat diluted by Mr Blair's winsome smile.

Their attitude to women is legendary (and substantially worse than anything that has been printed) which is one reason why they got on so well with the Conservative Party, Financial PRs and some members of the Press. Their lack of intellectual ability is equally well known.

Incidentally, most commercial lobbyists were aware of the asbestos problem and its potential impact on the Lloyd's insurance market in the early 1980s. One advised a family member not to become a Name because of this. As a result, it seems astonishing that apparently the Lloyd's hierarchy, and the Press, were not aware of the problems that have caused incalculable grief to thousands. From recollection, rumours hit the commercial lobbying industry during the passage of the Lloyds Bill (private legislation, 1982) which everybody knew would not work in the Names' favour; the minute the motor manufacturers started tacking 'asbestos' onto the reading lists (asbestos was in brake linings); and when Japanese clients of the lobbying industry, especially those who worked, or had worked, in the United States, asked about the problems in their monthly meetings .

Insurers handle very sensitive information which, apparently, on the grounds of either ineptitude or confidentiality, is not passed on to the various policing agencies. As a result, the industry can, for example, insure an incredibly dodgy nuclear plant on the Indian Sub-Continent that could become another Chernobyl, but nobody is to know about it. Meanwhile, spin-doctors are paid a retainer in case anything should go wrong. However, this refined sense of confidentiality does not always pertain. At one time the personal details of a woman scientist were all over the City.

Because of various City outrages, and the collective conduct of the financial community, the toothless Financial Services Authority is currently trying out a new set of dentures. As a result, the conduct of some city people, press, financial PRs and lobbyists is slowly being cleaned up. The real scandal is that it has taken so long.

Oil company executives live wonderful lives of make believe and are Very Important People. They are very urbane and rather enjoy political life since it seems very 'Mickey Mouse-like' compared to the real politics of the global business world and their own companies.

Their intelligence network is substantially better than anything government can offer. In addition, they have a better grasp of international relations since, unlike the banks and other financial institutions, they do not rely heavily on recycled 'diplomats' (MI6) to provide them with intelligence as an excuse for sitting on their boards. They are ruthless when it comes to humiliating, sidelining and emasculating other people, competitors, or citizens but are proving remarkably adept at meeting pressure groups, such as environmentalists, head on.

They are always well briefed before they meet the Press, and exhaust their commercial lobbyists who have to prepare endless dummy question-and-answers for them 'in case the Press should query such-

and-such which was raised in the House two years ago'.

Charities and **single issue pressure groups** have been helped by the fragmented and specialised media. As a result, they are able to communicate directly with target audiences, can be well organised and understand the new media well which is bad news for politicians and businessmen. Staff, however, can be dire. They know a great deal about politics since they are always having to watch their backs in the organisations that employ them.

Some charities are top heavy with important people and staffed by no-hopers. Sometimes, enlightened choices are made, particularly in the smaller charities, but this is rare. Many of the major charities are poorly managed, make shockingly bad employers, and have mind-numbingly awful old-fashioned hierarchies. This is a boon for some of the commercial lobbyists who offer sub-standard services to them. Basically, many charities are in an awful mess – which is good for their commercial lobbyists who can take advantage of them.

The publisher of this book spent a decade specialising in **transport** issues. This happened by chance. He applied for a job as Public Affairs Manager for the ports industry trade association. Up until then he had been working for a Conservative MP who, after the 1987 General Election had been made a Parliamentary Private Secretary at the Department of Transport.

Having impressed himself by beating off 120 other candidates to land the job, he was somewhat deflated to learn that rather than picking him for his intellectual ability and charm, his employers had chosen him largely because of the position of his former boss, thinking that he must therefore know his way around the Department of Transport and everyone in it. They were sadly mistaken, but he learned quickly.

In general, transport clients are interesting people to work for. They usually have a clear goal, although seldom a clue how to reach it or how to keep the public with them in the process. This is principally because of their historical arrogance in which arrogance they were supported by government. In the transport industry, the lobbyist becomes partly a management consultant and is included as part of the client's senior strategy team. This cannot be said for every industry. Transport clients can also be paranoid, particularly about a Labour government which, they assume, will adversely affect their businesses. Road hauliers are the worst.

They also think nothing of standing up at their Trades Association's annual bash and slagging off whatever government policy they happen to be against at the time, not thinking what their Guest of Honour Secretary of State might make of it all. Not that it is always their fault.

In 1989, the publisher of this book organised the British Ports Federation Annual Luncheon attended by 400 of the industry's leading lights. Cecil Parkinson was Transport Secretary. He started his post prandial address by informing the guests he had little to say about port matters – they were a bit boring anyway, weren't they? He then proceeded to speak about building new roads to a chorus of groans and murmurs from the assembled throng.

Which brings us to the **Civil Engineering** contractors. The smaller players are bemused by politics since they live in the real world, which is all about cutting corners. Privateers by nature, they have patriotic and generous hearts. However, much of their working environment is characterised by fraud, not least because of the conduct of the larger players. These all pretend that they are not involved in tax dodges and worse, but of course, they all are. They treat their staff appallingly and can be a risky investment.

Staff have lots of stamina, pride in their work, and are fiercely brave in working in environments that are physically and often politically dangerous, as well as lawless. The product that they offer is a sophisticated one. Sadly, they are often let down by their employers.

Politically, especially the family owned larger companies, they can make Mrs Thatcher look like a liberal although they are fond of saying that they are pragmatists and will work with anyone in power. Traditionally, however, they have had strong links with the right-wing and the security services (the latter because they believed themselves to be working in the public good rather than ideologically motivated). Many are still stuck in an ideological time warp, crushing those senior managers (usually the few from outside the family) who are not.

Their problems are two-fold. First of all there are too many of them so they are always trying to slit each others throats; secondly, because they are all so macho they do not like wimps. 'Wimps' can be anyone from those who vote Labour to those who vote Liberal Democrat.

They have still some way to go before women are treated properly in the industry, although those who have worked abroad are more modern in their outlook. Contractors, for example working in Iraq before the Gulf War, were struck by the number of high calibre Iraqi female civil engineers and, apparently, were embarrassed about the UK's record in this area. However, it is true to say that their attitude to all staff, irrespective of gender, is poor. This contrasts with their charm when dealing with their outside advisers and political cronies – especially when there is a possibility of a 'gong' for services rendered.

They are their own worst enemies and have yet to come up with a credible spokesman who can speak for the industry as a whole, or for parts of the whole. Like the defence industry, they are likely to come unstuck with 'ethical foreign policy' or value for money. But do not hold your breath.

Some of the larger companies are tied into the intelligence services and private security companies because they work on sensitive construction projects in the UK or the big defence programmes overseas. As a result they are as silly as the next organisation about classifying everything as 'top secret' even when it isn't.

It is impossible to make jokes about the civil engineering contractors who have worked all through the troubles in Northern Ireland.

Guarding construction sites has seen the taxpayer having to pick up the bill for the road protest movement i.e. private security guards need to be paid, and the taxpayer is doing the paying. This rather sticks in the craw since most of the contractors have been handsomely paid by the taxpayer already for concreting over the countryside. No doubt any number of them are worried that the government appears to be more switched on by rail – after all, the roads budget has been rather useful pocket money – but that is not to say that there is not a great deal of money in the railways for some of them as well.

Health and safety is an enduring problem although, contrary to popular myth, reputable civil engineering contractors do not leap up and down with joy every time one of their employees is badly injured or loses his life on site. Many of the contractors have admirable health and safety records, although this message has not yet got through in the Press.

Regrettably, the industry can be corrupt at every level. This is why it is amusing watching them trying to distance themselves from industries they perceive as corrupt i.e. chartered surveyors, the waste disposal people and the demolition boys. The latter are an exciting bunch of men.

Mavericks all, and much less complimentary words besides, they can get away with things we all know they ought not to but are willing to let them since they often have such a ghastly, and frequently, courageous job to do.

Management consultants always want something for nothing – particularly political information and contacts in government departments. Those setting up satellite communications for overseas clients all want to be spies (a bit difficult since they are all working for foreign employers) particularly now that the natives in the developing world have better skills than they do. They are pretty hopeless on European Commission matters, which they regard as regionally-minded, because they are so globally-minded (which is to say, American).

One can be forgiven for thinking that management consultants wasted their money on their education since they know everything any way. They are slick, juvenile, unfair, sexist, chippy, partisan, narrow, gossipy and fantastically speculative. The industry is without modern visionaries, and grander management consultants are immediately identifiable by their jargon filled conversation and group-think. They are incredibly chauvinistic, hierarchical and, get this, often ridiculously over-managed.

Lawyers send you reams and reams of detailed information on poor quality paper with faded print. This is so that when, unsurprisingly, you miss something, they can either sue you or claim a refund since you had 'all the information but did not act on it'. They are chaotically organised, chauvinistic, and completely unfocussed. They also always want to know what other lawyers are up to.

The big legal partnerships all have 'business development' departments these days which they loathe. The reason for this is that the business development departments are trying to get them used to IT, marketing and good business practice all of which is resisted by individual partners. As a result, many of the good business development personnel move on.

All lawyers enjoy slagging off barristers and think that former Lord Chancellor the Lord Mackay is a Saint for smashing the Bar. Getting anything done takes an age partly because partnership psychology is unwieldy and slow and partly because so many lawyers have friends at Westminster and are therefore desperately trying to out-compete their fellow lawyers. They never take advice and are overwhelmingly arrogant. They are staggeringly ignorant of Westminster and Europe and are so fine tuned to cracking legislation that they cannot get to grips with things before a legal text exists.

The partnership system means that there are an awful lot of duds around. A lot of them are funny trouser leg jobs i.e. freemasons with similarly 'funny' friends on the Continent. Their networks allow them to be both chauvinistic and racist since they are both judge and jury. The culture, however, is changing with many new initiatives, not least the Society of Black Lawyers.

Several law firms are now trying to market themselves as experts in lobbying, or even to form partnership arrangements with lobbying consultancies. These rarely work as one side ends up feeling used. Most lawyers know as much about lobbying as John Prescott knows about dieting.

You are not allowed to be rude about **farmers** many of whom have gone to the wall because of appalling government policies. However, there is some legitimate animosity towards them since any number of small businesses have similarly gone to the wall without the same hue and cry or subsidies. The foodies, for example the food manufacturers, are all in trouble now that MAFF is not allowed to be so cosy with them which means lots more dosh for lobbying companies.

The interests of the consumer are still not taken seriously and their interests are never likely to be the primary motivation of MAFF, farmer or food industry.

The **retailers** love lobbyists and consult them widely. But then they have to because they pretty well deal with every department of state, especially when they're winning various planning consents.

Working for **trades unions** is still fraught with problems although trades unionists have adapted rather well to using commercial lobbyists. However, it is not always difficult to understand why they, the Labour Party and some of the issues that they raise have had such a tough time in the Media. It was not solely to do with the Tory owned Press – although this certainly played a part – but with the fact that many trades unionists still look like thousand-year old toads with unbelievably dated views to match.

That is not to say that the unions do not have a future. They certainly do, moreover there is a growing school of thought which believes that the better the union, the better the industry – not that the Labour Party appears to recognise this. Also unions are beginning to reap the rewards of the EU – much to the chagrin of British business', which has not yet recovered from the Social Chapter union victory. Look out for anti EU and anti Union twaddle in the newspapers from now on. One or two unionists are superb Euro lobbyists.

Then you get all the clients, mostly publishers, running around trying to find lobbyists who will guide them through proposed **Freedom of Information legislation**. This offers lots of lucrative work for lobbyists and, a welcome relief, usually puts them on the side of the angels. A fairly rare occurrence in the industry. Unless, of course, they are working for those industries who are against freedom of information which is just as likely! The Government incidentally appears to be losing enthusiasm for the issue. No marks for guessing why!

Some clients always tell you that they have just jetted in from HK (Hong Kong) so are 'not yet up to speed' on one issue or another, when in actual fact they have spent days mugging up in the hope of catching their lobbyists out. The management consultants always play this game – and then pass your information on to their clients as if it were their own, which is why you and their clients are always kept at arms length. Those that really have come back from Hong Kong can be identified by how colonial they are and the gallons of carrot juice they drink for jet lag.

Others, such as top dog civil engineering contractors, fly into London by helicopter because their drivers all get snarled up in the London traffic and, as a result, are forced to use the tube, where they distinguish themselves by getting lost in the underground system.

Both have chips on their shoulders. The first lot make comments like 'I really cannot believe that London regards itself as an international business centre. Its transport problems are so bad. Frankly, if London doesn't watch out, it will be overtaken by Frankfurt.' Frankfurt? Who in their right mind would prefer an excuse for a city named after a sausage? Besides, any City whose airport contains three sex shops should be avoided by any self-respecting lobbyist.

The second lot either say 'You Londoners believe that you're so much better than anyone else'; or they say 'I don't know how you stand it – the air alone is terrible' pretending that they are all country boys at heart – which doesn't stop them hoofing it off to the big city whenever they get the chance.

Both are snobbish, one on the basis of their 'global' outlook; the other because, while reminding you of their working class roots ('I have real dirt underneath my finger-nails, lass') they are going out of their way to appear cosmopolitan. Actually, both lots can be rather provincial. The clients who are the most revolting are the ones who sing London's praises while choosing to live in the South of France to get away from the hoi-polloi.

Fees and Tendering

Public relations and other consultancy is a multi-million pound business under Labour. For example, this year, the Department of Transport, Environment and the Regions will spend £13.41m on external consultancies. Ministries considering the use of PR consultants have to be guided by such questions as to whether the project could be carried out by the Government's own employees.

All projects worth more than £90,000 have to be advertised publicly for tender. Often the contracts, although paid from public funds, are awarded through government agencies at arm's length from government departments. Big government publicity campaigns can cost about £170,000 – the top end of the fee scale. Some people believe that some of this money could be deemed for 'lobbying' purposes.

Following 'Cronygate' it was revealed that millions of pounds of public money was being poured into the lobbying companies from local authorities, to government agencies to privatised organisations. There was real condemnation of this in the press and Parliament – although, astonishingly, no-one seemed to point out that government's provision of information was at the heart of the problem.

Annual fees in the commercial lobbying companies are more typically in the region of £20,000 to £50,000, although large accounts are about £200,000. Ad hoc fees are in the order of £5,000 to £20,000 a month. These are usually one-offs. The lobbyist is both salesman and adviser which can be a tricky combination. The industry is fee rather than commission based which some believe makes it cleaner.

Some companies charge different clients a different rate for the same service. At one time it was not unusual to find one client being charged £1000, because that was all he could or would pay; while another was paying £10,000 for the same service because that was the fee he was prepared and had expected to pay.

Johnny Foreigner

Those who own the UK and/or invest in the country do not necessarily have the interest of the component parts and/or the UK as a whole as a priority or even as an interest. The Labour Party told the country that for years, although they do not appear to be these days, but the country still voted for Mrs Thatcher (who invited the foreigner in) anyway, on the basis that the multinationals bring us jobs in the short term, even if some sophisticated skills are located elsewhere as a result, which matters in the long term. Individuals, even patriotic ones, cannot always afford their principles. Nor, it seems, can New Labour.

The only thing to remember is that the American flag is not the British flag. Nor is the Japanese one. Nor is the French one, despite the fact we are in economic union with the latter (all those privatised waste water companies the French keep buying). To keep things in perspective, we should also recognise that as many British companies are multinationals themselves – and they have not had the local communities at heart either. It is rightly called modern imperialism or 'globalisation' for short.

Modern imperialism has provided financial bonus to many. Beneficiaries include ex public servants. Modern imperialism has also provided work for commercial lobbyists closer to home which is why the question at the beginning of the book as to whether you can lobby or work on behalf of a multinational, and still be a patriot.

To put the question is to go against the tide of internationalism that dominates the workforce. It is not meant to mean that many who work for the multinationals (excluding the commercial lobbyists) do not do so for good reason including the fact that the multinationals reward their skills, when British companies only reward their managements. Moreover, it recognises that now that British graduates are having to pay for their own education, rather than the tax-payer, they do not have a moral requirement to put their skills at the country's disposal. They can go to the highest bidder.

Commercial lobbyists however are different. Firstly because in beating the drum for the multinationals they can 'cheat' the taxpayer, and secondly because they maintain the charade that the multinationals for whom they work have 'British' subsidiaries.

An example of this is the commercial lobbying work carried out on behalf of the motor industry. The author spent seven years visiting car plants here and on the Continent with an All Party Westminster Group. None of the companies that she visited in this country were 'British' companies but subsidiaries of foreign parents. The politicians, however, whom she accompanied, all had to presume, for the sake of etiquette, that the chairmen they were meeting were chairmen of British companies.

This choked any number of them on both sides of the political divide since the reality was that the chairmen were nothing but glorified salesmen for their usually American masters and, as salesmen, had absolutely no say in the running of their companies nor any ability to defend British jobs or design skills.

The Americans themselves were rude to their locally employed staff – even ruder to locally employed Americans – and, unable to decide whether their best interests lay in the UK or on the Continent, exhorted the UK to play a leading role in Europe for US interests, while wanting the UK to act without Europe when it suited them, or going direct to Europe, without the UK, when that equally suited them. Meanwhile they employed countless commercial lobbyists, setting one off against another, and, in consequence, were advised by none. More often than not, they paid the penalty.

An example of this was when the author was working as a freelance consultant for an American multinational wanting to purchase a well-known British brand name. Believing that the largest cheque would clinch the deal, the Americans completely lost the plot. They had no idea how the country worked and moved around like royalty desperately trying to prove on the one hand that they were 'class' (the one really classy American happened to be an Eastern European who made HM The Queen sound common) while on the other hand being contemptuous of British 'class' which they found 'quaint'.

This 'quaintness' they presumed to be a pushover. While an important Secretary of State was (sensibly) on the golf-course when they wanted him, they almost stormed the office of a lesser Secretary of State (threatening his staff with the Ambassador and diplomatic ructions galore) unaware that their aggressive insensitivity would have the opposite effect to the one they wanted.

Their commercial lobbyists had to report to them a couple of hours later that the Secretary of State was, bunker fashion, under his desk in a steel helmet, and that, anxious to avert the impending diplomatic incident, was involving other secretaries of state in his problems. Meanwhile, back in the Americans' office, a private security company was sweeping the place for 'bugs', and checking all the waste-paper baskets.

Recognising that the whole of national government was now forced into taking a view on the matter, the Americans then decided that they needed local support. As a result, they swept out of Claridges in chauffeured driven limousines, and into the Home Counties. However, they were unaware that the constituency offices of most politicians are usually in tiny streets above even tinier greengrocers and that their cars would block such streets, which they did.

By the time they had got back to London they had pretty well offended everybody. It being a slack time in the Press, they had also begun to appear in the newspapers. A couple of days later they were dominating all media. Hysterical, they stopped their staff fraternising with local colleagues (which did wonders for office morale) in case any confidential information should leak.

It leaked anyway and the company completely freaked when a very sensitive document was posted back to them (in an ordinary envelope) by the distinguished lawyers of a rival bidder. By this time the tabloids were fighting the War of the Atlantic. Countless other companies, public servants and the like then all popped into the equation, some with dubious positions which the law of libel makes it difficult to even hint at, and the result was a complete mess.

In a recent book, former US Ambassador Ray Seitz appears to believe that anti-Americanism is based on the supposition that while Americans are much richer and more powerful, they are less intelligent than the Brits. Wrong, Ambassador. It is based on their commercial behaviour which may sometimes be characterised by the following adjectives – duplicitous, unethical, greedy, insensitive.

Unlike the Americans, the Japanese always listened to their lobbyists carefully. They were exceptionally loyal to these, never changed them, never expected them to compete with each other, and listened assiduously to all that they were told. They were voracious in their desire to know how the country worked, tried very hard to be sensitive about local feelings and never believed that information from the top (i.e. all the senior contacts they had within the national Government) was more important than information from the bottom.

Politically they were pragmatists, dealing with whoever was in Government. They did not accept that they had to deal with the Opposition prior to it obtaining office. Nor did they understand that ignoring the Opposition, at the time, the Labour Party, would be interpreted by some as political preference rather than pragmatism. Unlike the Americans they were not ideologically motivated. They wished to understand the 'form' so as not to give offence without in anyway wanting to be a part of the form. The Americans, on the other hand, did not wish to understand the form but did wish to be part of it so as not to show themselves up while at the same time looking down on the British.

Standards in Japanese business personnel declined as the years went on in proportion to their increased confidence. When they first arrived, and despite their then economic clout, they had an enormous inferiority complex. They wanted everything explained to them from a system that, for example, gave government a mandate despite not having the majority of voters behind it, to having the form explained to them at Wimbledon including debenture holders.

They were always puzzled that 'sex' could tumble Ministers and were similarly puzzled by anxieties over a politician's business interests. Given recent events in the Far East we now know why.

Those taking a European service were insatiable in their need for knowledge. In the early 1980s, they were a godsend to those specialising in Europe because they were the only ones taking Europe seriously. They soaked up information like human sponges. Their networking was phenomenal. Even Japanese students ran cuttings services and sent things back to Tokyo.

At Party Conference time they were extremely specific in their interests – health debates could not be fudged – they were interested in trade wars, the pharmaceutical industry, and anything to do with America. They were ruthless at downgrading but never sacked anybody. They had a total horror of dealing with someone new and did not understand that in the UK people change jobs.

Although all their information was pooled they were fiercely competitive among themselves and deeply resented it if the agency had a Japanese client additional to themselves. Basically, you could not work for two Japanese clients at the same time even if they were in completely different commercial sectors.

American multinational personnel disliked dealing with British Civil Servants because they found them immediately suspicious about their accents. As much as possible, they used English public school voices to deal with them. (Canadians complained bitterly that they were always confused with Americans!)

Both Americans and Japanese had different attitudes to corruption. The Americans, while being exceptionally correct about issues such as sexual and racial equality, were not so correct about corruption. Astonishingly, the reverse seemed true of the Japanese.

The tolerance of the former, given the swingeing anti-corruption laws in the US, seemed at odds with what they were saying in confidence.

There was a belief that since corruption can work in the West's favour (meaning America's), it was okay. There was no sense that corruption hurts us all, and no understanding that it is inextricably linked with the fabric of the national body politic as well as other national body politics.

The Japanese, on the other hand, talked openly about corruption in Japan which they claimed, even over a decade ago, would be their undoing. They talked even more openly about their shock in discovering that Britain 'was not as clean as we had been brought up to believe. We knew the British were corrupt in Hong Kong but we thought that was just Hong Kong.'

Working for the multinationals is dramatic and fascinating. However, unless he is very naive, the commercial lobbyist usually accepts that his rewards can be at the expense of his, or other's, countrymen.

Trade Associations/Employers Associations/Chambers of Commerce

Bread and butter money comes from organisations such as trade associations, of which there are far too many. This is because smaller and medium sized enterprises are predominantly concerned with their businesses on a day to day level and rely on organisations like trade associations and chambers of commerce to represent their political interests. However, these are often in the clutch of the largest donors so the interests protected are often only the interests of the few with little attempt to canvass opinion from the overall membership.

These stray into national politics – for example the attempt to influence the Terminal 5 debate on behalf of big business without consulting smaller enterprises, or seeking to swing its weight behind a part-time Mayor for London so that a member of the business community could run when the City of London had lost the argument – as if the latter could be trusted to promote anything but itself.

However, because many trade associations and the like are so dreadful, or because their needs conflict with the needs of other members, many companies are having to do the job themselves. As a result many trade associations have lost their constituency. In addition, it is difficult for such organisations to establish a consensus if trends operate to the disadvantage of some of their members, but not others, let alone the consumer and/or client.

Many of these bodies are run by elderly men and are therefore not as dynamic as they could be, especially internationally. This is because many have been recruited from the ranks of second division public servants, who fit in well with the deadwood already in employment with them. They always compare themselves to their opposite numbers in Europe who command enormous prestige, salaries etc. and therefore have the resources to develop research facilities but do not recognise that if the European model existed over here they would all be out of jobs.

Many are hopeless when dealing with the press, refuse to give the latter the stories they want i.e. that which is of interest to the wider public; rarely know how to write a press release, and lack all interpersonal skills which is why, with a few exceptions, they never make it on to out TV screens.

Many have cash-flow problems since they have no realisable assets. As a result some are trying to be more commercial in their outlook and services. However, since they refuse to promote the commercial at senior level, or bring such personnel in at an appropriately senior level, these are always unsuccessful – unless you consider renting out a couple of conference rooms, or organising a few conferences to be 'entrepreneurial'.

They are usually run for their senior staff rather than their members, who are always belly-aching about the rising cost of their annual subscriptions. Because many of these members are located outside London they have coronaries at the thought of how much is being spent on a secretary's salary. They are wholly unaware that they are paid peanuts as are most of the staff. Many of the staff are marking time before their retirement, have been in the same job for years and are as moribund as their organisation.

They make ideal employers for those with family commitments, and need a salary without having to do anything for that salary. However, they are bad news for commercial lobbyists because they waste so much time, and, if they have an in-house political specialist, resent having to listen to, and pay for, the outside advice usually bounced in on them by their larger members. Their character can usually be judged by their Director General. Questions to ask are a) has he been recycled from another equally moribund trade association or public service? b) Is he terrified of his senior members? c) Is he empire building and hoping that the director generalship will be a trampoline for something better? If the latter, recognise that your contribution will either be usurped or marginalised.

Their attitude to women is often older than Noah's i.e. there are any number of well qualified women at junior level but very few at senior level despite their substantially better qualifications. Ditto their attitude to Information Technology. And as for their attitude to those with entrepreneurial flair, especially those who have a vision to improve the whole, forget it. They might interview them (to prove something to their members) but never employ them.

They always resent the outside expertise, provided by commercial lobbyists, bounced on them by their despairing members. As a result, they usually do all they can to frustrate a decent result. They have the most awful tendency to be sycophantic towards ex-Tory secretaries of state and less than enthusiastic about Labour ones who, understandably , will not find the time to meet them.

They are also ridiculous snobs and adore gracing their top tables with a clutch of Royals, MoD brass, elderly peers or ex foreign office wallahs who will go anywhere for a free meal but do not add value to the industry. The fact that their members and poorly paid staff pay for such wasted hospitality is never an issue.

Their biggest problem is, however, that since they are sustained by their largest members, they are not independent. Another problem is that they are run by committee. This makes life difficult because a) things change every time the various committees meet, b) because those who sit around the table are often in competition with each other and c) believe that the small fry around the table with them should be grateful for the honour.

There is sympathy for both sides and many of the gripes have no solutions i.e. what is in the interest of larger organisations is seldom in the interests of smaller ones. The larger companies argue that they should not be expected to subsidise the minnows. Those who run the Committees are hardly the types to sort out the problems. And those who represent them to government are usually on the wrong side of ninety. Culturally – if not chronologically.

So what about modernisation? Desperate members are always on about this. As a result, new jobs are created in order to bring in the talent, modern ideas and business practice. The problem is that the new jobs created are actually the dustbin for all the jobs the existing moribund staff do not want to do – so the modernisers do not bother to join, or, if they do, leave immediately because they are blocked, or are terrified about becoming institutionalised like the rest of them.

So that their smaller members keep quiet, many have gone in for offering 'goodies' e.g. cut price BUPA, car leasing and so on. This does not distract anybody's attention – nor change the fact that they are still in the clutch of the big boys. There is a strong move at the moment to go in the direction of single umbrella organisations – this means that various Director-Generals are empire building – which is usually thwarted by all the lesser Director Generals who want to be on the same gravy train.

All Party Groups

The Secretariats of some of the All Party Groups are organised, sometimes at cost only, by commercial lobbyists. Others can be run by academics or retired public servants who can err on the naïve. Secretariat staff with commercial lobbying companies can have several employers (although they are usually only paid by one) i.e. the commercial lobbyists themselves, the clients who fund the Groups, often although not always trade associations or similar umbrella bodies, and the Joint Chairmen of the Groups who are always politicians. In the case of the Parliamentary Groups, outsiders also hold office. The result for commercial lobbyists servicing the groups is that the groups become both client and employer, a not always satisfactory mix. Many groups today, it should be said, are run internally by the funding organisation.

In those groups still being run by commercial lobbyists, usually, although not always, neither staff nor politician are paid an additional salary for running the secretariats, despite the fact that much of the work is done in their own time. However, the Secretary of the Group, sometimes a commercial lobbyist, often does command an additional salary.

In a well run group, staff maintain strict records of attendance and known expenditure (unknown disbursements can include payment to public servants over which the Secretariat has no control) including the provision of free office space and other hidden subsidy, meetings and questions, the latter of which, over time, develop into a comprehensive industry chronicle. However, as a rule, these records are confidential to the funding client and are not available for public scrutiny, despite the fact that the politician is paid by the taxpayer.

Secretariats run by outsiders, rather than by industry sponsor, are not usually put out to competitive tender. As a result the politicians of some groups have in the past been known to favour certain companies but not others.

Subordinate staff who run the Groups are usually just starting their professional lives. They are privileged principally because they have the opportunity to meet leading experts in their field and hear all the arguments of topical, commercial and national interest. As a result, a great deal of often conflicting information comes across their desks which they evaluate at several levels including a moral one.

The contacts that they make stand them in good stead later on in their careers since, in addition to meeting leading representatives of the business community, they also get to know representatives from, for example, US and EU political institutions.

In effect, the All Party Groups offer the best training an aspiring lobbyist could have. As a result of their involvement with the groups, the fledgling lobbyist is usually able to judge the quality of reporting of various issues, either in official government document or in the media, and how this impacts. This is especially helpful when a US/Japanese perspective is essential e.g. the importance of Europe for them, and how their viewpoints influence their national governments attitude in trade talks/wars. As a rule, the press reports Europe in a vacuum.

Many, especially politicians in both Westminster and the European Parliament, have a tendency to regard the staff of such groups as 'just the PR'. This is not always advisable since most 'PRs' can usually see through politicians oiling up to them. Most 'PRs' can also usually see which politician is after making a bit on the side – either out of the commercial lobbyists, the funding client, or the sponsors of a particular visit.

Tracking documents are usually maintained making a note of speeches and tabled questions, as well as questions raised in private meetings, and Secretariat staff usually acquire a 'feel' for what is/is not going on. (The author challenged one MP about an obviously planted question to find him bitterly hurt that she believed he had accepted money to table it – he had not. And another who told her that what he did 'as an elected MP was his business, not hers.' Her suspicions, incidentally, were correct.)

Problems when running an All Party Group are various. These include the fact that some politicians, because you are the 'PR', are disinterested/unaware of the other clients for whom you are working. This is not because the commercial lobbyist withholds such information but because the politician is often not interested in knowing in the first place i.e. you are only there to get him from 'a' to 'b'.

As a result, the politician might say something that is of interest to other clients. This information is usually passed on. 'Confidentiality' is a grey area. Such information, of course, can also be dud. One example is the information that a politician passed on about a manifesto commitment. Flagging up the positive aspects of one chapter, the politician omitted to mention the fact that the same comments were contradicted in the next.

Other problems can include demands being made on staff that are either inappropriate or do not conform to their personal convictions. An extreme example of this was the MP who wanted the lobbyist, when they were both on an All Party Group visit to Paris, to liase with both the Soviet Embassy and Aeroflot, the Soviet airline, on his behalf since he had been invited by the Soviet Ministry of Sport to attend the Moscow Olympics as the guest of the Soviet Government. The lobbyist had little alternative but to assist although she disapproved of his behaviour.

Other examples of poor conduct include Parliamentarians wasting other people's money – for example not turning up at airports and therefore missing airline flights, catching airline flights and then not going on the All Party Group visit but returning to the Group in order to catch the return flight home, falling asleep in meetings, to exhibiting poor personal hygiene, unkempt clothes, rudeness, chauvinism, racism and drunkenness. All these examples are witnessed by countless Civil Servants some of whom are relieved that they are not the only ones to see it.

One Civil Servant told the author about the man-hours, and waste to the tax-payer, when a group of Civil Servants spent days researching an oral answer for a minister, only to discover that the MP who had tabled it had 'forgotten' to turn up in the Chamber to hear the answer. This behaviour is almost as infuriating as the MP who is paid to table questions for commercial interests – until Tim Smith MP went and ruined all the fun – and in so doing uses the Civil Service as a free research department.

Hypocrisy can also be a failing, such as the need to charge the public high parking costs – without accepting that the special case they make for themselves (e.g. free parking in Westminster's deep car park, which is not regarded as a benefit in kind by the taxman) is unacceptable.

Despite the growth in private commercial interests, many of the politicians involved in the groups are commercially unsophisticated and know nothing about the strains and disciplines imposed by external considerations. Their problems, however, are usually based on ignorance rather than antipathy. As a rule, polarisation is a problem i.e. the Tories know many in management but no-one on the shop floor, and vice versa. This is changing with New Labour. Both, however, usually unite to see off any developing friendships with Euro MPs.

Attitudes to those taking part in All Party Group activities from the House of Lords depend on whether the Peer is a 'working' peer or not. Those Peers who are not, out for a 'jolly' or, more usually, the opportunity to mix with the business world for their own commercial gain, are usually despised by all. They can use the group as a training programme to provide them with informed industry knowledge and contacts . All at somebody else's expense.

The All Party Groups were considered by the now defunct and discredited Select Committee on Members' Interests. Their recommendations were inadequate in that they did not protect tax-payers, smaller clients of the funding organisations, or the staff. This is hardly surprising since they were principally designed to protect politicians and the reputation of Parliament and embarrass commercial lobbyists. As a result copious notes have to be filled in every six months by the lobbyist running such groups in order not to fall foul of the regime.

Other improvements could have included:-

- No Parliamentarian should hold office in more than one all party or Parliamentary group.
- Parliamentarians wishing to hold office in such groups should resign all commercial interests pertaining to the Group's remit
- All records should be maintained and available to public scrutiny, including itemised expenditure (bar bills etc).
- All work undertaken by the Group – visits, meetings in the House, delegations to Ministers, planted questions etc should be collated and available for public record.
- Self promotion, marketing, touting for business etc. while with the Group should disqualify any politician from further Group activities.
- No politician, or member company, should be allowed to use the Group's name without the consent of the Officers of the Group.
- Hosts, including foreign hosts, should be informed in writing that politicians indulging in commercial activity on their behalf or activity that may lead to commercial activities should be automatically disqualified from the Group.
- Qualifying rules of entry for commercial companies or outside bodies should be strictly applied.
- Entry to such groups should not be offered as a 'perk' or bribe by the

lobbyist running the Secretariat in order to attract new business to the lobbying company.

- Secretariat staff should have the right to refuse to assist a Parliamentarian should the assistance demanded not correspond with their moral/personal convictions.
- A complaints procedure should be established to look into allegations of sexual assault, harassment, or racism involving a politician and staff of the Groups
- A complaints procedure should be established in case politicians indulge in unauthorised commercial activity to the embarrassment to the Group
- No member of the Secretariat staff should have access to party conferences or Westminster in the name of the All Party Group if their principal purpose is other commercial activity.
- Programme/access selection criteria should be made available with 'alternative voices' to have right of access.
- The Secretariat should have the right to deny access to some politicians – for example those employed by a rival commercial interest to a host company
- The Secretariat should be able to sue a politician for missing an air-flight, and other costs incurred, unless genuine Parliamentary duties prevented his appearance.

Let's face it – some politicians join All Party Groups because they like to meet people, like hospitality and like to travel. Others however join the groups in order to improve their knowledge of certain issues which they hope will serve their constituents. The programme organised by many of the groups is both tiring and educational. On these occasions, Parliamentarians can be seen at their best.

For example, in the 1980s on a visit to Windscale, now called Sellafield, one group questioned a wonderfully sincere and frank senior member of staff who was not 'on message' corporately! Showing Parliamentarians the plants state of the art contamination chamber he said with a grin 'its only for show – if one of the fella's needs this, he's a gonner anyway!' Questioned about any personal anxieties about radiation he went on to say: 'Good grief, I'm not bothered. I've been here so long that I'm probably shining like a blooming light-bulb!' Much was gained by that visit although doubtless Windscale might not have thought so. (It should be said that the 'boldness' of the Parliamentarians evaporated. Tucking into a wonderful lunch, their forks stopped mid air in unison as they were informed that the fish that they were eating came from the stream running through the plant.)

The decent, the hard-working and the fair-minded are let down by those All Party Groups and some of their members who are none of these.

It is up to the system to sort the mess out.

Conclusion

Not all clients are as 'bad' as some of those detailed above, any more than are the politicians. Many are wildly enthusiastic, believe deeply in their industries and products, are motivated and wanting to motivate and enthuse others. As many politicians and other public servants are respectful of the responsibilities placed upon them, and the trust vested in them.

As a commercial lobbyist you will learn in time how to differentiate between the 'good' and the 'bad'. In the interim, there is only one rule worth remembering – cronyism, wherever you come across it, works against others and always goes hand in hand with sloppy standards and much more besides.

Good commercial lobbying is not about cronyism, although many of your clients believe it is, and would be prepared to pay for it, and as many companies would offer it if they could. It is about presenting arguments correctly and fairly in order to influence the political process.

Cronyism is anti-democratic. Good commercial lobbying is not. Make sure that you or your employers are offering your client the latter.

PRODUCT POLICING

Introduction – Bob Cryer MP – Some Examples of Bad Practice – Regulation – Lobbying (Miscellaneous Provisions) Act; Association of Professional Political Consultants; Establishment of an Ethics Council and Swearing of an Oath The Press: Political GALLOWS, SEA GULLS and HAWKS: Possible Joint Initiatives with the Press -Tribute to Commander Christopher Powell RN

Parliamentary operations by PR companies in and around Westminster had become so devious and underhand in the 1960s and early 1970s, that public use of the word 'lobbying' was deplored by some of those involved in public affairs consultancy.

Following its remarkable run of successful campaigns for local government in the early 1970s – well publicised in national and local press and local government journals – the chairman of Partnerplan, David Wynne-Morgan, decided to launch a specialist company – Partnerplan Public Affairs – and Arthur Butler, its Managing Director, produced its brochure which stated that among the services it would provide for clients was 'advice and assistance in lobbying at Westminster and influencing Government decisions '

The brochure was widely circulated and soon after its launch a letter arrived from the chairman of a professional association of public relations consultants complaining about the use of the word 'lobbying'. There was even a suggestion that the brochure should be withdrawn.

Butler and his colleagues were astounded. In their view, lobbying had an honourable role in the British democratic system. Partnerplan replied to the PR big-wig to that effect, adding meaningfully that so long as lobbying was conducted openly and above-board, no one need be ashamed to use the word in connection with their operations.

Bob Cryer MP

The politician who did most to raise political and public awareness about the commercial lobbying industry was the late Bob Cryer MP. A left-winger and former Labour Minister and MEP, he was killed in a car accident in 1994. Had he lived, there is no doubt that this upright man would have become a household name. His political career spanned several decades – one opponent remembers with a wry smile the day he snatched the microphone from Hugh Gaitskell at a student rally at Sheffield University.

Although at the time of his death, Cryer's position on commercial lobbying had altered slightly, he was by and large vehemently opposed to the industry, and wanted it outlawed on the grounds that its existence, and the conduct of commercial lobbyists in general, were undemocratic and frequently corrupt. He was also opposed to any politician accepting commercial interests, and was scrupulously even-handed in his condemnation of MPs on both sides of the House who did so.

Eventually, and reluctantly, accepting the near impossibility of outlawing the industry, he was the first politician to propose a register of lobbyists. In so doing, he recognised its limitations in that a register of approved lobbyists could create a cartel to which new members might be/might not be admitted for the wrong reasons. That is to say, he appreciated that it could, in effect, institutionalise and give credibility to those who did not necessarily merit it. He believed, however, that registration worked well in Canada and the US Congress, where he had noted with distaste that many lobbyists were former Congressmen.

The author first contacted Cryer in the 1980s on a matter unrelated to lobbying. She was subsequently to keep in touch with him on commercial lobbying issues, with both her and Cryer usually working through investigative journalist Mark Hollingsworth. Hollingsworth was a necessary party to the relationship, in view of the fact that Cryer loathed both the author's former employers, for whom she had a high regard and affection – as well as what she herself did for a living; while she was equally hostile to Cryer's position.

Not surprisingly, they both had different objectives. Cryer's was the dismantling of the industry at source. The author's, on the other hand, were consumer protection and the protection of staff in an unregulated industry. As a result, the politician was unable to entertain thoughts on consumer protection, the provision of state lobbyists for those without the means to lobby either in the UK or EU, or improvement in staff conditions. His antagonism was not reserved to the UK – as a former MEP he was equally against the conduct of commercial lobbyists in the EU.

Commercial lobbyists naturally took a stance against his position. This was not merely self-interest, although it certainly played a part, but also realistic. Those needing to access the European legislature (whether or not they were pro or anti Europe) could not always be expected to get it without employing lobbyists.

Other commercial lobbyists distrusted Cryer's agenda. They believed that he was anti-industry, and did not want industry's voice to be heard, since he regarded it as Tory and therefore untouchable for himself and his colleagues in the Labour Party. This, it was suggested, was one reason why he was also so vehemently opposed to the All Party Groups which gave industry a voice and, crucially, allowed it to meet members of the Labour Party, if they chose. Many did.

Views on Bob Cryer are so strongly held that it is next to impossible to judge who was right and who was wrong. However, many in the industry believed that, even if he was right on some issues, he offered only limited solutions, and those solutions were governed by ideology which sometimes appeared to ignore the validity of commerce and industry.

For example, he maintained that if politicians were doing their jobs properly (and had no outside commercial interests) neither industry nor citizen would have need of commercial lobbyists. He did not accept (or, if he did, he did not admit it to the author) that the growth in lobbying was due in equal measure to the incompetence, greed and intellectual inadequacies of many public servants, as well as the same inadequacies in national and European legislatures.

Nor did he accept that commercial lobbying, when fairly executed, enhanced democracy and gave thousands of outsiders access to the system. As a result, the limited relationship between the two was often determined by their intransigence. This was no doubt one reason why Cryer brought in the investigative journalist Mark Hollingsworth.

Hollingsworth had long been interested in the commercial lobbying industry and his cool and detached personality was exactly what was needed. He was neither a Press Luvvie nor a member of the Lobby, and therefore not compromised by the Lobby System. Nor, unlike many journalists, did he have any personal or financial interest in pushing one particular line or another. As importantly, he was not opinionated and therefore not intent on imposing his own personality on the agenda of either side.

As a result, he skilfully maintained a balance between the two and sympathetically insured that there was never any breakdown in communication. Throughout, he never betrayed the confidence of either, and, in consequence, never lost their confidence. This was quite something in view of the fact that, on the whole, both the politician and author had a poor opinion of some members of the press.

Largely because of Hollingsworth's unintrusive personality, the author and politician were able to deal with each other straightforwardly, in good faith and within their limitations. This was lucky since the very thought that Christopher Powell had been taking Private Members' Bills to Statute under his nose, understandably almost choked the politician.

He profoundly disapproved of the author's position – namely that Parliament should be more privatised not less, not least because of the poor quality of politician and political structures – and that more legislation of a technical nature should be drafted by outside interests with the appropriate drafting skills, rather than the reverse.

His attitude to Christopher Powell was exacerbated by the fact that he accepted that Powell was a noted procedural expert. (He admitted wryly that the reason why he had never wanted Powell to give evidence before the then Select Committee on Members Interests was because he would have been likely to give the industry a good name.) He also believed (wrongly) that Powell was corrupt.

Both he and the author were however united in their belief that some commercial lobbying companies (Cryer believed all) were abusing the system disgracefully, and both were united in their belief that some politicians and public servants were conducting themselves equally disgracefully. They shared a sense of outrage at what was happening, with what, at times, seemed to be the tacit acceptance of government and some members of the Press.

The author's abiding memory of the politician is his kindness to her. They were in close touch immediately before his death – he had tabled yet more Parliamentary questions on the conduct of commercial lobbying companies – and, in addition, at her suggestion, was due to address a seminar organised by a friend of hers, on his second great interest – the film industry. Regrettably, he was killed in a motor accident the week before that appointment.

Some Examples of Bad Practice

Some examples of bad practice in the industry in which Cryer took an interest are listed below. The mark of the man is that he was very careful when selecting questions to table, not to jeopardise the position of subordinate staff or innocent parties. This chivalry extended to a senior commercial lobbyist, whom otherwise he would have wished to target.

As a result, he was sometimes unable to table those questions which hit the industry hardest, although a lesser man would certainly have done so. In addition, he was the first to recognise the legal position of whistle-blowers.

Examples included :

— Subordinates expected to assist a political 'consultant' who did not know the difference between a Parliamentary consultant and a Parliamentary agent; nor the difference between a private bill and a private members bill.
— Subordinates expected to assist a political 'consultant' advising a water company who was unaware that there was one government bill, not two, for which advice large sums of money were being charged.
— Subordinates expected to assist a political 'consultant' consistently boasting about relationships with members of a Standing Committee considering commercially sensitive legislation
— Subordinates who witnessed the introduction of a naive client to a politician with substantial commercial interests, which, unbeknown to the client, diminished the politicians credibility
— Subordinates who witnessed the compromising of client confidentiality when a major company, in a sensitive industry, which did not wish to be identified, was meeting a Civil Servant
— Subordinates exposed to a clash of interests by senior personnel who, although ostensibly employed by a separate company, demanded the subordinate's assistance in the full knowledge that the subordinate was already contracted to a rival
— Subordinates expected to work for those bounced in over their heads whose ethics and/or political views they did not share
— Subordinates who expressed anxiety about company billing standards.

Regulation

Lobbying is big business, with large numbers of people working in it, many of whom, especially senior personnel, have no professional qualifications. They service a growing world market and charge enormous fees. Apart from bland and toothless voluntary codes and 'initiatives' it is an entirely unregulated market.

Those seeking to raise standards and lower fees have four problems:

— The public are relatively unaware of the industry, and what they do know is unfavourable.
— The consumer is ignorant of the standards that he has a right to expect from either Westminster or the European Parliament, let alone

the respective Civil Services, and at what cost.
- Neither Parliament/s nor Civil Service/s set the standard and/or name the cost and/or define the menu because to do so would be to admit that there is no public sector facility in this country or in the EU that is always equal to that provided by the private sector not withstanding the latter's inadequacies. This is a bit like pretending that the country offers no medical alternative to the National Health Service.
- Neither Parliament nor the industry offer standardised induction courses for those specialising or wishing to access political legislatures. One wonders what the academics have been doing.

At the time of writing the debate about regulation is, once more, in full flood. Many commercial interests who do not employ outside lobbyists are claiming that access to government is based on well argued position statements – yes, when the commercial interest is powerful enough to be heard. Other commercial interests, particularly those with senior personnel still after their knighthoods, are arguing that government's consultation process works best if the views of interests groups are channelled through their representative bodies.

This implies three things. First of all that representative bodies represent all their members' interests equally (they do not); secondly that there is always a representative and effective interest group (there is not); and thirdly that the conduct of representative groups is transparent, and accountable, especially their dealings with public servants (they are not).

As a result, it is easy to be cynical about the conduct of the debate, most particularly when the debate is limited to the conduct of the commercial lobbyists, and does not encompass all who lobby. For example, why should a commercial lobbyist, representing a small organisation, have to divulge and collate all the contacts to whom he has introduced the small organisation, in a public register, simply because he is a 'middle man', when, for example, an individual oil company is not required to collate such information and make it equally available to the public?

Perhaps here it would be useful to explain that one of America's definitions of a lobbyist is any organisation that spends a certain amount of money on trying to influence government; and includes any individual who spends 20% of their time so doing.

The main hold-up to UK regulation is the fact that it cannot be unfairly limited (although it probably will be) which means having to unravel too much, and the fact that only consumers, citizens and the industry's employees have anything to gain by regulation. Not of course, that any of the above is something that government would admit to. That is to say, for the regulation debate to go somewhere, the consumer and citizen would have to be provided with what the consumer and citizen need, not what the 'heavyweights' are prepared to give.

Full regulation, as opposed to knee jerk and limited regulation to make Parliament look good, means that Government has to do three things. First of all it must acknowledge that which we all know – 'democracy' has a price, and many consumers cannot afford to pay it. Government is both the market and the source of the market.

Secondly, the industry must outline what that price is. Private Members' Bills taken to Statute cost money. And thirdly, since the 'product' is democracy, and the 'retailer' the politician, government would have both to monitor the product and make the product accessible to all.

It is not just the politicians who are against putting the industry on a formal footing. Others lined up against the argument for regulation (albeit not in public) include some major clients of the industry. Most of the lobbying industry's larger clients, e.g. merchant bankers and stock-brokers, have strong regulatory constraints. As a result some have been known to find it helpful for their outside advisers not to be governed by the same constraints.

The lobbying industry itself has mixed feelings about regulation (or, for the moment at least, government's favoured option, self-regulation) for a variety of reasons. One, is that if the industry is to be regulated, such regulation should include everybody, not just the commercial lobbyists.

Regulation could only work if the industry as a whole was committed to proper standards. It is not. Many in the industry have no standards at all. Those that do, believe their reputations speak for themselves and have no wish to be dragged into the shabbier end of the market.

At a well attended meeting organised by the Institute of Public Relations in about 1976, members were given an opportunity to support a proposal for the introduction of a register for lobbyists to be controlled by Parliament in return for privileges granted by Parliament. It is a sad reflection on the standards of the time that instead of taking the proposal seriously they allowed its author, Arthur Butler, to be insulted by the IPR big-wig in the chair.

The meeting, held in the Churchill Hotel, Portman Square, was called to discuss a proposed register of clients from City PR firms following some questionable tactics in take-over bid battles, alleged insider dealing and conflicts of interests. Butler told the meeting that in his opinion there was an even more urgent need for a register of Parliamentary consultants and their clients, to be controlled by Parliament. (Before becoming a Parliamentary consultant himself, Butler had worked in Parliament for four national newspapers – the *News Chronicle, Reynolds News, Daily Express* and *Daily Sketch* – as lobby correspondent or political editor.)

In the light of his experience, he believed that Parliamentary consultancies were doing a more important job as communicators to the business world than the newspapers, which had ceased to provide detailed information on legislation and other Parliamentary activities.

He believed also that Parliament should recognise this. He proposed, therefore, that in return for having their clients and any Parliamentarians employed registered by Parliament, those consultancies that could prove they were in regular attendance at Westminster should be granted certain privileges enjoyed by newspaper correspondents. He did not rule out some form of payment for such a scheme, similar to agreements to cover costs made at that time by newspaper proprietors for the running of the Press Gallery.

Privileges could include: a daily free issue of published Parliamentary papers such as Hansard and Order Papers; easy access to passes to admit consultants to the public galleries to listen to debates (he acknowledged that the Press Gallery itself was already uncomfortably crowded); access to a bar, such as Annie's Bar used by the Press, to enable consultants to meet Parliamentarians on 'equal terms' over a drink; limited access to certain other useful areas.

Such an arrangement, Butler argued would hopefully put an end to the infringement of Parliament's rules by certain lobbyists and put the profession on a proper accredited basis. He also always recognised that facilities available to the citizen and small interest groups similarly needed to be considered within the arguments, and that many would balk at the idea of the tax-payer subsidising the corporate community. However, as he has always maintained, the corporate community, are also corporate citizens, and pay taxes too.

The PR big-wig in the chair, however, who had a Tory MP and former diplomat on his payroll, contemptuously brushed aside the proposal and added as a deliberate insult: 'If Arthur Butler wants to know how to get into the bars at Westminster, I shall be pleased to tell him.'

From the chair itself had come the admission that top PR people would prefer to go on bending or breaking the rules of Parliament rather than have the lobbying business regularised. Nobody in the large audience stood up to support Butler's proposal. He resigned from the

Institute of Public Relations soon after.

Today such a proposal would be laughed out of court, as indeed it was when Decision Makers' Maureen Tomison made similar suggestions in her evidence to the Nolan Committee, but at the time it might just have worked and helped avoid some of the scandals that have afflicted the industry over the last five years.

It is easy to lose sight of the fact that lobbying is not the only industry whose reputation suffers because of a few bad apples. Lawyers, accountants, management consultants, doctors, dentists and so on all have individual members or practices that shame their respective industries, trade associations and occupations.

These, despite regulation, are still in business. Which is to say, regulation, including self-regulation is not a cure-all. (Some lawyers, for example, believe that the Law Society could give way to a new independent regulatory body along the lines of the General Medical Council.) 'Abrogation of responsibility' is not meant to be a cure but is a way for government to avoid dealing with thorny issues.

Regulation only works if there is confidence in the regulator. And public confidence in regulators in general is at an all time low not least because there is no separation nor independence from regulator or affected interests. In addition, of course, even independent regulators have problems with policing and enforcing regulation.

Citizens, journalists, politicians and commercial lobbyists all recognise that the whole political machine both in this country and in Europe needs to be 'big banged'. The conduct of public servants, the waste of public money both here and in Europe (empty chambers, wasted electricity, incomprehensible and time wasting procedures and ceremonies, wasteful documentation – quite apart from laziness, fraud and corruption), the lack of facilities for those who serve us and the lack of facilities for us, require imaginative and speedy solutions.

Regulation of the commercial lobbying industry however would draw necessary, but, in the government's eyes, further unwelcome scrutiny to the indefensible deficiencies. It would also force Whitehall to come clean about its involvement with the industry – and other unregulated industries such as the private security/military consultancy industry – which it is reluctant to do.

Originally, commercial lobbyists were happy with the status quo since they believed that it served them and their principal market – government – well. However, they have now discovered that Government wants things both ways i.e. to avail itself of the services offered unless things go wrong when the industry can be dumped. That is likely to prove the greatest spur for the industry to seek a formal footing. 'Grey' areas, or plausible deniability, no longer work in their favour.

Lobbying (Miscellaneous Provisions) Act

One solution could be a *Lobbying (Miscellaneous Provisions) Act*. This could compliment future legislation, such as a new *Representation of the People Act*, and legislation already in the pipeline (e.g. anti-corruption legislation due in November '98). The Lobbying Act could establish a private/public partnership between the private and public lobbying sector, or some form of co-operation with public authorities. Any legislation, of course, would have to dove-tail with the EU.

A Lobbying Act would let government off the hook. It would not be forced to legislate for state lobbyists at local/regional/national/ European level, with allocation for costs should a citizen or small interest group, for example, be required to take a case to Brussels, but would legislate for the private sector. I

It would not be forced to provide access to the political world by supplying contacts or documentation via high street retailer at a price the citizen (consumer) can afford, nor would it have to ensure that local suppliers – Councillor, MP, MEP – were in a position both to supply such documentation as well as offering continuity of advice/contacts in local/national/European legislative matters but it would ensure that the private sector offering it were doing so in a transparent and accountable way.

In addition, the Act could require standardised training for both the private and public sector, legislate for such standardised training to be undertaken by both public servant servicing the public sector and lobbyist servicing the private one alike. It would establish a Register of those public servants (European Commission, Whitehall Mandarin, Civil Servant, Councillor, MP, MEP) qualified to give the public advice on all lobbying issues for free and it would establish a Register of those public servants able to undertake the above for commercial fee, thereby enabling them to advertise. This would recognise that which exists at the moment – with the merit that at least it would make the whole system transparent (particularly the conduct of Whitehall) if not accountable.

An Act would establish an additional register of all those public servants who do not lobby but are willing to acquire expertise in industrial or commercial enterprises without payment other than out of pocket expenses, as well as establish a new criminal offence for public servant/lobbyist for 'anti-democratic' conduct. It would establish an annual report of all lobbying activities in the UK and beyond its borders, to be available to the public, with a Government Minister responsible for answering questions in Parliament. This could include itemisation of those commissions paid to individuals, or companies, for successful participation in the government tendering process. It would establish a list of clients, most especially foreign clients and/or their agencies along the lines of American legislation as well as ensure that all those wishing to lobby declare all present and past relevant political or private commercial arrangements in a public register

Legislation, of course, costs money and time. There is no reason why the taxpayer should pay for this and a Lobbying Act could be an ideal candidate for privatised legislation. Enforcing legislation costs money and time. This, again, could be funded by the industry, since the costs of operating the above would not be inconsiderable. Therefore a levy, or lobbying tax could be a possibility although this is not ideal, not least because it could be construed as double taxation. Either way, the costs would inevitably be passed to the consumer and/or could put people out of jobs. Many lobbying companies are struggling as it is.

Such an Act would take much of the humbug and hypocrisy out of the debate by acknowledging that the present public sector, apparently provided by Whitehall/Civil Servant, local councillor, Member of Parliament and Member of the European Parliament, is lamentable. And accept that all public servants must be subject to monitoring – and charter marks – with those elected or appointed who are too stupid, or lazy to progress the consumer's concerns, to be appropriately penalised. How, for example, is an MP who never responds to a constituent's letter disciplined? Ideally, of course, such candidates should never be selected in the first place. But commercial lobbyists live in the real world and have to make do with things as they find them.

The above proposal would have two advantages. It would make the country more democratic and would introduce much needed outsiders of higher standards into the party political cartel now operating. Perhaps the present cartel could even be smashed?!

It would also accept that government had an educational function in specifying what people had a right to expect from their appointed and elected representatives, as well as informing them of how they could themselves become an elected representative outside the political party system. This, of course, would be another nail in the coffin of the present political party system, which frowns upon independents.

Penalties for non-compliance that could be written into the Act could include the withdrawal of licence to lobby or hold public office, the possibility of fines and/or imprisonment. In addition, a national body with sharp teeth could be established with the power to investigate and, crucially, the power to send in the hit squad when necessary.

Other clauses that could be incorporated could include:
- commercial lobbyists would not be allowed to concern themselves with, or intervene in, certain areas;
- the approval of the regulator would be required if the commercial lobbyist or his client wished to engage in other activities simultaneously e.g. a press campaign;
- rules of disclosure could also include the identity of directors and main shareholders, how these are rewarded, whether advantage is taken of offshore tax havens, any political affiliations or loans that could be deemed to be politically motivated, and any connections with outside organisations such as Think Tanks, Foundations and other independents such as some ideologically or commercially driven academics.

That is, of course, if there is such a thing as an independent academic.

In addition, it would be helpful if, at the top of all lobbying submissions to the appropriate authorities, including the press, there was a specific note of the arguments against the submission, what organisations or individuals had made them, and what had been done to accommodate them, if anything at all. This would enable all concerned to see such submissions in context, and allow, for example, the economic considerations of the submitting interest group, to be seen as one key factor in many, rather than as the determinant.

However, some of the above is delicate since conflicting national regulations could amount to unfair competition.

Finally, the Act could provide the equivalent of the 'Good Doctor Guide' naming those in both the private and public sector (i.e. lobbyist, Civil Servant, commissioner, councillor, MP and MEP) who had attained the required expertise and was qualified to lobby.

Because of the budget inadequacies of Parliament, the commercial lobbyists and the wider lobbying industry could contribute to the development of co-operation and joint ventures, in which Government (i.e. Parliament and the Civil Service) played a supervisory role. For example, in the interests of cost benefit efficiencies, outsiders could draft legislation or similar, under the supervision of Parliament. This would benefit taxpayers and consumers alike.

For such legislation to work, however, it would have to have the backing of the politicians and Whitehall as well as the industry itself. The precedents for this are not good. For example, there is now legislation on the Statute Book governing the conduct of estate agents.

However, because the industry could not have been more unhelpful when it was drafted, it is the most useless piece of legislation imaginable – reputable estate agents now wish they had been helpful first time around and want the legislation redrafted. Were this to happen, the citizen would have had to pay for things twice. Had the industry itself, of course, been forced to pay for the legislation in the first place, they would not have been so cavalier.

The above, of course, is not to imply that UK lobbying operates in a vacuum. Ideally, there could be dialogue at European level. This could increase public understanding of the commercial lobbying industry in the Member States. The audience could comprise not just the management and employees in the industry, but also its customers, enterprises which do their own lobbying in-house, public bodies, regulators, as well as the general public who could all contribute to the debate and establish appropriate mechanisms to ensure standards and compliance.

Standards, and quality, however, need to be a measurable element. This relates to quality/expertise of company management, quality of the organisation, procedures, and quality of the staff (education, training). The latter could be promoted if, by law, the wages of a new entrant to the commercial lobbying industry were not lower than the starting salary of, say, a trainee accountant or lawyer.

This is all the more important given the complexity of the business and the international legal environment in which employers and their clients operate. In view of the latter it is always astonishing how little time is spent on educating the staff. Employers are, apparently, unaware of the level of sophistication demanded. As a result there are very few compliance officers or departments in the industry to oversee and implement internal rules and procedures and ensure that all employees are adequately trained in the rules, most especially foreign laws and ethics. This would be exceptionally beneficial, for example, for some American or American style lobbyists, who appear to be unaware of some of the proprieties.

Competition between the various commercial lobbying companies should first of all be a matter of quality, including ethics, much less a question of cost. An effort could also be made to educate the client as the main purchaser of commercial lobbying services, in order to instil both a culture of probity and quality. For example, even sophisticated clients have been known to encourage poor behaviour if the lobbyist, in an unregulated industry, can get away with it; or, even if he cannot, so long as the client can distance himself from the poor conduct and keep things at arms length. Equally, any number of clients, are not sophisticated and therefore cannot judge the product and are not aware of the legal implications.

In Europe, the debate could concentrate on drawing up recommendations on best practices based on minimum agreed standards. In addition, research could be undertaken to help the industry to improve its services for customers, develop new service ranges, products and create new jobs.

The promotion of best practice should be a priority for the industry, as well as the contribution of staff to uphold fair and democratic procedure. The growth of the industry, and the extension of responsibilities that staff are expected to shoulder should mean high quality training in relevant aspects of both national and legislation. In addition, staff should be equipped with the skills that ensure that they are able to fulfil an important role in the public interest.

As importantly, clients of the industry must ensure that standards are maintained – including their own.

Codes of Conduct

An alternative to legislation could be a code of conduct with clearly effective sanctions for those who break them. For example, one of the lobbying industry's powerful sisters, financial public relations, is currently in touch with the Financial Services Authority to see how best to develop a regulatory structure for the financial PR industry. However, at the time of writing, the Financial Services Authority itself does not command wide public respect.

So, what exists at the moment in the commercial lobbying industry? There is the PRCA – Public Relations Consultants Association – whose members are supposed to adhere to a code of professional conduct, with proper regard to the public interest. They have recently launched a major consultation exercise of their members concerning a new PRCA public affairs code and register.

There is also the Institute of Public Relations – which, as already demonstrated, was less than helpful when Arthur Butler raised his anxieties about commercial lobbying twenty years ago. The Institute, now 50 years old, has since established a Government Task Force.

Finally, there is the **Association of Professional Political Consultants**. Regrettably, there are some divisions between those lobbyists who support the IPR Task Force and the APPC which cannot be explored in print without running the risk of lawyers being called in! Moreover, it recently had to reprimand two of its senior members over the 'Cronygate' business.

The Association of Professional Political Consultants was established in 1994. It has a code of practice for members and an annual report detailing which lobbyists represented which client companies. However, the association has no teeth. There are no real penalties whereby a member could be found in contempt for gross misconduct and barred from further employment in the industry. Moreover, the sanction, of course, only applies if you join, are eligible to join (for example, if you have been in business long enough) and agree to be bound by the Code.

It does, however, outlaw new business commissions and MPs are banned from sitting on the boards of member lobbying companies. Rules in other countries, however, are stricter – as Market Access, when in the process of merging with the American giant Omnicom discovered when the position of Lord Taverne (since retired) who sat on their board, caused a minor hiccough, through no fault of his own. Also, in the view of many, it is not the politician who causes the problem – Whitehall does, and the conduct of its Civil Servants pre and post public office is invisible. The APPC steers away from the Whitehall/commercial lobbying relationship completely, and similarly steers away from regulating lobbying companies connected with Think Tanks, political movements, foreign governments and other unregulated industries.

It was crucially wounded when it was formed because not everybody joined up. This was because any number in the industry did not like the founding members (for commercial, professional or personal reasons) and believed that their joining would confer legitimacy on those who did not merit it or, who were joining in the hope that they would be able to steal a march on the others i.e. in the hope that a cartel would develop.

The publisher of this book, Iain Dale, sat on the APPC's Executive Committee for a year until mid 1996. He well remembers the interminable discussions about the need for a pro active role for the APPC in educating the wider world about the merits of lobbying, but that is all they ever were – discussions. Nothing ever actually happened.

This was partly because most of the senior lobbyists represented at the meetings were only there because they felt they ought to be. They were understandably more concerned with running their own companies rather than devoting endless hours to putting a glossy spin on the industry they worked in. As a result, the work was left to the two instigators of the APPC, its Secretary Charles Miller (of the Public Policy Unit) and Chairman Andrew Gifford (GJW).

It was usually Miller who caught the brunt of any media interest in the industry – which, by definition, meant a media witch-hunt. Although he cuts quite a dash, and would win any award for Best Dressed Lobbyist, he is not a natural TV performer and should not have to shoulder the whole workload on his own. It is time for other APPC members to raise their heads above the parapet.

A measure of the APPC's failure is that at the height of the 'Cash for Questions' affair, it was unable to put up a spokesman for the industry as a whole. This may have been because one of its four founding members had been Ian Greer. As a result, they found themselves in untold difficulties. To his credit, Charles Miller defended Greer, his boss in the early 1980s, as much as he felt able, while the rest of the APPC were busily sniggering behind Greer's back and trying to pick off his juicier clients.

Because of this, however, the 'Cash for Questions' affair was able to rumble along in a vacuum with disastrous results for the industry's reputation. The same thing happened in 'Cronygate' for pretty much the same reasons. Nor, before or since, has the industry as a whole provided the press or broadcasters with a heavyweight spokesman able to speak frankly about the industry, and its importance to the public. This is probably because very few political consultants have been working journalists, and therefore have problems in getting items placed – quite a contradiction for an industry that prides itself on access.

Because as stated above, not everybody joined the APPC, those who did not were dismissive of it, particularly with clients and public servants, wounding it further. In consequence, clients of the industry generally did not and do not mind if the lobbyist is a member or not, and, more importantly, do not need to. Politicians have even less interest in the Association – most are unaware of its existence – principally because, again, they do not need to be informed of it.

However, the industry cannot blame the APPC for failing it. It is the whole industry that has failed to get its act together, clean itself up and establish its credentials. As a result, the whole industry has failed to offer:

– reassurance to the public
– public guidance as to what is/is not ethical practice including fair/unfair access to public servants
– provision or redress for consumers with a complaint
– appropriate education/training for their staff .

There are two reasons for such failure. Firstly, because many simply did not care. And secondly, because of the dishonesty of the debate.

Commercial lobbying should be transparent, but because of the political system fails any routine transparency test, commercial lobbying cannot be democratic. As a result, senior commercial lobbyists, understandably squeamish about taking on the blame for all democracy's ills, have tried to keep as low a profile as possible. In addition, of course, they wanted to keep quiet about some of their clients. Arguably, had those whose clients were acceptable to the public been more frank and aggressive in apportioning blame where blame lies, they would not have had to behave defensively.

Instead, and because, over many years, they have not found the courage to tell the truth, the product of democracy has fallen into the hands of producers servicing a market that exploits the lack of market choice. Those involved in it, especially public servants, at every level have got worse and the entire political machine less able to command the respect of the people.

The Oath and the Formation of an Ethics Council

All are pretty well agreed that 'something' must be done. This is demanded because countless clients:

- have been provided with a political service they do not need, at the expense of the service they do need
- have been offered no menu of prices, nor an appeal system, nor Lobbying Ombudsman
- have been charged fees disproportionate to the skills or services on offer while the staff of the commercial lobbyists have been ruthlessly exploited, and while countless public servants and members of the media have barracked both the industry and the players, as if their own industries are better.

All this barracking, of course, is purportedly on behalf of the public, and implies that, were the commercial lobbyists to be done out of jobs, the public would be better served by those insiders who remain. Bunkum and Balderdash, as Sir Bernard Ingham might say.

What could be considered to alleviate some of the problems above could be the establishment of a clearly constituted Ethics Council. Representatives from all parts of the industry could be invited to sit on it, including, for example, clients, public servants and the NUJ, representing the employees. This would assist with every day dilemmas, have both an educational and pastoral role, as well as provide the industry, and those working in it, with mentors. The problem about finding mentors, however, is that there are very few in the industry of sufficient standing and other attributes, who could act as mentors.

In addition, those seeking to work in the lobbying industry could be required to take an Oath, the swearing of which could be undertaken in formal and solemn surroundings to reinforce its gravity. This would require those wishing to work as commercial lobbyists to:

- Uphold Parliamentary Law
- Nurture Democracy
- Accept that they have a 'Duty of Care' for democracy by recognising the rights of others, acknowledging all moral obligation to individuals and correct and fair practice

and by

- Reporting any suspicion of wrong doing or fraudulent practice, especially that of superiors or public servants, using, if necessary, the protection offered by whistle-blowers employment protection, to independent regulators for investigation.

Our democracy deserves that at least.

Finally, no commercial lobbyist should be able to call himself such until he has met set standards of knowledge and expertise. This, for example, would mean that those new entrants from the Labour Party all presently running around calling themselves 'commercial lobbyists' would not be allowed to do so, any more than would, for example, former public servants. Nor, more importantly, would their new employers have been allowed to market them as such.

It remains to be seen where the debate goes, and what government and/or the industry decides to do. It is possible that anti-corruption and freedom of information legislation already on the cards might sort out some of the mess, so far as public servants are concerned. Other parts of the mess are also being tackled e.g. a code of conduct bringing financial information within the remit of the Financial Services Authority. Beyond this, as detailed above, a Lobbying Act could also be useful. As could legislation requiring all foreign clients to be registered.

As importantly, what is needed is an informed public debate. This is unlikely. Instead, discussions about what to do will probably be left to a small group of people behind closed doors. These, for whatever reason, will not recommend what is an essential prerequisite i.e. a Royal Commission into Democracy. Nor will they recommend that such a Commission look at the lobbying industry and its responsibilities in the correct context.

As always, the debate into modernising democracy will continue to be explored without reference to the public, and certainly without reference to commercial lobbyists. The public want it that way – because, living in a state of ignorance, the public has been informed that the industry is anti-democratic, when in fact, it is the market that the industry services which is undemocratic.

This is a crucial difference and not one that any of the public's information conduits has ever made clear.

The Press: The Political, 'SEA GULLS' and 'HAWKS'

At the moment, the Press appears to be in turmoil. For the most part its problems are outside the scope of this book but suffice it to say that there are a few brilliant signs of transformation. On the whole, however, the Press has either refused, or been unable, to come to grips with reform of itself. Coverage of national public affairs is patchy. Other examples include poor regional reporting of our great cities and foreign news.

Like our political system and those who govern us, the Press appear to have lost the plot years ago. Similarly, like our political system, it has also been engulfed by massive technological and commercial change, the impact of which is forcing the pace, not least because it can no longer rely on controlling the agenda. At the moment, there is no equivalent to the US Centre for Public Integrity, a non-profit, non-partisan organisation devoted to public service journalism.

In commercial lobbying, the press is, at long last, having to accept the industry's existence, even if it dislikes, and doubts its legitimacy or integrity. Hitherto, the Press has consistently tried to ignore it, and, as a result, has been unable to accept that:

- commercial lobbying is a response to the democratic deficit, not its cause
- commercial lobbying is a necessity in the EU because of the democratic deficit
- commercial lobbying is a lawful, commercial exercise – and successful too

In so doing, the Press has made no allusion to the fact that it has contributed to the democratic deficit, and insulted many of its own readers and viewers – from small businesses, to charities, to trade unions – who are clients of the lobbying industry. These, unlike the self-appointed opinion formers, are not hostile to the industry, but want to be better informed, and supplied with honest and independent information on products, standards and measurable achievement.

Refusal by the Press to cover the commercial lobbying industry has always perplexed practitioners, since they are in business to build relationships with their audiences and presumed that the press were too. Arguably, had the press been prepared to recognise the industry's legitimacy, it would have offered nourishment to those within the industry who were seeking to raise standards and ethics. Its failure to do so has contributed to many of the commercial lobbying industry's problems today.

One reason why some political journalists have been hostile to lobbyists is that in the past a small number inhabiting the Parliamentary Press Gallery have augmented their income by providing information for PR and Parliamentary consultancies. As far back as the early 1960s a senior officer of the lobby, now deceased, was assisting the Voice and Vision consultancy. And one Press Gallery member who pushed his luck too far was sacked by his newspaper for helping to front a PR Reception to which, unbeknown to him, his editor had been invited.

Journalists who were too honest to cross the line between reporting to the public and reporting secretly to public affairs firms naturally took a poor view of the PR man involved but failed decisively to tackle their less honest colleagues in the Press Gallery who were misusing the facilities and were the real culprits.

The race is now on for the press to reinvent itself so that it reflects the country's interests and needs in all their diversity. In informing the people, and encouraging them to be informed i.e. empowering the people, it is waking up to its responsibilities. The irony is that it is also teaching many that they need to be lobbyists – the manifestation of which in the private sector at least it has long denied.

In one's dreams one imagines seasoned hacks, sitting down with political representatives, professional communicators and commercial lobbyists in town halls all over the country offering bone fide assistance to individuals and small interest groups. But that is all it is – a dream.

This is a shame since the legislative system locally, regionally, nationally and in Europe impacts so heavily on all our lives that dozens of 'David Bellamys' of politics are needed to put up the sign-posts and point the way. Instead, journalists join commercial lobbyists and public servants on the lucrative conference circuit.

Recently, however, there is some evidence that the press is gradually becoming more responsive to the needs for balance when covering the industry.

The tabloids are leading the way in this and are often much more willing to be fair, and, more importantly, accurate than the broadsheets. This has implications for broadcasting since, as a rule, the broadcasters take their line from what they deem to be the 'serious' press.

It is difficult to explain why there is such an increasing difference between the two press types, although it could be that the tabloid journalist is more willing to acknowledge that he does not know the industry and is therefore willing to learn. Many in the so-called serious press do not take this line perhaps because they are busily making themselves comfortable in the ivory tower they share with ministers' advisers, thereby buttressing their respective egos.

Here they all feel like chieftains, oblivious to the fact that they are not. An example of this is a well known and justifiably well loved political figure, who retired from the Press recently. Throughout all his years of broadcasting to the nation via a well known news slot, he never once mentioned the commercial lobbying industry or its role in the political and legislative arena.

The commercial lobbyist's relationship with the press as a whole, but principally the written press, has improved. In the early years the commercial lobbyist watched the self-seriousness of the Parliamentary press gallery with bemusement, as besuited hacks, who thought that going to a ministerial briefing made them important, made no attempt to conceal their contempt for him. This, while the commercial lobbyist had contributed to the minister's thought process.

He was similarly bemused to witness some of the shenanigans in the Parliamentary press gallery and political press, none of which ever made it into the public domain. The hypocrisy of the latter is breathtaking.

While swarming all over individuals in commercial lobbying, politics, the police, Civil Service and so on, to expose misdemeanour or, in some cases, corruption, the press did not choose to similarly 'out' its own. It could be, of course, that it is saying that there is no misdemeanour or corruption among its ranks. Sure...

Whistle Blowers

The principal grievance that many in the commercial lobbying industry have against the press is that historically, with a few brilliant exceptions, it has never offered a home or a hearing to whistle-blowers. This is because had it done so, it would have been forced into accepting the legitimacy of some of the commercial lobbyist's work, as well as being forced into siding with them on many occasions.

This would have been awkward for the press since its own interests, bias and culture are firmly rooted in the status quo. An example of the latter is that any number of politicians whom it knows and trusts have a legal background. These have consistently denigrated the commercial lobbyists and members of the press have been more disposed to believe them than the outsiders who can challenge the legal cartel. In addition, some members of the press are influenced by academics who also deny the relevance of the commercial lobbying industry.

The result is that many young commercial lobbyists, who had previously believed in the independence of the press, began to question it. Such cynicism was exacerbated by the reading of primary source political documentation which showed the gap between what people actually see on television, or read in newspapers, and the truth. Forced, however, by some proprietors, employers and/or clients to be helpful to the press, hours were spent in assembling information demanded by the press, only to find that the journalist was apparently no longer interested.

As a result, while some members of the press distorted, suppressed, ridiculed, and tried to lose the commercial lobbyists their jobs, some younger commercial lobbyists were confirmed in their belief that the journalist was ignorant, arrogant and insensitive to other people's time. Others again talked about the full extent of press collusion with the political and administrative status quo, censorship, and, were one allowed to use the word, which, of course, one is not – corruption, be it of wallet, mind or soul.

The Present

What matters, of course, is whether lessons are learned from the past and whether maturity rather than self-importance and self-interest govern the future. For example, there are many joint initiatives that could be considered if the press were a) prepared to accept that others can be better at interpreting some political and legislative trends – especially commercial ones – and their relevance to people's lives, and b) are prepared to accept that in many areas it does not always have the monopoly of appropriate expertise to judge the impact of trends and legislation.

This would be asking a great deal. It would mean that the press would have to recognise some of its limitations, denting the ego (some would say not before time) of many of its number. These limitations, along with those of the political infrastructure, are what the commercial lobbyist has capitalised upon, and will continue to do so.

The press, for example, did not relate politics to the real world. The commercial lobbyists on the other hand took political information out of the vacuum and explained to their clients (not all of them wealthy) –how, for example, national or EU legislation or prospective legislation impacts; the government's position in the UK and EU; ditto the Opposition's; who the lobbyists are; whether in favour or against; what the other national governments/oppositions are up to; the NGOs, transnationals and so on.

As a result, commercial lobbyists provided information that organisations needed and, in addition, sought to influence the debate on their behalf. They provided information on Whitehall, local government, EU public servants and much more besides in the same way as they are now offering information on task forces and quangos. In addition, they drafted amendments and/or other prospective input into legislation.

Instead of recognising the legitimate role that the commercial lobbyist was fulfilling, the press blamed the commercial lobbyists for filling the information gap. Meanwhile, an entire press pack noisily congratulated a journalist for procedural knowledge that had led to the spotting of a 'planted question' in Parliamentary documents, ridiculously fanning the flames of an already big story, when this was something that a seventeen year old secretary in the commercial lobbying industry did every day.

Despite this apparent procedural knowledge, those same journalists did not 'spot' the scandal of the massive growth in private bill or statutory instruments work, where, over long periods, the odds were stacked against the citizen by powerful commercial interests and despite the fact they were constantly tipped off by the commercial lobbyists as to what was happening.

The result was that many commercial lobbyists came to recognise that many of the criticisms that they had against politician and public servant were mirrored by the press, which, in their view accounted for the conspiracy of silence. As a result, those who, arguably, were the best informed about massive corruption and incompetences in Westminster, Whitehall and the EU were completely overlooked by many in the Press. As importantly, the public were denied access to such information.

Joint Initiatives

Joint initiatives could be the way ahead. For this possibility to go somewhere, however, the press would have to recognise that many commercial lobbyists are the better communicators because they are in the business of explaining often complex arguments to laymen. The commercial lobbyist, as it were, makes his living from making issues both understandable and interesting.

In addition, they have to put things in context and present accurate overviews, because, in order to lobby on behalf of a client at all levels of political forums, they have to work out:

- Who is ranged against his client
- Who the client's opponents/allies are, including the opponents of their opponents, who, in consequence, are either neutral or prospective allies
- How their client's demands impact on various audiences
- How the press, including the different national press, will react

and how all might need to be seen against the wider background e.g. constitutional change in this country, or accompanying demands for change in other countries.

At the moment, and regrettably, unable to accept the skills of the commercial lobbyist, the press either call upon themselves to cover events, or academics, Civil Servants, politicians or organisations such as single interest groups. As a result, the public are not always provided with the arguments by those most qualified to give an overview, which is what is needed, nor are those selected to debate the issues always those most able to communicate them in as interesting a manner as possible.

Because of press hostility to the commercial lobbyist, much of which hostility is fabricated, he is not able to challenge his exclusion from the discussion — equitable air time and platform sharing appear to be alien concepts to journalists.

Joint initiative areas could include:

- coverage of **European issues**. The EU has been communicated in as boring a manner as possible despite the fact that what is decided at European level has enormous implications for all citizens. As a result, the public are not informed about the Euro-government that dictates their lives, or the politicians and bureaucrats that staff it. The commercial lobbyist, on the other hand, knows and lobbies all the personnel involved.

Of course, the press will argue that commercial lobbyists are not without bias, particularly now that the public are aware that some commercial lobbying companies are alleged to have been funded by pro-European groups. How different, however, is this to the anti-Europe agenda maintained by many in the press and funded by some Press Barons?

- **coverage of issues deemed to be 'boring'**. An example of this is the work done by librarians at the time of the Data Protection Bill. Among other issues, the librarians were anxious that the police should not have access to the public's reading habits. They argued that the citizen should have the right to read, for example, *Mein Kampf,* should he so choose, without any outside agency putting his name on a police computer. The implications of this small battle were enormous for civil liberties. However, the press decided that the issue was scarcely worth a mention since 'our readers are not interested in libraries or librarians'. The commercial lobbyist knew otherwise and, had the press allowed, could have presented it to the public, perhaps with a wider look at civil liberties in the UK.

- **coverage at Party Conference.** At the moment, press coverage of this is uniformly dull and homogeneous, which is hardly surprising when, for the most part, it amounts to little more than propaganda. There is little coverage, for example, of the lively and well attended fringe meetings. These are the 'alternative voices' that reflect some of the lobbies in society. Some fringe meetings are financed by commercial interests, some by charities, some by individuals and some by the marginalised. Many of these meetings are colourful and express valid, if sometimes off-beat points of view. Commercial lobbyists, who usually have to have a knowledge of the organisations hosting the fringe, as well as many of the players, know their way around them. The press do not – or, if they do, do not report them.

Party Conference is also, as everybody knows, one big drinking and food binge, usually with somebody else paying the bill. 'Interests' still, usually (although the market is changing) entertain in all the big hotels and restaurants, or hold cocktail parties. In the exhibition areas, those same 'interests' are placed, sometimes uncomfortably, side by side.

The press, while enjoying the hospitality, do not cover the networking, feuds, and friendships, nor do they cover how much a particular 'interest' is spending on entertaining/influencing, who they are influencing and why. Lobbyists do.

Some coverage of the above would bring Party Conference to life and be more relevant to the public and political process. In addition, it would be more interesting than the usual round of interviews with politicians or political 'anoraks'. At the moment some party conference coverage is dull because the press simply does not know how to interact with the whole political system. Lobbyists, on the other hand, are in business because of the whole. As a result they can identify all the players, including identifying those outsiders who sit on, for example, task forces, and who impact on the whole, some of whom are at party conference.

Another area for joint initiatives could be the great **State occasions**. At present, analysis of the legislative agenda following the State Opening of Parliament is usually confined to dull economic or even duller legislative analysis. The lobbyist, however, usually knows that behind the twenty-odd Parliamentary bills announced, are countless interest groups, who these are, and who will be disappointed. This would be of interest to the public.

The lobbyist also knows what legislation is needed and what is missing. The press, of course, know all the above too but do not communicate the various lobbies, including the citizen lobbies, enthusiastically nor make politics relevant to people's lives.

It is aware of this, and has started to make changes. Some of these changes however were so appalling that they can be dismissed. The way ahead is not dumbing down – insulting the public further – but making the debate interesting and relevant by inviting informed participation and comment from outsiders, including the commercial lobbyists. These know the lobbies involved and have a great deal more street-cred than boring economists, tired old commercially compromised academics, media personalities or embarrassed journalists stuck in a mid-night shop at 2.00 a.m., as one was at the time of the Referendum for a London Mayor, trying hard to find members of the public to interview.

Another area where the lobbyist has made himself relevant is in publicising Whitehall and Select Committee appeals for witnesses. The press could just as easily broadcast/advertise these appeals if it were so minded – and, more importantly, if the political process wanted the Press to, which it does not. It is amusing to note that while the Civil Service are now under some obligation to give equal time to opposing views and interests, the Select Committees are not. As a result, the public, who are often the better experts, are excluded from the consultation game, the political system, and the press, preferring those they already know, or those recommended by those they already know – although everybody madly denies this. Cronyism lives.

The lobbyist also knows when to widen the agenda if, no matter how erroneously, the core group is no longer commanding interest. For example, the commercial lobbyist would have widened coverage of the EU/British beef war to include the importance of avoiding a trade war with America over cosmetics and medicines (made from beef derivatives), introducing the public in the process to the work of the World Trade Organisation. The snapshot would have been important to the public since the story was, and is, jobs, jobs, and more jobs.

The lobbyist also knows when to lower the tempo. An example of this was the work done on behalf of Civil Servants at the time of the privatisation of the Royal Ordnance Factories. The privatisation of this was tied into the then prevailing political orthodoxy. Many Civil Servants were deeply opposed to some or all aspects of such privatisation and believed it to be in the public interest to fight it.

Their position, however, was constitutionally awkward because they were, quite rightly, expected to be politically neutral and were, additionally, signatories to the Official Secrets Act. Nonetheless, some, along with their unions, wished to lobby on some issues which they believed to be in the public interest. Some outsiders, including lobbyists and members of the press were organised to assist. Other members of the press, however, got wind of it and could have caused immense damage to those brave enough to be articulating their reservations.

The Future

In recent years, many commercial lobbyists have been astonished to find journalists belatedly going on about how short-changed the public are by our political system – a conclusion the commercial lobbyists arrived at years ago and wanted assistance in publicising, in the meanwhile offering an alternative solution.

They are also astonished by the fact that the Press does not acknowledge its own history in shoring up such inadequate political system nor that the growth in commercial lobbying was in part a response to the lack of information provided by the press at local regional national and European level. It will be interesting to see how this argument develops as new Mayoral offices and local/regional government begin to make headway in the UK. On its past history, the press is likely to be challenged by the information and knowledge provided by commercial lobbyists.

Today, writing about the press is awkward because the commercial lobbyist has a six way relationship with it. He is dependent on it because his clients are, because the political forums and personnel with whom he deals are, because the issues on which he lobbies are, because his own profession is itself an issue, as indeed is the conduct (or bias) of the press itself and crucially because the commercial lobbyist is so used to having a poor press, he no longer cares, although he makes all the right noises publicly pretending that he does care. The relationship is characterised by a lack of respect on both sides.

That having been said, the commercial lobbyists are comforted that there is a new generation around, and that generation is substantially more commercial lobbyist friendly. These days, politicians are married to lobbyists and journalists date them. They exchange gossip and diary items (for which commercial lobbyists can be paid). While this is an improvement on the past, it also has its dangers, not least because cosy relationships can result in issues being generated in the press by commercial lobbyists and willing journalists in order to stimulate business, giving new meaning to 'spot the planted question'!

Much more dangerous, however, is the fact that many commercial lobbyists no longer feel they need the press. If anything at all, some believe that the press need them. This attitude of course can depend on their clients' needs.

The explosion of multi-media mix has worked in the commercial lobbyist's favour, as has the arrival of the Internet with its ability to reach right into people's homes. Unlike the Press, the commercial lobbyist can set up a two way dialogue with their chosen audience using direct marketing techniques, and, again unlike the press, they can take advantage of the shift towards individual targeting rather than the scatter-gun effect of a big campaign, or the press' need to speak to a host of audiences, of different interests and abilities, at the same time.

The public's specialisation and growing sophistication has also worked in favour of the lobbyists and against the less specialised, tailor-made press. Newspapers and broadcasters are not customised; trade newspapers/magazines are, but, as excellent as a few of them are, they are often financed by interests with an axe to grind and therefore not independent.

The crucial reason, however, why the commercial lobbyists do not always need the national press is because of the development of the contract press. These magazines are not sold at news stands. They are, instead, produced for a select mailing list in half a dozen different languages. The UK is the most advanced market in Europe in terms of contract publishing, and with the advance in editorial quality, this is likely to increase. It is to these magazines that lobbyists are increasingly turning, finding friends and quietly influencing.

This is a shame since, like satellite and cable television, it can put knowledge of their work and how it impacts on the public out of reach of a significant proportion of the population. The commercial lobbyist cannot be blamed for going this route – it was the only route available. However, going above the heads of the people, and those who inform the people, is neither ideal nor healthy in a democratic society.

Whether their skills and knowledge are made more publicly known, and in consequence available to the public, is up to the press. To date, there is no sign of this. The ideal would be joint ventures, with particular emphasis on regional and local joint ventures, with lobbyists perhaps providing specialised columns in newspapers and slots on television to both inform, and assist small interest groups.

Whether such an invitation is ever made depends on the maturity of the press, and its recognition that it is in the public's interest for it to be in perpetual dialogue with the commercial lobbyists, within the understanding that both have a different job to do, jobs which can on occasion be complimentary.

The Political GALLOWS, SEA GULLS and HAWKS

Like many politicians and public servants, many journalists have an honourable history. So do any number of commercial lobbyists. However, on a daily and immediate basis, the people, for the most part, depend far more on journalism to inform and defend them, than on anyone else. Regrettably, however, many within the press appear to be unaware of their burdens or responsibilities.

Good political journalism is not merely about 'politics' but about being 'bound to the dogma of no master'. It is also about exposing private/public sector injustice and deception – about corruption and dishonesty, instead of being party to it either as a result of ignorance, fear or self-interest.

Most importantly it is about communicating and educating the public so that the latter can make informed choices, even if the political system does not provide them with the means to process such choices. It is also about educating the public about the various problems – in the political system, press and commercial lobbying industry, and what steps are being taken to put matters right and how long it will take.

The public is grown up. The press and political system, within which system the commercial lobbyists play a part, should do them the courtesy of recognising it.

There are three types of journalists. The bad ones are the **Political GALLOWS**. These are either all, or some of, the following: **G**lib, **A**buse confidence, **L**azy, **L**ure the naive, **O**verlook the truth, **W**reck lives, and are wholly **S**hameless.

Luckily, there are also two good types. These are the **Political SEA GULLS** and **HAWKS**.

The **SEA GULLS** are the best of the reporters. They **S**trike nimbly, have **E**xtensive background knowledge, report **A**ccurately, **G**rill the great and the lowly fairly, are never **U**nprincipled, are **L**oyal to those who assist them, **L**isten to other points of view, and are **S**teadfast in their responsibilities to the common good.

The **HAWKS** are the best of the investigative journalists. These **H**arass the public's enemies, **A**ttack those who seek to harm, dupe, or conduct their lives contrary to the public interest or ethics, are independent **W**itnesses for the truth, and **K**eepers of confidences. Sometimes, in seeking out the truth, they make the ultimate **S**acrifice, and lose their liberty.

The fact that the reputations of the Political SEA GULLS and HAWKS have suffered because of the appalling conduct of the Political GALLOWS is something for the industry to put right. It must also begin to accept that its loyalty lies with the public and not with itself.

Writing a long article in one of the broadsheets, a distinguished political journalist analysed where the modern lobbying industry had come from. The growth in modern times, he said, was as a result of the EU. That is not true. The growth was because of the conduct of public servants and administrative weakness in the political system, prior to the explosion of interests created by the EU. He knows it. They know it. The industry knows it. And all are responsible for employing disinformation to perpetuate a myth, or create a new one.

The journalist could have let the public into the secret too. Indeed, some would argue that that was his and his profession's primary duty.

If the press really wishes to take its responsibilities seriously it could look at the whole public affairs industry, its own dependence on it and its lack of forensic, specialist reporters. Meanwhile, there are two easy improvements and suggestions for the press. The first could be to ensure that its letters pages remain the domain of private citizens and not interest groups. The second could be to update the 'Court Circular'. A modern Court Circular could list meetings, including so called 'social' evening engagements, between elected and appointed government minister, or their representatives, and senior representatives of the business, charities and media world. This would assist citizens and small interest groups to have a clearer picture of what was going on and have some understanding of those who were denying them access. Transparency, if not accountability, must be a goal. Arguably, such an up-dated 'Court Circular' would be a great deal more relevant to the public than that which is covered today.

For the future, the political authorities, Press, major clients of the commercial lobbying industry and the lobbyists themselves must together find a way forward to enhance democracy. It would appear, however, that some believe themselves to have been burdened with an unwanted task.

Tribute to the late Lt Commander Christopher Powell RN, the UK's founding lobbyist

The founding father of modern lobbying, Commander Christopher Powell, died in 1989. The fact that the doyens of the political press, who believed that they knew everything there was to know about lobbying, had never even heard of him, is a good example of their limitations, and

Christopher Powell's effectiveness.

Although an arrogant man, he was deeply humble about democracy and Parliamentary governance, which is to say, his discretion and modesty were not due to secrecy but humility. Essentially a Parliamentary draughtsman, he was in his eighties when he took the last of his private members' bills to Statute in the 1980s.

He became a Parliamentary consultant (he hated the word 'lobbyist') because he could not afford to become an MP – at the early part of the century a private income, which he did not have, was a necessity. He arrived at Westminster in 1928 from the Royal Navy. During the Second World War he was a director of censorship at the Ministry of Information. In 1929 he joined forces with Charles Watney, a former lobby correspondent and Political & Foreign Editor of the *Daily Mail* then under Lord Northcliffe (Charles Watney could not stand Northcliffe and left when he could bear him no longer). The two of them set up the country's first Parliamentary information and consultancy business trading under the name of Watney & Powell. Charles Watney died in 1948 and Powell carried on as sole partner for twenty-five years before being bought by Traverse-Healy & Lyons and then moving under the then capacious umbrella of Charles Barker ABH, as Charles Barker Watney & Powell.

After the Second World War his work for the IPU enabled him to have an office in Parliament. However, he lost this when he was found to be using it for other work as well. He ran into further trouble when he was seen trying to stop a friendly MP from entering a Standing Committee on a Private Member's Bill, and, having got two entries in the 'Black Book', he failed to receive the knighthood he deserved.

Such minor misdemeanours – which Powell adamantly denied – came in useful at a time when lobbying was becoming more of an issue. After all, it allowed the State to deny his existence, something it was rather keen to do, since it did not want his work, particularly for small interests, to become widely known. He ran into trouble again when, working with Gerald Nabarro MP on a campaign to abolish purchase tax, he drafted hundreds of questions to the Chancellor of the Exchequer.

When he and Charles Watney first started their consultancy in 1929/30 they provided a secretarial service for quite a number of Conservative MPs who 'wished to avoid the trouble of dictating to a secretary or finding out the answers to all the complicated letters about War Pensions and Housing Problems and things of that kind.'

Christopher Powell explained: 'With the help of three or four competent secretaries we would dispose of the correspondence of up to

20 MPs in the course of a morning. The secretaries were trained to do the replies themselves to a large extent. Answers to the trickier ones were dictated by either myself or Charles Watney.

'Then the letters would go down to the House to be signed or sent to the members homes, where, in those days, many Conservative MPs spent most of their time – which is not surprising when you recall that at that period there were 472 Conservative MPs in the House, and that they and other MPs supporting the National Government numbered 556 against the Opposition's total of only 59! At least that way constituents knew their MP was doing something for them.'

In his eyes he was serving constituents – 'they deserved a good job' – far better than the MPs who represented them; clients who were not otherwise represented at Westminster; and the MPs themselves who were free to pursue their interests outside of Westminster 'and stay out of mischief.' All of this 'I liked doing, and for which I got paid.'

'Indeed, there was one Conservative MP whom we served, Sir Walter de Frece, MP for Blackpool, husband of Vesta Tilley, the wealthy and famous Music Hall Male Impersonator – who lived, whether Parliament was in session or not, at Park Palace, Monte Carlo. He would only return once a year to put on a Top Hat for the Budget Statement!

'However, all his letters were promptly and competently answered on the signed note-paper he left in London: Even written questions on subjects of interest to Blackpool frequently appeared on the Order paper and the replies, if interesting, were recorded in the local press.

'If there was an important division, he was paired by kind friends in the Whips' Offices – and he was considered quite a good MP by his constituents as a result!

'For my part, I found it an invaluable experience to see correspondence through the eyes (as it were) of a considerable number of MPs for a wide variety of constituencies, also to draft their letters to Ministers, their questions, as well as notes for their speeches and so forth. It also had the advantage that I never had to pay for anything since I had up to forty sets of Parliamentary documents. I gave up providing secretarial services to MPs because the new generation of MPs preferred to dictate their own letters or were able to afford individual personal secretaries.

'In those years, too, we provided a compact and comprehensive Election Handbook for Conservative Candidates at Election time. This was before the publication of such Handbooks by Conservative Central Office. We used to sell about 500 at £5 a copy, which, in those days, was quite good business!

'I accompanied many delegations to Ministers – some were annual rituals such as that to the Chancellor of the Exchequer by the Theatre Interests about Entertainment Duty. Sir Oswald Stoll, I remember, Chairman of the Stoll Theatre, would set up his notes on a kind of small music stand and read them in a steady monotone to a bored Neville Chamberlain in his splendid Treasury room overlooking the Horse Guards.

'Some very effective delegations were organised by the Parliamentary & Scientific Committee, (of which Powell was Founding Secretary – see below) – for example when the Minister of Technology, the Lord Privy Seal and the Minister of State for Education and Science met us to talk about our Report on the Abstraction and Retrieval of Technical and Scientific Information.

'I recall another to the Minister of Transport, then Alan Lennox-Boyd, from the British Road Federation asking for the speed limit on lorries to be raised. The Minister said "But I'm longing to do it and if only you'll make your campaign a bit noisier and ensure that I get support for the necessary Regulation in the House of Commons I'll do exactly what you want" – and shortly afterwards he did!

'Special Meetings are my favourite way of influencing – I recall a clause in a Children & Young Persons Bill – a government bill, incidentally – which sought to raise the age at which children could appear on the stage. This greatly upset certain Pantomime producers, schools of ballet and dramatic art, circus proprietors and so forth. So, we engaged a really star cast for the purpose and the largest committee room in the House of Commons was packed to hear artistes like Nervo and Knox and Ivor Novello testify that they would never have achieved the success they did if they had not been allowed on the stage at the age of 12 or less.

'We also had some attractive ballet and adagio dancers with us, to give similar testimony. At one stage the Chairman had to refuse a rather unparliamentary demand for some of the adagio dancers to give a practical demonstration on a Committee Room table! However, the point was made and the Bill was suitably amended in Committee!

'What I call a "campaign" is the work I did for the Port Wine Trade Association who were worried about the low and falling sales of port. They attributed this in part to the then high customs duties on heavy wines such as port and sherry, which at that time were four times as high as those on light table wines – the dividing line being about 14% of alcoholic content. This was a legacy from Sir Stafford Cripps when Chancellor of the Exchequer at the end of the War. He was a vegetarian and a tea-totaller. He grudgingly agreed to lower the wartime duties on light table wines but could not bring himself to reduce those on heavier wines.

'I said it might take about three years to achieve success and that is precisely what it did take. We got out an excellent case on paper including graphs, which showed how the high duties on port were providing less revenue whilst the proceeds of the lower duties on table wines were going steadily up. Then we had to exploit the case with Customs & Excise and Parliament. Customs & Excise were tepid so we concentrated on Parliament.

'For three years, twice a week for three or four months before every Budget, I took 3 or 4 Conservative MPs or 3 or 4 Labour MPs out to lunch in the City back parlours of all the Port Wine Shippers to discuss our case. It was wonderful!

'These functions became extremely popular especially as the shippers took pleasure in showing their best vintage ports as well as other wines in which they specialised: the Port Wine Lobby quickly became one of the most popular in the House!

'The Chancellor was being badgered about the case constantly both by questions in the House, amendments to the Finance Bill and chat-ups in the Smoking Room. After three years he capitulated and I had a splendid testimonial from the Port Wine Association, plus several cases of classic vintage port and two visits for the helpful MPs to the Douro Valley in Portugal.

'Alcohol always went down well, as it were! I was involved in the Scottish Licensing Bill too, a long time ago now, reforming licensing laws in Scotland. The Scottish Licensing Trade, for which I was acting, were unhappy about some of the provisions, although it went a long way towards liberalisation, and we evolved a series of amendments with good briefs supporting them.

'We were fortunate in finding several Scottish MPs on both sides of the House who were sympathetic to the views of the licensed trade and were quite eager to help. At various stages in Commons and Lords, the Government were obliged to accept quite a number of these amendments.

'Luckily, it was not a party issue and up to a point the Government was prepared to give way gracefully. At the subsequent Annual Dinner of the Scottish Licensing Trade, I was delighted to receive a two minute standing ovation from 500 Scottish publicans, mostly in kilts. A very impressive sight!'

He did not like what he called 'modern' words, such as marketing, although he certainly believed in it! Recalling one occasion, he said: 'I remember when purchase tax and chocolate biscuits were an issue. These were dutiable if chocolate covered a certain number of biscuit-millimetres. One very big manufacturer with very popular chocolate biscuits was caught but most of his main competitors were outside the limit. We sent all the secretaries in the House of Commons a letter explaining the absurdity – and a special packet of chocolate biscuits – and calling for remedial action. There were immediate questions on the Order Paper and Amendments in the Finance Bill. Success!

'One of my first contributions in Parliament was to get a debate staged on a Motion concerning the Channel Tunnel. In 1930 a Cabinet Sub-Committee Report in its favour had been turned down by the Government in a White Paper. I had just been asked to become Secretary of the All Party Channel Tunnel Group and, by spending many long evenings in the lobby and enlisting the aid of Tunnelist MPs, I managed to get some signatures to a Motion deploring the government's attitude. It was finally selected for debate later that year.

'We went down 178 votes to 170 (Winston Churchill and Aneurin Bevan, I am glad to say, being amongst the 170) – but we kept the Parliamentary group going to encourage and support the project and in 1975 – i.e. forty-five years after the Motion I mention, nearly got the enabling legislation through all its stages in Parliament until Harold Wilson's unilateral decision to withdraw.

Despite all his efforts, the Commander began to fear that the Channel Tunnel would not be built in his lifetime.

'My Channel Tunnel Group still survives – and the Channel Tunnel Project is far from dead. And there will probably be more Motions, and more Debates, and more Bills. But NO Channel Tunnel in my life time, I fear!'

Imagine his delight, therefore, when Prime Minister Thatcher signed the Channel Tunnel Agreement with France. He was flushed with pleasure, and philosophical, although hurt that few remembered how closely he had been involved.

Private Members' Bills provided him with a special amount of pleasurable work and achievement. For some organisations, such as a well known animal charity, he helped to get a dozen or more Bills on to Statute – dealing with such matters as Slaughter of Animals, Regulation of Pet Shops, Animal Breeding Establishments, Riding Establishments and so forth.

At the time of his death in 1989, and in view of increasing anxiety about the commercial lobbyists, his very real achievements were played down. The bulk of his work – i.e. private and private members legislation – was not mentioned at all, least of all in the long obituaries published in both *The Times* and the *Daily Telegraph*.

One of these newspapers did not even name what many believe to have been one of his greatest achievements, the Parliamentary and

Scientific Committee, of which he was Founding Secretary. He helped to establish this body in 1939 (handing the reins over to his admirable successor Arthur Butler in 1978) so that those involved in science, and subsequently technology, particularly in industry, could have some input into the political system.

Instead, the newspaper referred coyly to the fact that he had been 'invited' to reorganise an existing committee which was 'relaunched' under 'a slightly different title'. Powell was deeply and rightly proud of the Committee which had a mixed membership of Parliamentarians from both Houses, and representatives of certain Scientific and Technical institutions, in addition to a limited number of large industrial groups and undertakings which had a big interest in R&D.

The use of the word 'and' in its title was insisted by upon by the Speaker so as to distinguish it from Committees with membership solely confined to Parliamentarians.

He was delighted that HRH The Duke of Edinburgh, an honorary member since 1958, addressed it again on the occasion of its fiftieth anniversary in March 1989 and, more importantly, became its President for that year. He was similarly proud that so many members remained in membership following their appointment to government – including two future Prime Ministers, James Callaghan and Margaret Thatcher, who at one time rented a cottage from him when she and her husband were looking for a property to buy in Kent in the 1970s. Both the Thatcher's were close personal friends.

Lady Thatcher's signed photograph remained in her one-time cottage in the grounds of his home, and it was always hoped by those who put his name forward for an honour that, as a scientist herself, her government would recognise publicly the contribution he had made to the public good. It was not to be.

The formation of the Committee was a 'milestone in the relations between Parliament and Whitehall and the scientific community' (Lord Shackleton, President, 1977 – 1980) and, among other things 'can legitimately claim to have won from government the principle of tax relief on expenditure and research and development' (Lord Wakefield).

In addition, it 'helped to bring about the establishment of the House of Commons Select Committee on Science and Technology in 1967' (Lord Shackleton) all of which, Christopher Powell, as Secretary for thirty-nine years was central to and during which time 'he did more than any other to set the tone' (Lord Shackleton).

The Committee became a unique lobby and pressure group and its activities and membership were carefully recorded in the book he co-authored with Arthur Butler, on the occasion of its fortieth anniversary.

During his years of stewardship, as science was 'transformed from an almost peripheral activity…into the engine of modern society' the Committee 'was one of the channels through which the change of attitude was brought about'.

Still in existence today, it is regrettable that a once vigorous committee, on the cutting edge of all great scientific debate, has now fallen victim to much that is dull and mediocre. A sign of the times, perhaps. He always quoted J.D. Stewart (1958) that "pressure groups (e.g. the Parliamentary & Scientific Committee) are essential to the government of our complex society" and himself said that 'the coherent expression of opinion they render is vital. They are the only means by which many individuals can contribute to politics. Without them discontent would flow and valuable knowledge be lost. It is important that the system of government be such that their role can be carried out with responsibility.'

Other influential committees with which he was associated included the British Group of the Inter Parliamentary Union (IPU) in the immediate post-war period. When he gave this up he continued to service one of its sub-committees, the Franco-British Relations Committee which decided to become independent.

Coyness about his work at the time of his death was in marked contrast to the dinner organised at the House of Commons in 1978 to celebrate his half century at Westminster, attended by the then Prime Minister and fifty Parliamentarians from both Houses and both major parties.

He was constantly checking through the Acts and back copies of Hansard, and his knowledge of Erskine May was second to none.

He complained bitterly that younger lobbyists did not do that enough: 'None of you are taught these days', he used to say. He could not believe it when informed that a well known commercial lobbyist did not have a single Parliamentary procedural reference book, let alone copies of the Acts and back copies of *Hansard*. The other reference book he used constantly was *Whitakers Almanac*.

He seldom needed to consult *Dod's Parliamentary Companion*, since he had an encyclopaedic knowledge. He did not write 'biographies' of Parliamentarians – indeed he despised them – but he was always happy to give his opinion which invariably meant a chapter and verse recital of their competencies/histories.

He had an enormous range of clients and knew industries well – the oil industry were 'do it yourself merchants these days – they only pay us so that we queue up for the brown book for them'. Government bodies 'like to forget they are paying us' – which was the only explanation he could come up with, with a chuckle, when one of his old clients in a government quango refused to come to the telephone when he was monitoring two 'animal' bills (at that time in both Houses of Parliament), insisting instead on 'private' meetings.

He worked closely on behalf of his clients with the Parliamentary agents – for whom, at one time he had an enormous respect, until their drafting and other standards dropped – and was always anxious about whether a private bill might end up a hybrid. He was dismayed at the growth of the private bill system which he believed to be deeply undemocratic.

He never apologised for what he did for a living and saw no reason to. 'MPs and Peers are not all lawyers. So why should they be expected to know anything about legislation? My little Opticians Bill (1980) is a hard-working little bill. But it is entirely uncontentious. Why on earth should Parliamentary time be devoted to it? Far better that the Opticians pay me to do all the work.'

Powell was the only one to take such bills regularly to Statute. The Parliamentarians in whose name they were piloted – who were never able to give credit where credit was due because it would explode the system – were generous in their praise of him. It was usually they who came to him for private members work or to table

Parliamentary questions that he had drafted, all of which they did without charge. It never occurred to Powell to charge his clients what lawyers, accountants and PRs charged – which, in his eyes, was extortion. His fees were always modest.

He always agonised where and how to introduce his bills – under standing order procedure, ten minute rule or in the Lords – since the Ballot is 'only for the sexy'. He believed that the House of Lords was not used enough (true at one time, until the explosion of European legislation hit it). And noticed the increased workload in the Lower House commenting unhappily 'some do all the work as usual'.

He was saddened by the ever increasing workload of both Houses who were dealing with European issues. 'Its not fair to expect the Lords and Commons Committees to have to take responsibility for so much' and was worried about the numbers of Statutory Instruments 'I've never SEEN so many – who is behind them all?'

He was absolutely gleeful when Sunday Trading went through – he had seen debacle after debacle – and was horrified at the amount the lobbyists had charged. When told that there was another inquiry into lobbying he chuckled and remarked 'Are you sure the Politicians WANT people to be helpful?' He asked about the Committee, its composition, and who was giving evidence. He also wanted to know if the House of Lords was involved in the inquiry and was relieved to find out that it was not. In his view people were elevated to the Peerage because they still had a job to do for the country – he did not like to hear of their commercial interests – nor did he like to hear about their involvement with the All Party Groups in case 'everything comes tumbling down'.

His comments on the Parliamentarians with whom he had to deal brought Westminster to life, particularly when, during the 1980s he was heavily involved in animal experimentation legislation. 'A hoodlum'; 'A bit of a spiv these days. His father went the same way'; 'A nasty little man'; 'A thousand year old toad'; 'A sweetie'; 'An honourable Socialist'; 'An old-fashioned Tory'; 'A bright young man'; 'A serious young man'; 'A clever girl. Had to go into politics, husband's so dull'; 'A tiresome girl'.

He was always the first to recognise that, for many, the only contact they had with the political system was through their local MP, who was frequently not the best ambassador for Parliamentary democracy. "Mine" he commented dourly 'is only interested in sheep. And I do not have any sheep.'

He followed Parliamentary legislation closely and was able to identify everyone involved – including those noticeable by their absence. His friendships – he had no 'contacts' – were across the political, social and generational divide. 'He'll do as he's told – he's a friend' or 'he's not as a daft as his father' or, as often, 'he's STUPIDER than his father'.

For some of his enemies he had an enormous respect – 'The worst kind of Socialist. A competent one.' – and affection 'that naughty little trouble-maker, always popping up and down.' He was appalled that Parliamentarians were being paid by lobbying companies and taking on more and more commercial interests. 'That is quite wrong. None of those who worked for me asked for money, let alone took it. They just did as they were told and were happy to.'

He was quite clear that MPs and Peers should be made to register all their business interests and activities but not their investments which he saw as an invasion of their privacy. Nor did he feel that it was sufficient to record an occupation e.g. law – the nature of which might include client activity of a non-Parliamentary nature but which nevertheless represented powerful commercial interests. He was dismayed at the amount of business politicians were accepting – he could always tell which questions had been tabled by such interests in the Order Paper – claiming that politicians 'should only have one or two commercial interests at most'.

He would certainly have been dismayed by the words of Dudley

Fishburn, until May 1997 a Conservative MP, that 'fellow backbenchers advised me "to get a job" so now I act as a consultant to a bank, an American law firm and am a director of a public company.'

Powell always said that the country got far too much out of 'competent' politicians and was the first to recognise how few of them were appreciated or even understood. He believed that for them the pay was bad, the hours of work terrible and the demands, emotional and otherwise, far too much to ask. 'The few bad ones ruin it for the rest of them'.

He thought very little of the Press – especially the Parliamentary Press – 'Don't they realise how hard it is for the Select Committee to get noticed. And that its important for people to understand what the Committee is trying to do? The problem is, they don't understand the issues.'

He was particularly anxious about the growth of Parliamentary lobbying and lobbying Whitehall. The latter he felt was quite wrong since it was up to the Minister 'whom it is RIGHT to lobby' to deal with Civil Servants. He disliked the growth in the All Party Groups – partially because he thought that he was the only 'outsider' who could run them with due regard to the Parliamentary system and partially because he resented equally both newcomer or old competitor. 'He's anxious I'll pinch the business back' he was known to observe about another lobbyist of not quite similar vintage.

Nor did he feel that Parliamentarians should be paid by individual companies since he believed that All Party Groups were lobbies and it would be unfair on other companies. He was particularly anxious about lobbyists or MPs running the Groups because it disadvantaged clients of other lobbyists or MPs who were excluded. In his eyes the Parliamentary group as opposed to the All Party Group brought disparate outsiders together, as well as Parliamentarians and Whitehall.

He had an enormous respect for the Civil Servants who ran Westminster – 'if the Civil Servants can't find the answer, nobody can' – and was appalled at the work demands placed on them.

The behaviour of the public relations world also shocked him as did the conduct of some MPs whom he euphemistically referred to as 'growing increasingly erratic...' (By that he meant greedy) – '...Can't even put it down to the freemasons!'

He loved Parliament and adored his friends, following the troubles in their lives – and various indiscretions – with discreet, unjudgemental (and therefore sympathetic) indifference. He adored France but preferred Italians 'they never want to marry the staff' and was, in his own way, very much a feminist 'It is always an inconvenience when a girl marries. It means the workforce loses the intelligent half of the pair.' He never believed that marriage and children 'were enough for an intelligent girl'. One of his memorable grievances, however, was with women who smoked. Harking back to the 1920s, when, according to him, young women took up the habit in large numbers, he would look at his female staff sixty years later and comment meaningfully as they lit up: 'Women should not smoke. It makes their ears smell. Such a pity in my view'.

He was arrogant, opinionated, and treated some people badly. He liked to teach however – he read everything he was given – and was prepared to instruct anyone who did him the courtesy of listening. He floated in and out of Westminster as he chose, making sure his letters got into members' pigeon holes or meeting politicians in the inner members' lobby. In addition, all his (usually) female staff had to say to get into Westminster was that she was 'one of Commander Powell's ladies...'

He did not take a client on unless he liked him personally and he felt that he could help, and it never occurred to him to 'use' his client's ignorance by overcharging or providing a service he did not need. He was the same about issues and one of his greatest prides was the work he did for the inheritance rights of illegitimate children.

He was philosophical about 'political' honours since he recognised that the parties had no other way of showing appreciation to their servants. On being told that his old friends were still trying to win one for him he was deeply touched. He was deeply hurt by the system's refusal to recognise his work and achievements but bore such hurt with dignity and discretion. He only once departed from such discretion, commenting with a mischievous smile, 'I should have been a freemason!'

The fact that he was not a freemason, incidentally, proves that although the freemasons were well-represented in Parliament, it was possible (contrary to popular belief) for some to succeed without them. Many of Powell's friends, however, were freemasons, especially in the Lords 'but I never felt the need for it'.

He always refused to be drawn on 'secret societies' confining himself to the disparaging comment 'what on earth is the point of a 'secret' if you need a 'society' to keep it ?' It is because the Honours System cannot be defended that he should have got one. He did not because this would have drawn attention to the deficiencies, and therefore conduct, of Parliamentary democracy over decades. He set out his memoirs when he was too old to do the story justice and too loyal, as he always was, to want to. These he dictated to Annabel Lloyd, one of his most beloved assistants, who despite a heavy work load and family responsibilities, absorbed most of his burdens in the last years of his life.

He died in 1989 without sentimentality and with typical style. Confined to a wheel-chair, and told that he needed to have his foot amputated, he responded 'Cut it off. I have no further use for it.'

Those who loved him were delighted that he died peacefully in his sleep the night before the operation

CONCLUSIONS

Many lobbyists have conducted themselves with flagrant disregard for the proprieties and taken advantage of democratic deficit. Many others have sniggered on the way to the bank as Parliament, a once glorious institution, totters on the edge of bankrupt authority and decay.

All of these, hypocrites every one, no doubt stand to attention on the eleventh hour, of the eleventh day, of the eleventh month, for The Glorious Dead who gave their lives for the corruption of cronies.

An apology is owed. But how can you apologise to the dead, without putting things right for the living? And to whom is an apology to be made? Arguably, only to the People. These, on discovering the existence of commercial lobbying, are now treated by public servant and press alike as victims in need of bereavement counselling. Did the People really have such a high opinion of the 'democracy' on offer, and who were the ones who denied them knowledge of the commercial lobbyists in the first place, particularly in view of the fact that some of these have helped outsiders access democracy for decades? Certainly not the commercial lobbyists themselves.

The industry might be revolting and many of the players even more revolting but the public has the wit to recognise that commercial lobbyists are not a cause but a symptom. Moreover, a symptom that can also offer some amelioration.

Who else should apologise? Perhaps some members of the business community who could be deemed to penalise those commercial lobbyists who do not offer anti-democratic practice for considerable fee in favour of those who do. This is a little like choosing as your accountant, the guy who offers tax evasion rather than the guy who offers tax avoidance. Both might be reprehensible but one is at least lawful – for the moment anyway.

Who else is responsible? The Press, whose conduct over decades is the one big unreported news story. Who else? Government, both elected politician or adviser, as well as public servant here and in the EU. The whole system stands accused of arrogance, deeply flawed planning and a failure to dispel the power of elites created by many years of both corruption and mismanagement.

Not that the press or government appear to be worried about this – after all, all they need to do is blame the commercial lobbyists, apparently wholly unaware of exactly how cut off from the public they are. It is like going to a doctor with a broken leg and being counselled because you lost a false eye-lash when you fell over.

Interestingly, nobody has asked them to apologise to The People. However, various politicians have asked that the commercial lobbyists apologise to Parliament (naturally wearing the laurels of The People's Representatives, which, as we all know, they are not.)

Whatever for? There might be some nice people in Parliament but the majority are duds. Duds, indeed, who let the commercial lobbyists represent The People during Labour's almost two decades in the wilderness. Or have they forgotten already?

As for 'Cronygate' – and Parliament anxious that government treats it with contempt – Parliament has a point. But that point is not with the commercial lobbying industry. If Parliament wants to be taken seriously it has to offer leadership. This is next to impossible since most of its number could not lead an old bumble bee to a honey pot unless the bee was going in that direction anyway.

It is impossible to respect even some parts of the whole, let alone the whole itself. Not in the old guard, not in the new. Altruism and decency did not exist yesterday, and they do not exist today. The system is organised to block the decent so that, except in rare circumstances, only the worst get through. To assist in the 'getting through' organisations, small or large, employ commercial lobbyists who can be far more competent and cost effective than bumble bees.

Parliament, however, has reacted rather badly. As a result, knee jerk reactions are now the norm. While government on the whole is well and truly sticking to a few commercial lobbyists, some in the Cabinet are banning staff from dealing with them – except of course those 'outsiders' who secure massive contracts for government, and those Parliamentarians who are sponsored by, say, a trade union, who of course are not lobbyists!

How pushing the commercial side of the industry back into the shadows does something for transparency is the typical logic of fools. It could also be anti-competitive. Not of course that disinterested academics, politicians and journalists currently pontificating about the industry know anything about this, any more than they know anything about commercial lobbying's wider environment – Europe and world markets.

You are the leading lobbyist on a multinational campaign, in which national government has an interest? Good on you. Deal with Commission representatives (all on the commercial lobbying conference circuit, along with journalists and other public servants) and ministerial departments of other countries within/without the EU – but, once back in London, ooops, stop lobbying. Ship over the client's chief executive from Rio instead because a Cabinet Minister will not speak to the client's appointed agent (a transparent arrangement) i.e. his commercial lobbyist. Although, of course, some of his other Cabinet colleagues will.

And what will happen when local government and the new assemblies are up and running. What? No lobbyists? Tough, then, when local Civil Servants want the re-cycled politicians elected to them educated to a level where they can understand difficult arguments. Even tougher when your small interest group that does not know how to articulate its needs, despite its validity, loses its case because the lobbyist as advocate is not allowed to represent him.

Old cynics like to believe that the more cynical they seem, the more idealistic they are. That is just not true. It is how they comfort themselves that they did so little to put things right. Despite 'Cronygate', and no doubt similar scandals to come (EU/European Parliament watch out!) commercial lobbying is here to stay, and, thank goodness it is. The commercial lobbyists at least are not humbug merchants nor do they deal in the sentimental twaddle of political inadequacies.

They deal with real life. More importantly, they represent modern life. Until such time as our political system is doing the same, commercial lobbying remains. Join the industry yourself if you are looking for an interesting career. It is one that will take you into the twenty-first century.

The commercial lobbyist might not have a place at democracy's debating table (government and press will see to that) but the industry will prove itself closer to the people in the longer term. Economic trends might be global, but this country is ours – and our democracy must be ours too. It cannot be left to politicians.

To make it ours, outsiders such as the decent commercial lobbyists give assistance to those who need to know how to get the best from it, when the powerful seek to deny it. The heavyweights, meanwhile, will offer only what they are prepared to deliver, not what we all need and want. We are all lobbyists now. And for that, no apology is necessary – unless, of course, those who dish up and seek to defend the limited democracy on offer care to make it. Do not hold your breath.

In choosing a career in the industry, you can look forward to a lifelong passion in politics, ideas and cultures. It can be an awful career too – one member of the media, joined the industry because she found the media so dire. She found the commercial lobbyists even worse and went back to the media. It often lacks a certain cerebral quality. As often again, it does not. Most importantly, if you are lucky, it can also be an exhilarating career.

You can sit at the hand of those who are gods in their respective powerful worlds. Or you can sit at the hand of those who are not gods, seeking to challenge the powerful.

Political insider dealing is unfair, in the same way as financial insider dealing is unfair. The difference is that in the one, the source of the insider dealing are those whom we either elect or appoint to protect us. There is, and always has been a large, unelected cadre, no doubt always oiled by young men with too much testosterone.

Today, its manifestation is those who move from Think Tanks to lobbying companies to government as special adviser. In the old days it was those who went to public school together, including the Opposition, or were related to each other by marriage. This, of course, is anti-democratic if democracy is about representative government. Since, however, democracy is not merely about representative government but about modernisation it is scarcely valid.

Commercial lobbying as a career is a challenge. It is, for example, difficult to stay in the industry beyond a certain point if you find yourself agreeing with your client's opponents more often than you agree with your clients or if you find yourself unable to respect or trust your employer and changing employers only means more of the same.

It is also difficult staying in the industry beyond a certain point if this means accepting managerial responsibility, which in turn means accepting the decisions made by management even if these do not correspond to your moral code. As management you see much and hear more – not least that some of those setting the agenda, commercial lobbyists, bankers, politicians and the rest, have no respect for democracy and even less understanding of how precious it is.

It is not always easy to be a moral person, and work in the corporate world at the same time. Nor is it always easy to escape the conclusion that commerce and democracy are fundamentally incompatible.

Some of you may decide to quit. If you do, you will not have lost anything. Rather, you will have gained much. In particular you will have learned a skill that will last a lifetime – knowing when to press on, when to make the right noises, and when to be patient. The keenest skill of all that you will have acquired is that lobbying is a long game – which for some, who want results today, if not yesterday, is a completely alien culture.

Lobbying teaches you to 'line up your ducks', a process which can take years. Once these are in place, however, you can target them one by one. Knowledge of the long game is vital to survival. Quit commercial lobbying, and you will know how to make your point of view heard (whether you are fighting a planning decision which wrecks your and/or your community's built environment, or working for a commercial interest) when, so often, the 'heavies' would prefer to pretend that neither you, nor your point of view, exists.

On the other hand, if you decide to remain in the industry or join it now, an exciting decade is ahead of you. The new millennium and technological change will see to that – as well as industry anxieties about modern mores, which are now on your side. The fight against poor standards and ethics, is no longer a lonely one . Those who do fight will no longer be an isolated voice internally, nor will they be on their own externally.

Internally, this is because 'ethics' now make good business sense for some, although certainly not all. As a result, some employers are beginning to pay increasingly greater attention to conduct, as well as 'ethical' accounts and accept that valued members of staff can refuse, without damaging their careers, to work on those accounts that do not correspond to their own codes of conduct. Externally, it is because while many vociferous members of the press remain implacably opposed to the industry, as many recognise its validity. There is a mountain to climb, but it is happening.

There comes a time when chaos reaches such a pitch that the only thing to do is put a line under the past, and go forward. Contrition is necessary. And forceful modern institutions to regulate the unregulated, so that 'politics' becomes merely an accessory to lobbying, modern technology its engine, democracy its core.

Policing of the industry, is needed with an identifiable chain of command. Many of the employers in the industry have no idea of the difference between right and wrong. Many of these, in their forties and fifties, are the industry leaders and learned their trade in the moral fog of the 1970s and 1980s.

Whether you become an industry leader is determined by two things – your choice of employer and colleague.

Meanwhile, industry practitioners' continue to seek to defend themselves by ducking and diving all over the place, hiding behind trendy new doctrines that declare the end of politics and tradition, and the emergence of the 'Risk Society', they talk typical hogwash. They make it popular to speak in terms of the end of political parties and politics post-political party as if politics was once all embracing which it wasn't – that's why commercial lobbyists had a job in the first place – and life was free of risk. It was not, is not and never will be.

As for tradition, those same industry practitioners appear to forget that new ones emerge all the time, and that some traditions, minus theme-park pageantry – decency and fair play to name but two – never die. Tradition reflects the diversity of our people rather than the conventions of yesterday which crushed them. Whether commercial lobbying is accepted by the public as a tradition worth keeping will be determined by how the commercial lobbying industry responds and conducts itself in the future.

Twenty years ago not even friends and family understood what a commercial lobbyist did for a living. Today, market penetration, if not acceptance and understanding of the product, is high. Twenty years ago, most commercial lobbyists could not work for an overseas tea council without enormous debate, now more and more work for foreign governments. Unlike in the United States, there is no legislation requiring them to list the foreign interests that they serve.

Twenty years ago, commercial lobbyists could not say they took Private Members' Bills, outside the Private Members' Ballot, to Statute (the politicians in whose name the Bills were piloted were unpaid) – although they did – and were forced to run the gauntlet of intimidation and downright subterfuge. Today, were such a service being offered they would advertise it.

Six changes in particular are noticeable.

Firstly, the change of market focus. This was at one time all about Westminster and Whitehall. Now it is about Europe and beyond, as well as established, or soon to be established local and regional governments. A spin-off from this is a newly acquired ability to shoot above the heads of politicians and Mandarins. In this, great causes are often assisted by campaigns taken up by the Press.

Secondly, the political culture. This has lost its mystique and not before time. But it has also acquired a nasty, furtive quality.

Links with some Think Tanks, academics, commercial operations and so on do nothing to dispel anxieties. Meanwhile the quality of public servant declines.

Thirdly, corruption and fraud. This was in evidence in Westminster twenty years ago and was equally in evidence in the European

Parliament and Commission. Today, it is a growth industry in Europe; much less so in the UK – the conduct of many councils besides, which have overtaken Westminster in the corruption race. The problem remains that, that which the citizen deems to be corrupt is not regarded as corrupt by those in a position of privilege. In this deceit many remain lawfully protected.

Hundreds of millions of pounds of taxpayers' money is lost through fraud and incompetence. In a national audit office report in February 1998 it was noted that financial controls had collapsed in 46 ministries and government agencies with 'fundamental failures and weaknesses' in one department in ten. There are similar problems in Europe.

Fourthly, the position of women, gays, the disabled and ethnic minorities. Twenty years ago the political system, quite literally, loathed them. The commercial lobbying industry, however, historically, has been good to women principally because in the early days the work was very poorly paid, so few men were interested. Womens' ability to use the new technologies gave them a further boost. Today, the picture is patchy. In politics, some women have made headway in this country but hardly in Europe. In commercial lobbying, they have been sidelined by some of the larger male dominated consultancies (especially those that have grown out of financial and corporate PR) but are doing exceedingly well in others. The whole political system, and commercial and legal worlds, however, are so 'male' that even where women are well placed, the environment is often still 'masculine'.

Regrettably, the ethnic minorities – who could do well commercially by setting up something like an Ethnic Commercial Lobbying Company – are scarcely perceived to exist. This is a travesty. It is also commercially short-sighted in view of the professional, educational and inter-personal skills that many representatives from the minorities possess, let alone the commercial opportunities and contacts they possess overseas.

As for the disabled – the breakthrough made by Alf Morris MP in 1969 with his Private Members' Bill, and his appointment as Minister for the Disabled in 1974, has not been sustained. Their exclusion from the work place, and, of course, all other areas of life, including commercial lobbying, was, and remains, shameful. The gay community, on the other hand, despite recent and relatively minor setbacks, is at long last beginning to make some headway.

Fifthly the extreme left-ultra right debate. This had to be monitored because of the impact the debate's marginalised representatives had on workforces. Twenty years ago the commercial lobbyists could see it at first hand in Westminster, in Europe, and in the Press where the ultra-right had more friends than the extreme left. Today, both groups remain ready to promote mayhem, retain their supporters in the workplace, and have well developed links here and on the Continent. In so doing, the honourable right and honourable left may be unfairly drawn in by association.

Sixthly, the class battle. This remains firmly in place – social fluidity is not the same thing as equality – although it does not seem to be such a determining factor. As a rule, all elites promote their own and the present government has proven it is no exception. The difference is that the new 'class' believe that they will only be around for a short time and therefore seek to capitalise fast, accelerating the rate of greed, while seeking to control the rate of inflation.

The naiveté of characterisation is almost quaint. Conservative voters, who may or may not be 'classy' are all greedy, prissy and repressed while those who vote Labour are not. Above all, the latter are anxious about the trodden on. Both pictures, of course, are a nonsense. It is no longer correct to talk in terms of the battle between left and right (although in its very simplicity, it is appropriate). Instead we are encouraged to think in terms of materialists versus moralists as if the right-wing cannot be moral or the left-wing cannot be materialist. We are never presented with the true picture. That is to say, the corrupt v those who are not corrupt.

Commercial lobbyists, entering this political world, can look forward to a life of casual, brutal carelessness. A profession where getting results is solely determined by the unfairness of money is always especially brutalising. On the other hand they can also look forward to The Great Debate – modern democracy – in which their industry may play a part.

How we wish to govern ourselves, who is to be responsible for such government and how we wish to employ those who govern us – including 'outsiders' some of whom may be lobbyists. These, until recently, have felt themselves protected by an assumption of impunity, not least because a culture of complicity was fostered by a powerful state in which huge payments were made. Today such impunity has all but evaporated. Commercial lobbying will be all the more vigorous, and healthy, for it.

At a time when commercial lobbying and the commercial lobbyists were at their highest levels of probity, the State refused to sustain such standards since that would have been to jeopardise the laissez faire of its own. In consequence it was strangely oblivious to the world in which lesser mortals lived. Hard ball tactics (the dirty, the sleazy) were widely admired when all these did was trash, and did so wickedly. If there is a loathing for the commercial lobbyist, let there also be understanding that the industry is no more, nor less, than a reflection of politics and the market itself.

Today, change is belatedly on the way. Whereas at the moment, what you see is what you get – ambition and banality – tomorrow it is likely to be a different story. Even commercial lobbyists – who made no attempt to address and eliminate public hostility – have been shocked at the loud cheer that greeted their ascent end in crashing descent. The public – and who can blame them as they watch the ridiculous, self-conscious, vulgar and grasping prosper? – have had enough.

None seemed to have a love of politics nor sense of altruism and public service. Discreet Old Masters such as Christopher Powell have not been replaced. The industry that was once exhilarating has become home to mercenaries and lost souls. Dominated by greedy leaderships, its most faithful lieutenants have been those in need of a bit of humour, and irony, to give themselves personality and depth and an understanding of what democracy means, what people sacrificed for it, and what people continue to sacrifice for it. They had no understanding of the spirit of democracy.

But that problem was not confined to commercial lobbying. The entire political world was, and is, characterised by the mind-numbingly boring and energy sapping back-stabbings of small minded greedy creeps who simply cannot begin to comprehend how big an idea democracy is. These block, and have blocked for decades, those who know what is wrong, and want to make things better.

As a commercial lobbyist you will skim the surface of other people's lives and laugh at the Political Pilgrims on the Damascus Road, all looking for St Paul and all vainly wishing to find a St Paul that listens (to them but not to others!). There are no longer any secret lovers. Where once upon a time, for commercial lobbyists to be effective, they – but not their work – had to be invisible, now they are visible while their work is ever more hidden. The former was not furtiveness – in the hands of the right people, it was humility. In an increasingly tacky universe, there is no last remaining outpost of integrity.

Change is our collective responsibility – and that goes for commercial lobbyists too. And change is on its way.

Of course, improvement in industry standards, in the same way as improvement in politics as a whole, depends on us. It depends particularly on commercial lobbyists because the product of democracy is now in the hands of professional communicators – and these professional communicators own the commercial lobbyists.

That is why there is a good news too. The commercial lobbyists should be reaching out to the electorate, and to a limited degree they already are. In reaching out to the electorate they are introducing into democracy the modern, two way dialogue of direct marketing technique. Targeting people individually, rather than the random scatter-gun effect of a big campaign, in addition to the arrival of the Internet with its ability to reach right into people's homes, is good for democracy. The future lies in direct politics where, rather like direct marketing, and, admittedly for a fee, the citizen will be able to ring up for advice.

That is not to say that the avoidance of moral scruple in pursuit of profit has had its day – it has not. Human nature is fundamentally selfish. Those making big bucks will continue to do so. There will always be a gap between rhetoric and conduct and beneath the sophisticated veneer there will always be a hoodlum lurking. No-one who wishes to survive in commercial lobbying will be able to be quiet, respectable and gentle. However, there is a strong possibility that commercial lobbyists who make money will also be on the side of the angels.

The debate has matured. The public is maturing. The commercial lobbyists have only to catch up and prove themselves worthy of that maturity. Characters come demanding different things. Things start off consensually and end up in unmutuality or divorce, where the only reliable instinct is that all participants betray each other. The commercial lobbyist can, at worst, limit the betrayal, at best ensure that there is pragmatism and, more importantly, healthy respect for opponents offering different opinions and solutions.

Commercial lobbying is like a series of one night stands – sometimes a wonderful memory that lasts a lifetime, but, more usually, venal, unmemorable, sordid, feeding on those looking for the moment. Its future lies in the quality of its 'love' affairs – and in its 'lovers' – as well as in its ability to sustain such love affairs indefinitely.

Go into the industry knowing that whether commercial lobbying is at the sordid end of the 'love' affair market – or at the glorious, quiet, decent end – is up to you. Commercial lobbying can be undemocratic? So, for example, can representative groups. Do trades associations always ballot their members? Of course not. Many are controlled by their majors. Smaller interests have no outside advocate – which is where the commercial lobbyist can come in.

The Public are against the industry? Explain to them that if they knock out the commercial lobbyist, the Public Affairs Director of a major bank will continue to wine a minister, and the Chief Executive of a leading charity will continue to dine a Civil Servant, and the Director General of an employers organisation will continue to hob-nob in Brussels and sit on a pal's Task Force. The only people not in the loop will be small interests. Some of these employ commercial lobbyists – and are grateful to them for the service they provide.

Similarly, ask the public who has most to gain if the commercial lobbyists are knocked out? Vested interests such as public servants and so-called academics busily feathering their own nests as 'independent' authorities – although of course they are paid whopping sums of money by those who determine their 'independence'. People must be aware of the issues. They must also recognise that their best advocate is frequently the 'outsider'.

And that is what the commercial lobbyist is, and always was.

Commercial lobbyists illuminate the doorways to other outsiders – and push their clients through those doorways – so that their valid and honourable voices are heard against the powerful. Sometimes, those clients who the commercial lobbyist assist lack appropriate knowledge and/or interpersonal skills to recognise the fob-off. In which case, the commercial lobbyist goes through the doorway with him to help articulate the problems, and ensure that he not only recognises the fob-off but short circuits it too.

Sometimes the client cannot afford a lawyer to help him draft his needs or, as likely, the lawyer himself has no knowledge of Parliamentary drafting. The commercial lobbyist drafts, amends, and inserts. Does so quietly, and at a price that the client can afford. That is the reason why so many powerful institutions loathe them. Commercial lobbyists can be, after all, quite good at their jobs. And that is the reason, and much else besides, why the honourable commercial lobbyist has nothing on his conscience.

The public are owed an apology. But not from those commercial lobbyists who conduct themselves honourably.

To lobby, you have to follow the chieftains who control the agenda. To be a lobbyist, you have to know how to throw the agenda in favour of your client. Democracy is all about sharing it. Never allow yourself to believe you are a chieftain, even if you are, because those who do never understand how easy life is for those who control the agenda – and come unstuck when others wish and/or succeed in dictating it. Chieftains overlook the character of the people of these islands at their peril. That character has been sleepy for a not inconsiderable time. But, once roused, it is fiercely free spirited, anti-authoritarian and gloriously wilful.

And who will be doing the dictating and forcing the pace? Democrats. Radical ones. Lively ones. Humourous ones. Passionate ones. Let cynics and mandarins talk about the death of ideology, they never knew much anyway. Meanwhile, watch as demands for modern democracy increase. Democracy is not a new ideology but it is an idea whose time has come. Commercial lobbying has a part to play in this new ideology in the same way as it has a part to play in both public life and public service.

It is of course by no means certain, however, that the commercial lobbyists will be asked to participate in such an altruistic exercise.

If they are not, the leadership of the industry has only itself to blame.

BIBLIOGRAPHY

One Man's Word, Ian Greer, Andre Deutsch, 1997

MPs for Hire, Mark Hollingsworth, Bloomsbury 1991

No Hiding Place – Business and the Politics of Pressure Control Risks, 1997

Managing Communication in a Changing World: Annual Report Institute of Public Relations 50th Anniversary

Soundbites and Spin Doctors, Nicholas Jones, Cassell, 1997

Practical Techniques for Effective Lobbying, Charles Miller, Hawksmere, 1998

The Parliamentary & Scientific Committee Lt Cdr Christopher Powell and Arthur Butler, Croom Helm, 1980

Lobbying Lt Cdr Christopher Powell (Speech to the Libraries Association, 1980)

Legislating the Criminal Code: Corruption Law Commission No 248, 1998

The Invisible Persuaders, David Michie, Bantam Press, 1998

Lobbyists for Hire, Kevin Moloney, Dartmouth, 1996

Committee on Standards in Public Life Nolan Committee, HMSO, 1994

Public Affairs News Letters (various)

PMS Guide to Pressure Groups 1997